EVOLVING VISIONS OF THE PRIESTHOOD

10/21

Evolving Visions
of the Priesthood

Changes from Vatican II to the Turn
of the New Century

Dean R. Hoge
and
Jacqueline E. Wenger

LITURGICAL PRESS
Collegeville, Minnesota

www.litpress.org

Cover design by David Manahan, O.S.B. Photo by The Crosiers, Gene Plaisted, O.S.C.

1	2	3	4	5	6	7	8

Library of Congress Cataloging-in-Publication Data

Hoge, Dean R., 1937–
    Evolving visions of the priesthood : changes from Vatican II to the turn of the new
century / Dean R. Hoge and Jacqueline E. Wenger.
        p. cm.
    Includes bibliographical references.
    ISBN 0-8146-2805-2 (pbk : alk. paper)
        1. Catholic Church—United States—Clergy. 2. Catholic Church—
United States—History—20th century. I. Wenger, Jacqueline E. II. Title.

BX1912.H588 2004
262'.14273—dc21   2003009623

Contents

Preface

The studies contained in this book by Dean Hoge and Jacqueline Wenger continue a series begun in 1970. In the 1990s the National Federation of Priests' Councils initiated a process that would become a "trends study" to provide the Church in the United States with trend data on the priests of the country over the last forty to fifty years. Twice it sponsored research repeating portions of the landmark 1970 survey.

This is important data because it traces the movement of the Church in the United States during the first forty years of the implementation of the Second Vatican Council. In this research on priests, the gradual introduction, reception, and implementation of the prescriptions of the council can be known, thus giving the Church in the United States a good picture of itself and its struggles during the postconciliar period. These studies are important also for what they tell us of the priests who were bringing the theology of the council, with its unfolding understanding of the Church as the people of God, into the everyday life of parishes and faith communities. By following the movement of what has been happening, we get a glimpse of the future that beckons.

For the purposes of the National Federation of Priests' Councils, the data offers issues for the setting of an agenda. The clearly identified problems which surfaced in this latest study and are reported here give the National Federation of Priests' Councils and the bishops a clear picture of what the priests are feeling and thinking, of how they are disposed to lead the local faith communities, and what specific problem areas need further research, clarification and attention.

Given the struggles of the scandals confronting the Church in the last year, it will be helpful to search through the data to see if there were indications of why the particular problem of pedophilia and ephebophilia arose so suddenly and so much related to a given time frame.

As in the companion volume, *The First Five Years of Priesthood,* commentaries in this book, provided by six distinguished scholars and pastoral leaders, will assist in furthering the discussions we hope this book will provoke.

I commend *Evolving Visions of the Priesthood* to you for reflection, comment, and study. It is the wish of the National Federation of Priests' Councils that the findings of this work would help further the investigations on priestly life and ministry taking place in the United States today.

The National Federation offers thanks to Jackson W. Carroll and the Pulpit & Pew: Research on Pastoral Leadership project funded by the Lilly Foundation. Their assistance has made this project possible.

Rev. Robert J. Silva

President, The National Federation of Priests' Councils

Foreword

There is little doubt that the pedophilia crisis has presented the Catholic Church—its bishops, priests, and laity—with one of the most serious challenges of its long and venerable history. How the Church comes through this crisis, what kind of changes will emerge on its far side, are at this writing very much up in the air. The authors of this important new book on the priesthood, writing during the crisis but drawing heavily on survey data collected just prior to it, faced a considerable challenge: how to describe "evolving visions of the priesthood," as the title promises, when the present situation is so fluid, so much in turmoil.

By not ignoring the crisis but at the same time taking a much longer view of continuity and change in the priesthood, the authors have met the challenge admirably in calling attention to important long-range trends in the Church's priesthood. Such trends will no doubt play an important part in shaping responses to the present situation, but they continue to be important in their own right, the pedophilia crisis notwithstanding. The authors' analysis, buttressed by recommendations from interviews with priests and commentaries by distinguished Catholic leaders, makes an important contribution to the Church and to all who are concerned with the future of pastoral leadership today, Catholic or Protestant.

Pulpit & Pew: Research on Pastoral Leadership is both privileged and pleased to have been a cosponsor, with the National Federation of Priests' Councils, of this research. This is our second joint undertaking, the first being a companion volume, *The First Five Years of the Priesthood*, also published by the Liturgical Press. Both projects were under the competent direction of Dr. Dean R. Hoge of Catholic University of America, joined in the latter book by Jacqueline E. Wenger. *Pulpit & Pew* is a multifaceted study of pastoral leadership, both Catholic and Protestant, being undertaken at Duke University's Divinity School with funding from Lilly Endowment, Inc. Its purpose is to provide credible research findings about pastoral leadership today and the changes impacting it. Three central sets of questions guide the various studies:

- What is the state of pastoral leadership at the new century's beginning, and what do current trends portend for the next generation?
- What is "good ministry?" Can we describe it? How does it come into being? Do its characteristics vary by denominational tradition? By congregational context?
- What can be done to help "good ministry" to come into being more frequently? And how can it be nurtured and supported more directly?

This book adds much to our understanding of these questions, especially as they apply to Catholic priests. Although many of the trends and insights are specific to Catholics, many issues cross over to Protestant clergy as well. Although Protestants do not have a clergy shortage nearly as critical or dramatic as Catholics, several U.S. denominations are experiencing a declining number of ordained clergy who are willing to serve as pastoral leaders of congregations, especially over an entire career. They have particular difficulty in meeting the leadership needs of their many small congregations— smaller by far than most Catholic parishes. To do so, they are increasingly turning to trained, but non-ordained, laypersons, many of whom are part-time. Although not faced with the requirement of celibacy, Protestant pastors, like Catholic priests, complain of loneliness and the difficulty of sustaining close relationships with other clergy. Also like their Catholic counterparts, they express dissatisfaction with their spiritual life. Therefore, although Catholics will be the book's primary audience, Protestants can nevertheless learn much from the research and from the wise reflections of the priests and the commentaries by Catholic officials.

For the staff of Pulpit & Pew, I join with the National Federation of Priests' Councils in commending it to you. I also invite readers to be regular visitors to our project website, www.pulpitandpew.duke.edu, where other project reports and news of the project are available.

Jackson W. Carroll

Director of Pulpit & Pew
Ruth W. and A. Morris Williams Professor Emeritus
Duke University Divinity School

Introduction

I was a priest in those early days and there was this tremendous excitement about becoming more relevant to the world and to do things to make the church very much a part of the world situation. There was a great sense of activism. We were out to be very much involved in the community.

—An older priest in a focus group

I think what is really exciting in my generation (it's kind of fun to see) is that there is a sense of rediscovering some of the stuff that got buried after Vatican II. I really don't get emotional over Vatican II.

—A 32-year-old diocesan priest

The year 2002 marks the thirty-seventh anniversary of the closing of the Second Vatican Council. Older people today remember the changes introduced by the council and the excitement that followed. For most Catholics in America, the postconciliar years were full of excitement, anticipation, and hope among priests and laity alike. Younger people today, by contrast, see the council as something remote, simply history. They never experienced the pre-Vatican II Church or the struggles of the '60s. What they know of the Church is what they see today. The priesthood today, even more than the laity, includes both types of persons. The existence of these two types of priests today is the principal topic we researched for this book.

Some hopes generated by the council have been realized, others have been dashed, and a few expectations have turned out to have been unrealistic from the outset. It has often been noted that the innovations of the council were at the level of parish, diocese, and nation, but not at the level of the priesthood. The energies of the council were directed elsewhere. Moreover, the innovations that emerged from the council documents put priests in a relatively passive posture of being more acted upon than acting.

After the council, priests experienced a season of uncertainty. They asked themselves: How distinct are we priests? Should we have a unique social status? Will a celibate priesthood continue in the future? They also took action in response, beginning in 1966 and 1967. American priests began organizing themselves into self-governing organizations, while at the same time a large numbers of others chose to resign. The situation was alarming to church leaders.

In 1968, the American bishops decided to invest in a large survey of priests to learn the facts about priests' satisfactions, dissatisfactions, and problems. They specified that the survey should also gather data from newly resigned priests. The National Opinion Research Center (NORC) at the University of Chicago was commissioned to do the survey; Andrew Greeley and Richard Schoenherr were put in charge.

The NORC team carried out a masterful survey of active and resigned priests in 1970, published in the book, *The Catholic Priest in the United States: Sociological Investigations* (NORC, 1972). This book was one of a three-volume set, the other two being on psychological and historical investigations. Eugene Kennedy and Victor Heckler wrote *The Catholic Priest in the United States: Psychological Investigations* (1971), and John Tracy Ellis edited *The Catholic Priest in the United States: Historical Investigations* (1971).

The 1970 survey remains to this day unsurpassed in scope and thoroughness. It has served historians and sociologists as a benchmark for assessing later trends, and it has done the same for us. In 1985 and 1993, teams of researchers headed by Dean Hoge replicated questions from the 1970 survey, using identical questions and equivalent samples, in search of trends. The findings were described in the 1994 report, *Project Future Directions*, published by the National Federation of Priests' Councils. In 2001, the National Federation of Priests' Councils received financial support from Duke Divinity School's Pulpit & Pew Research on Pastoral Leadership initiative to carry out another survey, continuing the series of priest surveys at eight-year intervals—1985, 1993, and 2001.

The 2001 Priest Survey

The National Federation of Priests' Councils nominated an advisory committee to help design the 2001 survey. To get trend data the committee decided to repeat most of the earlier questions, unchanged, but also to delete a few and add several others. Thus we designed a questionnaire repeating about 100 earlier questions, and we sampled the same 44 dioceses and 45 religious communities as in 1985 and 1993.[1] We sent questionnaires

---

[1] The sample was a random selection of dioceses and institutes from the larger list in 1970. We wrote to the dioceses and religious institutes sampled in 1985 and 1993. All but two of the dioceses sent us the names of their priests, including retired priests. We made substitutions for the other two. Of the religious institutes only 24 responded,

to random samples of diocesan and religious priests. The response rate was very high (71%).

In late 2001 and early 2002, after the survey was finished, we carried out 27 personal interviews with priests, and board members of the National Federation of Priests' Councils convened seven focus groups. Finally, with the help of many advisors, we wrote up our findings.

Independent of our research, the *Los Angeles Times* carried out a survey of American priests in the summer of 2002. They mailed out 5000 questionnaires to a random sample of priests and received 1,854 completions, for a 37% response rate. Many of the topics they asked were the same as we studied in our survey. Their lower response rate makes their findings less precise, yet the overall outlines of their results seem convincing. Also the relationships between variables in their data, which depend less on a high return rate, are credible. Generally the *Los Angeles Times* survey agrees with our findings, and specifically we will point out the comparisons in later chapters. (See *Los Angeles Times*, 20 and 21 October 2002.)

Throughout the project, our foremost goal was to gather and convey reliable information on the priesthood. The ultimate goal of the research program is to inform the practical decisions of church leaders, although we have left to others the task of spelling out practical recommendations. The National Federation of Priests' Councils asked six key Catholic leaders to give us their views of the research's implications; these six commentaries appear at the back of this book. Thus we co-authors have kept our own reflections to ourselves, except for a few statements which we have included in chapter 7.

The Sexual Abuse Crisis

Early in 2002, when our research was more than half finished, revelations about priests' sexual abuse of minors splashed across the nation's newspapers. The dramatic stories astonished and angered many Catholics. Long articles appeared in magazines, including cover stories in *Time* and *Newsweek*. Now in autumn 2002, as we are writing this book, the continuing sexual abuse crisis is being analyzed every day in reports in newspapers,

---

but the 24 included all of the large ones. Between April and July 2001 we sent out 1,200 questionnaires to a random sample of diocesan priests and received 858 back for a response rate of 71.5%, not counting undeliverable questionnaires. We mailed out 600 surveys to religious priests and received 421 back for a response rate of 70.2%. The 1985 and 1993 surveys were similar; the 1985 survey had 1,062 questionnaires for a 86.8% response rate, and the 1993 survey had 1186 for a 69.5% rate. In analyzing the data we used the same weighting formula employed in each survey beginning in 1970. The result is a true random sample of diocesan and religious priests.

magazines, and television. The new circumstances leave us, as researchers, in an awkward situation, since we are utilizing pre-2002 data to depict the identities, joys, and problems of post-2002 American Catholic priests. At the time of writing, we have no way to know the duration and outcome of the present-day turmoil; we are still swimming in the middle of it. Yet everyone agrees that after spring and summer 2002 the public perception of the priesthood changed, and priests themselves have made changes in their lives.

The only way for us to proceed under these circumstances, we believe, is to separate any discussion of the post-crisis priesthood from the body of our findings. We appraise as best we can what has changed as a result of the crisis in the epilogue of this book.

In chapter 1 we set forth the historical context of the priesthood today. In chapters 2 and 3 we introduce the new survey findings. Chapter 4 quotes at length the views of six of the priests we interviewed, to illustrate two distinct viewpoints. In chapter 5 we discuss specific issues facing priests today, including problems of the image and role of the priesthood, difficulties of conveying the Church's moral teachings, and sharing ministry with laity. This is followed by chapter 6, devoted to one specific concern: homosexual subcultures in seminaries, dioceses, and religious communities.

In chapter 7 we try to answer the questions as to why the theology of the priesthood has changed and what its effect will be on the Church. Finally, chapter 8 summarizes the principal practical recommendations made by our interviewees. The epilogue discusses the sexual abuse crisis, and it is followed by six commentaries.

Acknowledgements

During the whole project we benefited from outstanding help. We thank the National Federation of Priests' Councils for encouraging us and helping us make key decisions all along the way, especially the president, Robert Silva, the executive director, Bernard Stratman, and his assistant, Alan Szafraniec. We thank Dr. Jackson Carroll of Duke University Divinity School, director of Pulpit & Pew Research on Pastoral Leadership program, for including this study in the program.

Our advisory committee included Cletus Kiley, Melvin Blanchette, Michael Cronin, Ted Keating, Stephen Rossetti, Mark Hession, Dennis Beeman, Canice Connors, Ellen Doyle, Robert Leavitt, Robert Silva, Christa Klein, Lynn Levo, and Katarina Schuth. We also received valuable advice from Paul Philibert, Eugene Hemrick, James Garneau, Mark Latcovich, and Aniedi Okure.

We thank our interviewers, especially Tom Butler, Rick Krivanka, Carol Stanton, and James Ivers, plus our transcriber, Rosalind Grigsby. We thank the priests who convened focus groups: Douglas Doussan, Gregory Peatee, Kenneth Przybyla, Owen Korte, David Toups, Jack McEvilly, and Donald Sterling. We appreciate the good work by our research assistants at The Catholic University of America: Kounian Ding, Andrea Johnson, Ann Kasprzyk, and Florence Cole. We hope the result is of genuine value to the Catholic community.

D. H. and J. W.
Autumn 2002

Chapter 1

The American Priesthood after the 1960s

What did people go into the priesthood for in the 1950s and before that? The choices in my little Western town were policeman, fireman, and priest. I chose the priest—the best job!

—*A 59-year-old religious priest*

This book contains rich information on the state of the Catholic priesthood today. Nearly all of it was gathered in 2001 and 2002. In order to convey the new findings convincingly, we need to pause a moment at the outset to sketch the historical context. Today's priesthood does not exist in a vacuum—it is riding on some long-range social trends.

Future historians of American Catholicism, looking back at the twentieth century, are bound to identify the 1960s as a turning point. It was a time of rapid-fire change. Pope John XXIII gained the papacy at the end of 1958 and quickly convoked the Second Vatican Council, which ran from 1962 to 1965. His 1963 encyclical *Pacem in Terris* was received with acclaim throughout the world and was quickly established as "the most beloved text in modern Catholic thought" (Weigel, 1993:69). *Pacem in Terris* argued for new international institutions which would have authority to constrain the actions of individual states and could promote basic human rights worldwide.

John Fitzgerald Kennedy was elected president of the United States in 1960. The election of the nation's first Roman Catholic president in itself signaled a new era of acceptance and self-esteem among American Catholics. Their euphoria was unlike anything seen heretofore. The subtheme of Kennedy's election was "Catholics have arrived. We're as good as anybody else." Posters and wall hangings appeared in religious article stores showing the Pope on one side and John Kennedy on the other. The twin elections in Rome and here at home were affectionately nicknamed the "John-John" event.

The Second Vatican Council was a world-changing event that received constant coverage in the American secular press. The most important achievement for Americans, in the opinion of many historians, was the promulgation of *Dignitatus Humanae* (Declaration on Religious Liberty) in 1965. It aligned the Church with America's constitutional commitment to religious freedom and removed a festering source of suspicion over the Vatican's motives felt by many American leaders. The innovations that touched Catholics themselves most directly were the changes in the liturgy—the use of English, the singing of hymns, the repositioning of the priest so that he now faced the people throughout the Mass, and the elimination of kneeling at altar rails. In the years after the council, a great wave of institutional change swept the Church in the United States. Dioceses established priests' senates and personnel boards. In some places, team ministry replaced the pastor-curate relationships. Sisters became parish associates, and deacons and lay ministers were added. Ecumenical discussions were begun in numerous places. These innovations provoked two different reactions from Catholic clergy and laity alike: from some, joyful acceptance, and from others, determined resistance (Hennessy, 1981:315).

As if these changes were not enough, American society, both Catholic and non-Catholic, was then in the midst of political turmoil and cultural revolution. The civil rights movement, the anti-war movement, the women's movement, and the sexual revolution all took off in the 1960s. For everyone in America it was a decade of change; for Catholics there was a double dose.

The rapid-fire changes in the Church produced strong feelings among priests—in both directions. Young priests tended to rally behind the innovations as a source of new fervor and faith in the institution. By all accounts, they felt empowered to find new ways to celebrate the faith and to reach out to non-believers. There was even a sense that the definition of the priesthood itself would soon be changing—including acceptance of optional celibacy for diocesan priests. As a result, when the Vatican put the brakes on institutional changes at the end of the decade and especially when Pope Paul VI issued *Humanae Vitae* (On the Regulation of Births) in 1968, a hush fell over the priesthood. The Church was not going to change its long-held teaching about artificial birth control after all, and furthermore it became clear that the Church itself was not going to change. The priests were admonished to toe the line. (Some observers, including sociologist Andrew Greeley, believe that *Humanae Vitae* had as much emotional impact on the American priesthood as the council itself.)

The End of the Immigrant Era

Observers in the 1970s and 1980s called the 1960s "the end of the immigrant era" in American Catholicism. In strictly demographic terms this was true, though it would not remain so. More accurately, it was the "end of the *first* immigrant era." Most Catholic immigrants arrived from Europe beginning about 1860 and continuing until immigration was curtailed by Congress in the early 1920s. The highpoint of immigration was 1900-1910. Hence by 1965, most American Catholics were well-settled third and fourth generation Americans, and very few were new immigrants. It was true that the immigrant era was over—temporarily. Nobody knew in 1960 that the McCarran-Walter Act would soon be amended (in 1965) to eliminate national quotas, opening the gates to a second major wave of Catholic immigration.

After World War II, American Catholics moved up and out. More attended college than ever before, partly with help from the G.I. Bill. They moved from their old urban neighborhoods into the mushrooming new suburbs. Catholic parish life inevitably changed when suburban Catholics found themselves living side-by-side with Protestants and worshiping in newly-built modern churches that looked just like the other churches in their subdivisions. Economic and demographic trends like this one are slow and often unnoticed, yet they have subtle effects on all social institutions—including parishes and including the decisions young men make about entering the priesthood.

By the 1970s, about three-fourths of American Catholics felt that they had "made it" in America. Only the immigrants arriving in the second great wave—mostly Latinos—remained on the social and economic margins.

The Priesthood after the Council

The years after Vatican II were a time of uncertainty for priests. On balance, they had as much to lose as to gain from the council's actions. Its emphasis on the "priesthood of the laity" and on the church as "the people of God" demanded that the role and identity of the priest be reconsidered. The council's *Presbyterorum Ordinis* (Decree on the Ministry and Life of Priests) disappointed many because it lacked a clear theology of the priesthood. Many priests now felt confused, since their earlier role and their secure status were lost; large numbers resigned between 1968 and 1974. Historian Scott Appleby concluded that "there was a widespread loss of confidence in parochial ministry in the 1960s" (1990:59).

The earlier model of the priesthood, entrenched for two or three centuries, was severely challenged. It was named the "cultic model" by priest theologian and historian James Bacik because of the central importance it places on worship and sacraments (Bacik, 1999). That is, it saw the priest as mainly a provider of sacraments. This sacred role was underlined by the priest's distinctive lifestyle. The priest remained celibate, lived in a rectory, brought the sacraments to his parishioners as much as possible, wore distinctive clerical garb, and kept a certain distance from everyday social life. In the era of the cultic priesthood, parishioners placed their pastor on a pedestal, as a mediator between themselves and God. Priests administered large Catholic parishes, many of which had their own schools. Solely by virtue of their office, priests were accorded high status and influence in the immigrant communities (Bacik, p. 51). They saw themselves as a separate clerical caste.

Seminaries fostered this concept of the priest as a "man set apart." In keeping with it, both minor seminaries (high school and college level) and major seminaries (theology level) employed a paramilitary approach to formation, especially during the 1930s, 1940s, and 1950s. It was a highly regimented system designed to produce a uniform product—"soldiers in the church militant" (Appleby, 1990:9). It emphasized obedience to hierarchical authority, formalism in spiritual exercises and devotions, conservatism in doctrine, and self-control in all things. Seminary life was regimented from morning to night, with definite times for rising and eating, assigned seats in classrooms and dining rooms, and lights out at 9:30 or 10:30 p.m. Students were not allowed to leave campus without permission, and all reading material, religious or secular, had to be approved by the administrators. In some seminaries, radios and newspapers were forbidden. Seminaries were "total institutions" in the sociological sense of the word, designed to build character, obedience, spirituality, and camaraderie.

A seminary system that seems intolerably regimented by today's standards was, nevertheless, a welcome step up for thousands of boys from immigrant families. Appleby tells what seminaries meant to many:

> The simple fact that the seminary provided three square meals a day guaranteed happy memories of their time there for many depression-era seminarians. The seminary also encouraged camaraderie (while discouraging personal attachments), organized recreation, an advanced education, and a structured lifestyle—no mean accomplishment in the 1930s and early '40s. And the Roman priesthood meant job security and lofty social standing in the majority of towns and cities in the United States. . . . In the same way, the religious world of preconciliar Roman Catholicism, the hallmarks of which were moral clarity and theological certainty, promised spiritual security of a sort to the man who had given everything to follow Christ. (1990:22)

This cultic model of the priesthood was already beginning to change prior to the council, but the conciliar documents gave the main push. A new model of priesthood arose, sometimes called the "servant-leader model." This vision, summarized by historian Robert Schwartz, saw priests as sharing the human condition with all of the baptized (Schwartz, 1989). It received its energy both from the council and also from the democratic spirit of the '60s. It de-emphasized the priest's separateness and special status, placing himself in the twin roles of servant and leader within the community of believers. The Church itself was now defined, following the council teaching, as the people of God, a community in which the clergy-laity distinction was much less important. A priest's distinctiveness now came from his spiritual and institutional leadership within the community, not just as a matter of ontological[1] difference coming from holy orders. Moreover, the earlier concept of "ministry" as the domain solely of priests was now redefined as the work of all baptized Christians, both priests and laity. Now nobody had to become a priest to do ministry.

The servant-leader model called for different training and different sensitivities. Because it included *leadership* of the community, in practice this meant leadership of the faithful in parish life requiring collaboration with laity and, specifically, with cadres of professional lay ministers helping to administer schools and parishes. The line separating the priest from the laity was blurred. This was made vividly clear, in symbolic terms, by the removal of altar rails in many churches and, later, by the practice of inviting lay eucharistic ministers (who help to serve the bread and wine of Eucharist) to step into the sanctuary space and move around the altar. Before Vatican II this would have been unthinkable.

Inevitably, the priests in any diocese tended to divide into those embracing and those resisting the new vision.

> In many of these [dioceses] the presbyterate was divided into various factions according to the approach taken toward reform—and the expectations of competing groups as to how far and how rapidly the reforms should proceed. The controversy, and the accompanying sense of "the priesthood under siege," was sustained precisely because the drama of the council and its aftermath had aroused in many the expectation that the priesthood would be significantly reformed. For some this meant the introduction of optional celibacy; for others it simply meant a greater share in ecclesial self-determination. For still others, it meant the right to publicly question the teaching of the Church. (Appleby, p. 76)

Older, pre-Vatican II-era priests generally found the servant-leader model baffling and threatening. They argued that it changed their whole

---

[1] The theology of ontology refers to an understanding of the basic nature of a person. Ordination produces a permanent ontological change that makes the priest different from the laity.

way of life, and anyway, they were never trained for it. They had not become priests for this. Young priests adapted much more readily. By 1970, young and old held vastly different views of what a priest is and what he should do. For example, in the 1970 Greeley survey, priests were asked if they agreed or disagreed with this statement: "Ordination confers on the priest a new status or a permanent character which makes him essentially different from the laity within the church." Of all priests age 35 or younger, 52% agreed. Of all 66 or older, 95% agreed. On the statement, "I feel that I am most a priest when I am saying Mass and hearing confessions," 56% of the priests 35 or younger agreed, compared with 93% of those 66 or older. Young and old lived with different visions of what they were doing.

Younger priests in the post-Vatican II era faced a choice. Either they needed to buy into the dominant servant-leader model or suffer marginalization by other priests. The tensions of the years 1965 to 1975 produced a bulge of resignations from the priesthood. For those who embraced the new model and strove to embody it in parish life, it was a source of joy and hope that the Church was entering a new era. They prayed that the change would be permanent.

Yet it was not to be. Already by the 1980s many newly ordained priests wanted a change, and they adopted elements of the cultic model of priesthood. Bacik describes what happened:

> A few years ago, commentators were predicting the gradual demise of [the cultic] model as older priests retired and died. But now it is clear that many recently ordained priests favor the cultic model and have adopted the traditional clerical lifestyle. They see themselves as part of a separate clerical caste and resist the more collaborative approaches associated with the reforms of the Second Vatican Council. They generally espouse a traditional classical theology, which separates them from the priests who are more attuned to the pluralism of contemporary theology. Older priests, who have worked their way through the profound changes of the council, often find it unsettling to be confronted with a new vision of a style and approach they left behind. Younger traditionalists often are not comfortable with clergy who have tried to adapt their ministry to the needs of the modern world. Unfortunately, these tensions can lead to serious polarization within a diocese and great stress and confusion within parishes. (1999:54)

By the early 1980s, tensions began to emerge over the models of priesthood. A different model came into favor—which some saw as preconciliar and others saw as a new synthesis, but which in any event was close to the cultic model. Older priests were frustrated. Why were the new priests so drawn to the model sidelined by Vatican II? Did they not grasp the vision of the council and the post-conciliar generation? In fairness to the new priests, we must clarify that the documents of Vatican II were not uniform or decisive in preferring the servant-leader model. Support for both models is clear in the conciliar documents. Yet the post-Vatican II priests were dismayed. The result is a polarization over the theology of the priesthood (and more broadly, proper ecclesiology) that pits older and younger priests against each other to this day. Each faction stands firmly and confidently on a well-established theology of priesthood and Church. The shift in ecclesiology beginning in the 1980s is visible in survey research, as we will see below.

Sexuality and Sexual Misconduct

As if the turmoil of the Council and the shortage of seminarians were not enough to deal with, new controversies erupted in the 1990s. Two are important to mention here—the debate about homosexuality and the problem of sexual abuse of children.

Homosexual men have been in the priesthood since time immemorial, even if this was not publicly acknowledged. The official theology of the priesthood holds that celibacy is a gift of God, and that once a man is ordained, sexuality of whatever kind will not be allowed to interfere with his devotion and his ministry. Of course, all humans have sexual urges, but, so the teaching holds, they can be managed, controlled, and sublimated in ways that contribute to ministry. From this point of view, the difference between heterosexuals and homosexuals was not enough to worry about: all priests were to lead celibate lives whatever their sexual orientation.

In the 1990s, several voices raised questions about homosexuality among seminarians and priests. The topic was handled gingerly by church decision makers. One concern was whether homosexual seminarians in some schools tended to separate themselves from other students and thus formed a distinct subculture—even becoming dominant in the student culture of some seminaries in a way that left heterosexuals feeling intimidated. In a few schools there were charges and counter-charges about how members of the faculty condoned such a separate subculture or even took part in it.

A second issue was whether the Catholic priesthood was acquiring a public reputation—whether deservedly or not—as a haven for homosexuals, so that all priests, regardless of their actual sexual orientation, would feel that the general public suspected they were homosexuals. It was argued that an association of priesthood with homosexuality would weaken the authority of priests generally. In chapter 6 of this book we address the issue of homosexual subcultures, but nobody has accurate information on how many homosexuals are now in the priesthood. How many are sexually active? Is the number of active homosexuals the minority that it seems to be? Is anyone certain? Does it matter? More clarification is needed on these questions.

The Decline in Numbers

The bishops who took part in the Second Vatican Council were proud of their work. The majority agreed with the new directions and anticipated a strong future for the Church. They were surprised, therefore, when the numbers of new seminarians, priests, and nuns took a clear downturn a few years later. During the 1970s and 1980s many seminaries closed. The decline in seminary students has continued until the present day.

In 2001 there were 46 theologates still in operation in the United States (including American-sponsored seminaries in Louvain, Belgium and in Rome), with 3,483 priesthood candidates enrolled. This was a major drop from 8,159 candidates in 1968 (Froehle and Gautier, 2000). By the year 2001, only eight high school seminaries remained open, with an enrollment of 816. By 2001, 15 freestanding and 24 collaborative (that is, as part of a Catholic college) college seminaries remained open, with an enrollment of 1,594. The number of ordinations dropped from 771 in 1975 to 533 in 1985, 511 in 1995, 442 in 2000, and 509 in 2001. The downward trend in ordinations was about 3% to 5% per decade during the 1980s and 1990s.

In 2001 there were 30,223 diocesan priests and 14,968 religious priests, according to the *Official Catholic Directory*, for a total of 45,191. This compares with 57,317 in 1985, or a decline of about 12% to 14% per decade. The ranks of religious priests are thinning faster than those of diocesan priests—about 20% per decade, compared with about 9% for diocesan priests (CARA Report, 2001). The number of sisters declined from 179,954 in 1965 to 78,094 in 2001, or about 15% to 17% per decade. Religious brothers have similarly declined.

Meanwhile, the numbers of deacons and lay ministers were rising. The Vatican Council reintroduced the office of permanent deacon, and soon American dioceses were training and ordaining them. There were 12,851 in 2001. Even more important in the long run was the increase in professional lay ecclesial ministers in parishes. Most commonly they are directors of religious education, pastoral associates, directors of music, and youth ministers. Their numbers rose after the 1980s, and a 1997 survey estimated that 24,146 were in service. This number is close to the estimated 27,000 priests active in parish ministry. Between 1992 and 1997 the numbers of lay ministers rose by 35%, and in the next few years it will grow to exceed the number of priests working in parishes. The future will see additional increases. The 1997 survey found that professional lay ministers today are about 82% female, and the average age is 50 (Murnion and DeLambo, 1999).

Changes in the Catholic Community

The number of Catholics in the United States has risen continually over the past century. In 1970 the estimated number was 47 million, and in 2000 it was about 61 million. We should expect continued growth in Catholic membership partly due to the new immigration, which is heavily Catholic, and partly due to the higher fertility levels of recent immigrants. We should plan ahead with an expectation of 8% to 12% growth per decade. The priest-to-laity ratio is rising and will continue to do so. In the year 2000 it stood at 1: 1,257, up from 1:652 in 1950.

The levels of education and affluence have risen in the past and will continue rising in the future. In the mid-1920s, about 6% of all American Catholics had college degrees, and in 1980 it was 28% (Schmalzbauer, 2000). This increase is not unique to Catholics; indeed it occurred among Protestants to a similar extent.

Barriers separating American religious communities have gradually fallen since World War II, and we should expect even more to fall in the future. Surveys measuring anti-Semitism and anti-Catholicism have shown that both have receded among Americans generally since the 1960s. The American tradition of religious toleration and goodwill, which has been constant in the last half-century, got new impetus from the terrorist attacks of September 11, 2001. After the attack, American leaders from the president on down called on everyone to show goodwill to religious groups other than their own—especially toward Muslims, and judging from the thousands of local religious dialogues, forums, and cultural events in the following months, this summons was answered in communities across the nation. Today more than ever, Americans are being urged to show acceptance and goodwill to all religious groups. An important by-product of this emphasis will be greater ecumenism and less insistence within the Catholic community on maintaining strict boundaries between those inside and those outside the community. It is reasonable to expect an era of blurrier boundaries as well as increased concern about Catholic identity, both institutional and personal (D'Antonio, et al., 2001).

Overall Changes in American Society

What we said about the impact of the 1960s on American Catholics also holds true, though to a lesser extent, for all Americans: the 1960s were a turning point and a launching pad for further social innovation. Numerous social trends have taken place since then, too many for us to catalog here. However, four of them deserve mention because of their pertinence in understanding the shifting context of priestly ministry.

1. Greater Pluralism and Cultural Awareness

Americans today are more aware of the different religious groups in our nation, and more aware of world religions, than ever before. Catholics have become better acquainted with the practices of Protestants and Jews, and vice versa. At the end of the twentieth century everyone has become more familiar with Muslims.

The level of education of Americans rose during the last four decades. In 1960, only about 8% of adults (age 25 or older) had a college degree, but in 1998 it was 24% (Caplow, et al., 2001:53).

One indicator of cultural awareness is how much individuals communicate with persons outside their immediate family or community. Telephones have now penetrated almost all American households; in 1940 about 36% of households had them; in 1960, 78%, and in 2000, 94% (Putnam, 2000: 167). Television sets increased in numbers, such that by the late 1990s, three-quarters of all U.S. homes had more than one set. Internet use rose until 51% of all households in 1999 were connected (Putnam:223).

An indicator of cultural contact is the amount of travel abroad by Americans. International travel skyrocketed after the 1960s. In 1960 about 2 million Americans went abroad (not counting trips to Canada and Mexico); in 1980 it was 8 million, and in 1997 it was 22 million (Caplow, et al.: 130).

Under these conditions, no religious community can prevent outside influences of all kinds, beneficent or not, from influencing its members—especially the young.

2. Declining Trust in Institutions

Public trust in institutions has been monitored by Gallup polls since 1973. Figure 1.1 summarizes the trends. It shows a long-term withdrawal of trust in most institutions—but not in the military, which rose in public confidence during this period. (The figure does not show all of the institutions studied by Gallup polls.) Organized religion has enjoyed a high level of public confidence the whole time, but its rating dropped a moderate amount after the early 1980s.

Public opinion surveys have also shown a decline in generalized trust in other people. The most common measure is a survey question asking the respondent to choose between two options: "Most people can be trusted," and "You can't be too careful in dealing with people." This question has been asked in dozens of American surveys, and the result has been a gradual decrease in persons choosing "Most people can be trusted." In 1964, 54% said that most people can be trusted, and in 1995, 35%. Another repeatedly asked question was, "How much of the time do you trust the government in Washington to do the right thing?" The percentage saying "Just about always" or "Most of the time" dropped from 76% in 1964 to 25% in 1995 (Morin and Balz, 1996).

Figure 1.1
How much confidence do you, yourself, have in each one of these institutions in American society? Gallup polls, 1973–2000.
(Percent saying "a great deal" or "quite a lot")

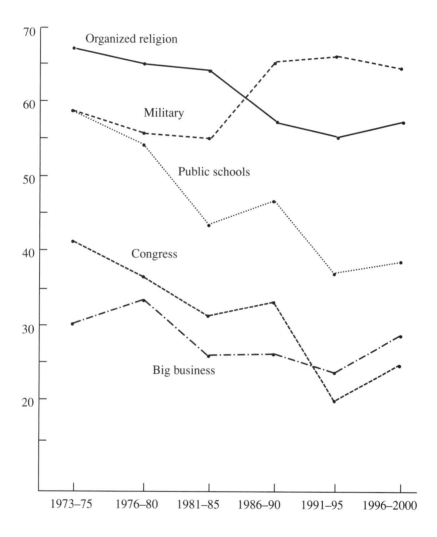

Source: *Sourcebook of Criminal Justice Statistics*, 2000.

3. Sexual behavior became more open and more widely tolerated

Sexual openness became more prevalent in the early 1960s, as shown by the growth of *Playboy* and other men's magazines. Demands for more personal freedoms in the 1960s and the new availability of birth control pills had an effect. The trend continued, and it included greater tolerance of premarital sex and changing gender roles for both men and women.

The feminist movement gained momentum in the 1960s and continued growing all during this time. It emphasized self-determination of women and re-examination of traditional gender roles. The number of women in the job force rose. A review of sociological research on attitudes from 1960 to 1988 found that during these three decades the view that adults must get married and have children grew weaker, while tolerance of divorce and support for changes in traditional gender roles grew (Thornton, 1989). In annual polls of first-year college students, the percentage saying that "activities of married women are best confined to home and family" fell from 48% in 1970 to 28% in 1999 (U.S. Census, 2000:187).

Youth experimented more and more with sexual behavior. The percentage of 19-year-old women who have had sexual experience rose from 29% in 1960 to 51% in 1980 and to 74% in 1991 (Caplow, p. 71). In the General Social Survey (a reliable series of attitude polls), the percentage saying that sex before marriage was "not wrong at all" rose from 27% in 1972 to 44% in 1996 (Caplow, p. 77). Cohabitation of unmarried couples increased.

These trends in sexual attitudes and behavior took place among Catholics as well as other Americans. Many of the trends are contrary to official Catholic moral teachings about sexuality and marriage, thus increasing the distance between Catholic laity and church positions.

4. Organizations began to use more collegiality and less hierarchy

This trend is not easily measured in surveys, since it took place in specific organizations. It is most vividly seen in the best-selling books about management and human relations, such as *Theory Z*, by William Ouchi (1981) and *In Search of Excellence*, by Thomas Peters and Robert Waterman (1988). The message has been that management of large organizations can best be done by consultation, collaboration across levels, teamwork, and reduction of line authority.

Clearly the social and cultural context for priestly ministry has changed greatly since the 1960s. The effects are gradual, often going unnoticed until some surprising occurrence forces us to take notice—and then sociologists are brought forth telling the public that unnoticed social trends are a major explanation. The trends have affected the lives of priests, as we will see in chapter 2.

Chapter 2

Characteristics of Priests in 2001

I think the priesthood, because of the shortage of priests, is getting identified with the sacramental. We're becoming sacramental machines and I think that is a terrible thing to be reduced to in the priesthood.

—*A 49-year-old diocesan priest*

We now turn to the findings of our 2001 priest survey. In this chapter we look at priests' ages and ministry positions, as well as their attitudes about their seminary training, satisfactions in their priesthood, problems in everyday life, and future plans.

We begin with age. The average age of priests has been rising, both because a smaller number of men are entering seminary than previously and because students are coming to seminary at a later age than before. In 2001 the average age of priests (including retired priests) was 60. For diocesan priests it was 59 and for religious, 64. (For details see table A.1 in the appendix.) Twenty-six percent of the diocesan and 39% of the religious priests were 70 or over. Figure 2.1 illustrates the age distribution.

In the *Los Angeles Times* survey of priests, the average age was found to be 61. The survey found that 88% of the priests were non-Latino whites, a figure higher than the white percentage among lay Catholics.

The average age of these men's ordination was 29. Bear in mind that this is the overall average for all priests today of all ages. Recently the average age of ordination has risen; those ordained in 2000 and 2001 averaged age 36 at their ordination. By contrast, back in 1970 the average age was 27. Another difference: many fewer seminarians today attended high school seminary or college seminary (in past years called "minor seminary") than earlier; instead, many more attended Catholic or public high schools and colleges. Few priests today are in their twenties or early thirties; in the 2001 sample only 4% were age 35 or younger, compared with 22% in 1970.

Figure 2.1
Age of Sample Members
(In percents)

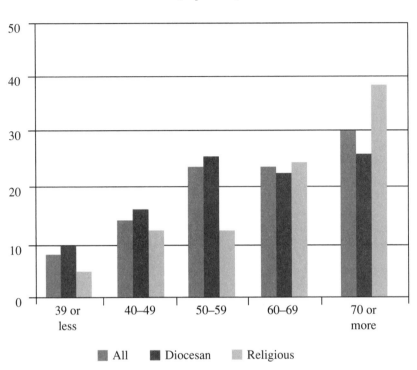

The proportion of retired priests in the sample grew fivefold—from 3% in 1970 to 16% in 2001. The changing age distribution from 1970 to 2001 is depicted in figure 2.2, and changes in the ages of ordination are shown in figure 2.3.

What positions do the priests currently hold? As noted, some are retired—19% of the diocesan and 12% of the religious. Forty-eight percent of the diocesan priests and 12% of the religious priests are pastors; 13% of the diocesan and 10% of the religious are parochial vicars. Twenty percent of the religious priests have educational apostolates. (For details see table A.1 in the appendix.)

Criticism of Seminary Education

The priests in our survey were fairly critical of their seminary education. Of the five possible criticisms mentioned in the questionnaire, the one most commonly agreed with was "few attempts were made to help the

Figure 2.2
Ages of Priests

DIOCESAN

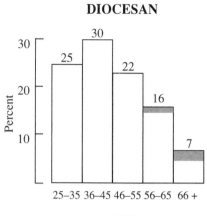

1970

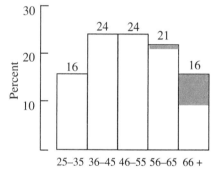

1985

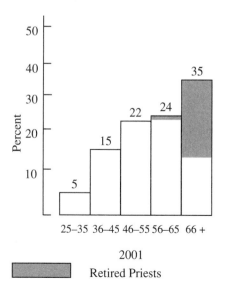

2001

RELIGIOUS

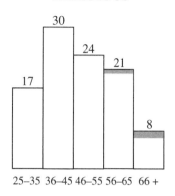

1970

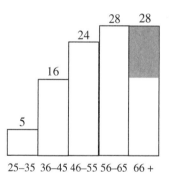

1985

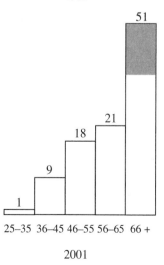

2001

Retired Priests

Figure 2.3
Ages at Ordination
(In percents)

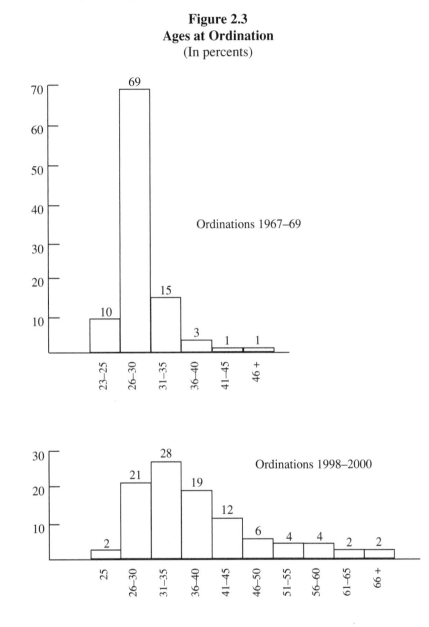

Source: National Opinion Research Corporation and Catholic University data.

seminarian learn how to deal with people." Generally, the priests' criticisms concerned training in the human and practical aspects of seminary preparation more than the academic coursework (see table 2.1).

Table 2.1
Criticisms of Seminary Training (In percents)

	All	Diocesan	Religious
Do you agree or disagree with each of the following statements about your seminary experience? (Percent who agree)			
1. Most of the courses were too theoretically oriented.	39	41	34
2. Too many courses were superficially presented.	27	29	24
3. Many of the courses were irrelevant to modern pastoral needs.	42	44	36
4. Few attempts were made to help the seminarian learn how to deal with people.	59	63	52
5. The seminary was too sheltered from the mainstream of life, intellectual and social.	47	48	45

Older priests were much more critical than younger ones, especially in two areas: lack of help in learning to deal with people and being sheltered from life's mainstream. The difference between older and younger priests' responses was noticeable on item number four, which criticizes seminaries for not helping students learn how to deal with people. Seventy-three percent of those ages 56–65 agreed that they did not get enough help with this while only 29% of 25–35-year-olds agreed.[1] On the fifth item, criticizing

[1] A statistical note is needed here. Throughout this book we report no significance tests on data tables, solely to make the text more readable. Nevertheless we have carried out significance tests for all the trends and comparisons, and in the text we write about "trends" or "differences" only when they are significant at the .05 level. This is the normal convention in data analysis. If any trends or differences are too weak to be

seminaries for being too sheltered, the percentages agreeing in the five age groups ranged from a low of 15% for the youngest group to a high of 64% for the oldest groups, with criticism getting stronger with age. Young priests made relatively few criticisms of their seminary training.[2]

Questions about seminary education were asked repeatedly beginning with the 1970 survey, and the level of criticism has dropped over this time. To illustrate, figure 2.4 compares 1970 responses with 2001 responses averaged on the five statements of criticism. (We removed the 1985 figures for the sake of simplicity.) All five criticisms in 2001 were lower by 15 or 20 percentage points from their levels in 1970. The decline in criticism could be a product of improved seminary training over the 30-year period, or it could be due to recent seminarians being less skeptical and more ac-

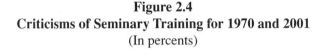

Figure 2.4
Criticisms of Seminary Training for 1970 and 2001
(In percents)

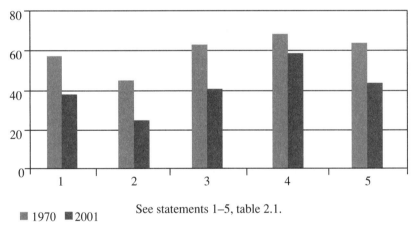

■ 1970   ■ 2001   See statements 1–5, table 2.1.

---

significant at .05, we describe them as too small to be reliable. In the total sample of 1,279, differences in responses to separate questions which are less than 5 percentage points are too small to be significant and should be seen as nonexistent. For example, if when assessing sources of priestly satisfaction, responses to satisfaction A and to satisfaction B were less than 5 percentage points different, the two should be seen as tied. In comparing subgroups such as diocesan versus religious priests, differences of less than 7 percentage points should be seen as nonexistent.

[2] We looked at the number of years since ordination to determine if it was time of ordination, not age, that affected responses. The pattern of responses was not affected by the number of years since ordination. Thus, we can accurately speak of "age differences" as an indicator of change throughout the book.

cepting of authority. Probably both are true to some extent, but from this survey we have no way to assess the impact of each factor.

From historical accounts, we are certain that seminary training has improved since 1970. Numerous innovations have been made, including pastoral years during theology, clinical pastoral training, less military-style discipline, more personal freedoms, and smaller class sizes. We are also certain that students back in the late 1960s were more rebellious against church structures in general than they are today; indeed the National Federation of Priests' Councils was born in 1968 out of the unrest felt by many priests. Again, while both seminary changes and shifting attitudes of students very likely contributed to the higher contentment with seminary formation today, our own guess based on our experiences is that the changes in seminaries account for most of the drop in criticism.

Sources of Satisfaction

For its ministry to be vibrant and effective, the Church needs priests who feel energetic and well-supported in their ministry. Do priests today feel more encouraged—or more demoralized—than in the past three decades? Table 2.2[3] gives the responses to a question asking about sources of satisfaction in the life and work of priests. It shows the six most important sources. (The complete questionnaire included a series of eleven choices; see table A.2 in the appendix.[4]) Clearly in first place is "joy of administering the sacraments and presiding over the liturgy." In second place is "the satisfaction of preaching the Word." These functions are similar: both take place in the Mass, both are personal performances in public, and both are sacred duties that may be carried out only by priests. They are the occasions when the priest is in his most unique priestly role, so it should be no surprise that they are the most satisfying of all. Other research has found this to be the case as well (for example, Walsh, et al., 1995).

Following these two in importance are "opportunity to work with many people and be a part of their lives" and "being a part of a community of Christians." Thus, personal relationships and community bonds are the second most important source of satisfaction; usually such relationships occur in a parish, but it could be in another religious grouping.

---

[3] The questionnaire listed eleven possible sources of satisfaction and asked the men to rate them in importance. Results of the top six are shown in the order of their reported importance, not in the order in which the questionnaire presented them.

[4] The appendix contains tables with responses to several series of questions not discussed in the text of this book. The topics include the level of confidence the priest has in Catholic leadership at the diocesan, national, and international level; level in interest in presbyteral councils; and a comparison between priests and other professional persons.

Table 2.2
Six Sources of Satisfaction (In percents)

	All	Diocesan	Religious
There are many sources of satisfaction in the life and work of priest. Would you indicate how important each of the following is as a source of satisfaction to you? (Percent saying "this is of great importance")			
1. Joy of administering the sacraments and presiding over the liturgy.	90	94	82
2. The satisfaction of preaching the Word.	80	80	79
3. Opportunity to work with many people and be a part of their lives.	67	65	72
4. Being part of a community of Christians who are working together to share the good news of the gospel.	62	59	68
5. Opportunity to exercise intellectual and creative abilities.	55	53	59
6. Spiritual security that results from responding to the divine call.	51	51	51

The sixth-ranked item, "spiritual security that results from responding to the divine call," describes a dimension of the priestly life that is on another level from specific roles or responsibilities—it is the feeling that solely by being a priest one is responding to God in ways that offer spiritual assurance for one's life now and in eternity. This spiritual comfort underlies everyday life and can provide staying power even when frustrations are at their worst. This is suggested by the fact that it was rated much higher than "respect that comes to the priestly office" (rated tenth of the eleven satisfactions). Respect for the priestly office from society is relatively less crucial. Other sources of satisfaction (not shown in table 2.2) are, on average, less important, including "living the common life with like-minded priests," "administering the work of the Church," "respect that comes to the priestly office," and "engaging in efforts at social reform."

Diocesan and religious priests differed in their responses to these questions in six areas. Using as a rule of thumb a 10-point minimum difference, diocesan priests rated four items higher than religious priests: (1) administering the sacraments, (2) the challenge of being the leader of the Christian community, (3) the satisfaction of parish administration, and (4) respect that comes to the priestly office. (See table A.2 in the appendix for details.) Religious priests, by contrast, rated (1) the well-being that comes from living with like-minded priests and (2) engaging in social reform as both of more importance than diocesan priests rated them.

Priests' ages appear to be of no significance concerning the six sources of satisfaction, with one exception—"spiritual security that results from responding to the divine call." The oldest age category—66 or older—gave spiritual security a much higher rating than all the other age groups. Spiritual security of this kind means more to the oldest men than to the others.

All of the questions about satisfaction listed in table 2.2 were asked (except item #2) in every survey since 1970. Only one clear-cut trend occurred over the 30-year period: on the first item, "joy of administering the sacraments and presiding over the liturgy," the percentage saying it was very important rose from 80 to 90. This points to a growing importance of sacramental ministry to priests ordained more recently.

In the *Los Angeles Times* survey of priests, the clear majority said they are satisfied with their lives. The specific question asked, "Are you satisfied or dissatisfied with the way your life as a priest is going these days?" Seventy percent said "very satisfied," 21% said "somewhat satisfied," and 6% said "somewhat dissatisfied" or "very dissatisfied." This question is different from the questions in our 2001 survey, but the results agree in indicating a high level of satisfaction.

Satisfactions in the priestly life were not only measured by the survey but also discussed at length in our interviews and focus groups. The following excerpts present statements made by several priests. The quotes included here were chosen because they reflected the opinions of the majority of the priests interviewed; we have avoided minority or idiosyncratic attitudes. (Throughout the book we have followed this practice.)

A 37-year-old diocesan priest:

> The best part of my experiences has been a lot of the sacramental work. Saying Mass, hearing confessions. Confessions are wonderful. Being sacramentally present to the people, being priest for the people. Trying to be Christ present to them, that's always a good, wonderful thing. And to be able to point the way to God and say, "Look, this is the way we all need to go as spiritual people." And preaching too. That's all wonderful.

A 36-year-old diocesan priest:

> I love being a priest, wouldn't want to do anything else. I can't believe I ever did want to do anything else. What's good is the notable influence that you have on people's lives, and what's bad is the notable influence you can have on people's lives [laughing]. One thing I've really learned is that people may have higher expectations of a priest as far as how someone is going to treat them than they would someone who is not a priest. They expect kindness from everyone, but they expect more kindness from a priest.

A 40-year-old diocesan priest:

> I remember hearing confessions for the first time. It was the most humbling thing, and realizing that you can never be prepared for someone to come in and bare their soul to you. I went in there like, "Yeah, I can't wait to do this. I'm going to sit in my confessional and I'll really help people." And when I walked out of there I thought, "I never want to go back into that booth, that confessional, again." I prayed over that. "Okay, God, give me the courage to say what needs to be said. Give me the wisdom to speak your words." But it becomes a very humbling experience. And you can practice in the seminary as many times as you want, but when somebody truly comes in baring their soul, it's different. And that was probably the most difficult thing, ministry-wise, that I had to do. You just don't realize how people really come in and bare their soul to you.

The survey asked several questions about happiness. First, we asked a standard question about happiness that has been used in dozens of polls over the past forty years: "Taking all things together, how would you say things are these days—would you say you're very happy, pretty happy, or not too happy?" The wording of the question and the responses are standard. (See table 2.3, first item.) This allows us to compare our results with other polls. The priests in our survey reported the same level of happiness, on average, as was reported during the 1996–2000 period by college-educated American men (ages 30–79) overall. Of the priests in our sample, 45% said they were "very happy," while the average of these American men in polls was 43%. If we limit the American sample to men ages 30–79 with a *graduate degree,* their level of "very happy" responses was about six percentage points higher than all men with a college degree or more.[5] We conclude that priests have the same level of happiness and morale as other educated American men their age. If there was in fact a "morale cri-

---

[5] Data were from the General Social Survey gathered annually by the National Opinion Research Center. This is a well-known high-quality survey measuring indicators of American attitudes and values. In the General Social Survey responses, levels of happiness of American men changed little between the early 1970s and the late 1990s.

sis" in the priesthood in 2001—and we have heard this assertion many times—the response of the priests certainly does not show it. Possibly the situation has changed with the sex abuse crisis in 2002.

Table 2.3
General Question on Happiness (In percents)

	All	**Diocesan**	**Religious**
Taking all things together, how would you say things are these days—would you say you're very happy, pretty happy, or not too happy?			
Very happy	45	44	46
Pretty happy	49	49	49
Not too happy	6	7	5

As mentioned, the question in table 2.3 was asked in 1970, 1985, and 1993, as well as 2001. The percentage responding that they were "very happy" rose steadily, from 28% in 1970 to 39% in 1985, then 39% again in 1993, and finally 45% in 2001 (see figure 2.5). The rise in the total samples was largely due to a large rise in happiness among younger priests—the 25–35-year-olds and the 36–45-year-olds. Older priests also rose in their reported level of happiness, but only slightly. Whereas younger priests had lower happiness ratings in the earlier surveys, in 2001 their responses were the same as those from older priests.

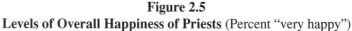

Figure 2.5
Levels of Overall Happiness of Priests (Percent "very happy")

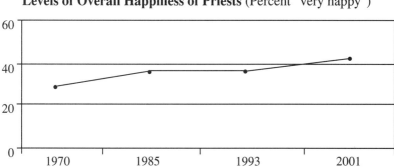

Research from the 1960s helps to answer the question as to why, at that time, younger priests were relatively unhappy. It was largely due to feelings of being unduly subordinated and underutilized while serving as curates. In a survey of curates in 1966, Joseph Fichter found that many were downcast because of poor pastor-curate relations and an excess of routine duties that did not at all require seminary education:

> The following complaint by a curate in his late thirties from an eastern diocese is paraphrased by others: "The daily work in the parish is piddling for the most part: writing Mass cards, unlocking the school door for the Boy Scout troop, copying baptismal records. The pastor always lays stress on being here to answer the door and the phone, and this is the main service to the parishioners. This is what he wants, but as a function for one's life career it is a maddening process. We cannot act on our own initiative because he controls us and the entire operation of the parish too closely." (Fichter, 1968:132)

A 1966 curate in his twenties:

> It is difficult to sit in a rectory waiting for sick calls that never come. About all you can do is to think of some way of pushing yourself into special work. It's almost the only way to use your talents while you're still young. I don't think our bishops have any idea of the frustration felt by their young priests. (p. 132)

The 1960s problems of overregimentation and underutilization are gone. Today, the fact that the number of young priests is so limited and the shorter period of service before promotion to a pastorate or other office mean that young priests are rarely left feeling like doormen or secretaries. Some investigators have suggested that the small number of young priests today might itself be demoralizing to the newly ordained. But we can see that small numbers do bring some benefits. Newly ordained priests feel needed today, and they are happier and more energized than they were three decades ago.

We asked the priests about eight specific conditions often mentioned by observers of priests as affecting their happiness. How important did the priests consider these conditions? Table 2.4 lists them in the order of their importance in the priests' responses. In first place, clearly ahead of all others, was "your sacramental and liturgical ministry," in agreement with priests' sources of satisfaction (table 2.2). Priests were moderately happy with their living situation, present financial situation, and personal spiritual life. They were less happy about other items, listed at the bottom of the table. Three of the bottom four items have to do with church governance in the diocese, institute, or international level, and lowest of all—in reality, a great frustration—was the image of the Catholic priesthood in the American public today. The relatively poor image of the priesthood in the American public, exacerbated by the sexual misconduct crisis, is probably a burden on these men.

Table 2.4

Happiness with Specific Conditions (In percents)

	All	**Diocesan**	**Religious**
How happy are you with the following specific conditions? (Percent saying "very happy")			
1. Your sacramental and liturgical ministry	55	59	47
2. Your present living situation	45	46	43
3. Your present financial situation	30	29	34
4. Your personal spiritual life	22	22	21
5. Conditions for ministry in your diocese or religious institute	22	19	29
6. Practices of governance in your diocese or religious institute	15	13	21
7. Practices of governance at the international level in the Church	11	11	10
8. The image of the Catholic priesthood in the American public today	4	5	2

In general we can say that *local* conditions were a greater contribution to happiness than diocesan, regional, or international conditions. Under these circumstances, since local conditions are more gratifying, we would expect priests to invest more of themselves in their ministry locally. Also, local living conditions and financial circumstances were, on balance, not problems for these men.

Diocesan and religious priests differed on two items. Diocesan priests were happier than religious priests with sacramental and liturgical ministry (first item), while religious priests were happier with the conditions for ministry in their religious institute.

Age groups showed differences on three of the items. Concerning "your present living situation" and "your present financial situation," priests of the 66-and-older group were much happier than those in other groups. On "practices of governance at the international level in the Church," the opposite pattern occurred. Overall, the young priests were happier than any other age group with the conditions of their priestly life. Again we see that the young priests are more satisfied with the Vatican and the Pope (seventh item in table 2.4).

Problems Facing Priests

We asked the priests to rank certain problems—those that observers have talked about as troubling priests today—according to how much they affect them personally. The questionnaire listed twenty problems, and the ten rated as "a great problem to me personally" by the most respondents are listed in table 2.5. (This was one of four possible responses, the others being "somewhat of a problem," "very little problem," and "no problem at all." The total list of 20 problems may be found in table A.3 in the appendix.)

Table 2.5
Ten Problems Facing Priests (In percents)

	All	Diocesan	Religious
There are many problems which face priests today. Would you indicate how important the following problems are *to you* on a day-to-day basis? (Percent saying "a great problem to me personally")			
1. The way authority is exercised in the Church.	24	23	27
2. Too much work.	17	19	13
3. Unrealistic demands and expectations of lay people.	13	16	8
4. Loneliness of priestly life.	13	14	12
5. Being expected to represent church teachings with which I have difficulty.	13	12	16
6. Celibacy.	11	12	8
7. Uncertainty about the future of the Church.	10	10	8
8. Relationship with the diocesan bishop of the diocese in which you work.	8	9	6
9. Relationships with superiors or pastor.	7	7	7
10. Difficulty of really reaching people today.	7	7	6

The items are listed in the table in the order of their predominance. The percentages are relatively low (the highest being 27%) because they reflect only those priests saying "a great problem to me personally." Thus the *intensity* of a problem is not indicated by the numbers in the table—only its *relative* importance. Of most widespread concern was "the way authority is exercised in the Church." The problems ranked second and third were similar issues (and might even have been combined): "too much work" and "unrealistic demands and expectations of lay people." The items ranked fourth and sixth were "celibacy" and "loneliness of priestly life." The fifth-ranked problem was "being expected to represent church teachings I have difficulty with." These were the most common serious problems facing priests.

The questionnaire listed many other possible problems that we hear talked about, but the responses indicate that many of them do not weigh heavily on priests today. They include "difficulty in sharing authority" (rated as a great problem by 1%), "difficulty of working with women" (by 1%), "too little work" (by 2%), "conflict with parishioners or laity" (by 3%) and "lack of a clear idea of what a priest is" (by 3%). Even if we make some allowance for respondents' possible defensiveness or unwillingness concerning self-disclosure, we still must conclude that these latter problems are not widely felt. We can be thankful for that.

Diocesan and religious priests revealed noteworthy differences on only two of the problem ratings. One was "unrealistic demands and expectations of lay people," a problem diocesan priests were more apt to list than religious. The second was "the way authority is exercised in the Church," which religious priests were more apt to list than diocesan.

Age differences showed up only for the top three items. Older priests were somewhat more troubled by "the way authority is exercised in the Church" than were younger priests—with the highest rating in the 56–65-year-old group. For their part, younger priests were more troubled by "too much work" and the "unrealistic demands and expectations of lay people." This was especially true among priests ages 36–45. Apart from these issues, age differences were small.

Because the same 20 problems have been asked in the survey since 1970, one can observe changes over the decades. Three items have shown significant shifts since then. First, the proportion of priests reporting "too much work" as a great problem has nearly doubled since 1970—from 8% to 15%. The proportion citing the "unrealistic demands and expectations of lay people" as a great problem also nearly doubled (rising from 7% to 13%). Here is more evidence that the increased workload and the higher expectations of laity have become more burdensome today. Third, the percentage citing "difficulty of really reaching people today" *fell* from 16% to 7%. This was an unexpected finding, the meaning of which is unclear to us.

A 68-year-old religious priest talked about problems with authority structures:

> With diocesan priests, I've noticed that as there continues to be a diminishment in the numbers of priests, it has caused a sense of tension and anxiety, and "How are we going to do all these things?" Our cardinal—the sad thing was—up until a year and a half ago he would not allow anyone to address or openly speak about it, because he just said, "There is no problem" about the diminishment of priests. "We're handling this problem, There's no problem." But a year ago is when he finally acceded. Okay. And he set up a committee that studied the issue of the diminishment of priests. They have since come out with their report and what we need to do in this diocese. I think that issue, for diocesan priests, is a very critical one. So many diocesan priests are living alone, and they feel a tremendous burden of trying to be a good priest in the face of so many things that they have to do in their parishes. And I think that they feel terribly discouraged that this issue, a very central issue for them as priests, was not tolerated as a topic to discuss in this diocese. With the cardinal, there are certain issues which you do not bring up. He doesn't want to hear about them.

A diocesan priest, age 37, tells about a lack of archdiocesan vision:

> In this archdiocese the parishes really are becoming more and more owner-operated franchises. I don't feel there is a full-blown mission or a vision in the archdiocese. I really feel like I'm operating a franchise. We're suffering in this area from closings, this and that. And parishes are closing because they don't have enough money. But there isn't a mission plan that says we're going to close these ten places and we're going to open these five. I don't see that. I don't see the vision. So my connection to the archdiocese is working here, to make this an owner-operated franchise.

The problem of overwork was discussed at length in our interviews. The priests discussed it as being related to the fewer priests and the rising expectations of laity.

A 36-year-old diocesan priest:

> Priests are doing too much. That's what you're seeing in the priests right now. I'm seeing it. Too much is being asked of them, and there's not enough assistance or support. Or there is a refusal on the part of the parish and the diocese to address the situation, and there are not enough of us to go around. And the same method of operation that was present fifty years ago—even with Vatican II, we haven't moved or challenged people to move out of that mode of being. So the same pressures, the same expectations are placed on priests, and there are half as many of us to go around. Fifty years ago it was fine. Father was waiting by the phone because he didn't have a lot to do. He

had plenty of time to pray, and you'd find him in church. You'd meet him on the street, and he'd have time to talk to you. And now there are half of those priests present today, and yet the same expectations are being placed on that half. And we're killing ourselves in trying to meet those expectations.

A 49-year-old diocesan priest:

The one thing I've definitely seen is more and more talk about the shortage of priests that is developing and the denial that most bishops are in about this. My bishop would deny to high heaven that we have a vocation shortage, and yet we do. More priests are talking about that. And also about the aging of the priests. So it's a sign to me that things are really shifting fast. It's a sign to me that I'm going to have more work already, but very quickly in the next five or so years it will be even more work, because a lot of these guys will retire or die or whatever else. So there is a great shift in attitude and pre-occupation about this even among many of us younger fellows. And I'm not even that young myself. I'm 49. There are many guys who don't even want to be pastors any more and have to put up with all the hassles, because it's just too much. They'd rather be an associate or a parochial vicar and let the pastor worry about all those problems. A part of the reason for that shift is that the American church, because of all of our personnel guidelines and rules and requirements of professionalism and all of that having to do with finances and stuff, it's become more and more difficult to administer a parish. Because you have all these things you have to abide by, including dealing with the government on FICA and all of those things. Priests just find that it's so wearing and tearing on them that they don't want to do it. Now, some of the guys that are in parishes that have enough financial re-sources can hire an administrator to take care of all that. But the largest part of the rest of them can't afford it, and some don't believe in doing it. So that's been a big, big thing.

A young priest in a focus group:

Many of us live alone. And it is very, very difficult to get appropriate relief help—people who have faculties, who can do the sacraments. Sometimes you have to wipe out everything for a week, because you can't get another priest. Or you have paraliturgical services. But just to be able to get away! Many times I feel trapped. Can't leave. Can't take a day off, or feel guilty when I've done so.

A 64-year-old diocesan priest with much experience in giving retreats reflected on whether priests are overworked:

If by "overworked" you mean that your own interior space is really shut down, that is, you can't reflect and you can't take breathers, I would say they are overworked. First of all, when you're in a parish, if you've got a funeral or two and you've got a regular Mass scheduled every day, you have a couple of things coming at you and you're on the run the whole time. That can go on seven days a week without stopping! And what happens is, you can become just a pure functionary unless you take time off to step back from that. And also, you don't have anything to give the people after a while, if you don't do any real reading or any type of reflection, or you're not bouncing ideas off of other people—if you're only going, going, going.

Let's look at the predicament out there. You're the only one in charge in this parish, and Mrs. Smith is sick. If you take that day off, she might die, and she would want the priest there. Well, there are priests who operate off of that guilt complex. "If I leave, something could happen, and therefore I won't be there and I won't be serving these people." My own feeling on this is, then you go see the person the day before, you anoint them and make sure that if you aren't there, they're prepared for death. If some emergency comes and you're not there, well, that's life. That's Providence. You can't be every-where at all times. You've got to get rid of the messianic complex.

A diocesan priest in a focus group called for rethinking parish structures:

One of the problems is that we're not open to new structures. We've got to pastor the Church in the same way that we've done for so many years. I think we need to be open to different types of ways of pastoring the Church. One of the things in our diocese is that only a priest can be a pastor. I think we need to look at that. I don't know what the options are, but I think we have to be willing to look at other options, because I think there are other ways of doing it that might even be better, that the people might even be served in a better way with a different structure. Like the priest who said, "I took a big parish so I wouldn't have to pastor three parishes." [laughter] I think one thing that we're doing that is very destructive to Christian commu-nity is making mega-parishes. Some of the parishes that were closed were really the ideal size. If they're financially viable, why can't we find a differ-ent way to pastor them rather than creating a monster that is going to destroy a priest who is asked to pastor maybe three or four parishes.

Everyone agreed that the expectations of lay people have risen.

A young priest in a focus group:

The most difficult thing for me is the great variety of sense of expectations. There is really a lot of demand on us. For myself, that's what makes me most weary. It has nothing to do with whether a person is conservative, liberal, or whatever. It has to do with the expectations. I made a list the other day. I listed nine people I had disappointed. [general laughter] I counted them: I know I disappointed nine people. [laughter] That's the most difficult thing for me, living with that.

A 68-year-old religious priest described the changes in lay involvement:

> I've experienced changes myself where I'll say something and someone will
> say, "Well, Father, that's a good point but . . . ." And I'll say, "Yeah, you're
> right, I hadn't thought of that." Whereas in the past it would have been
> "Father has always said . . . ." That happened to me as recently as just yes-
> terday. I have a business manager, and we're redoing a chapel. And he was
> opting for something and I said, "I think that's not so good." And he said,
> "Well, let's take another look at that." And we did it several times. In the past
> that would have been unheard of. So I said, "No, let's hear your view. What's
> your point?" In the past, if Father had spoken, that was the end of it. I see
> this all the time now. We priests are taken as someone they respect but they
> also say, "We're professional people, we're people who are educated. We
> have an idea here too, and we're going to say it."

A 37-year-old diocesan priest discussed changes in lay attitudes toward
priests:

> Everyone talks about how there is less respect now. I would say something
> more—there is just *less thought* about the priest on the part of the laity. I
> think we're much more marginalized in their minds and much less thought
> about. I think there is a much greater sense that they can hold us account-
> able, which is both good and bad. Sometimes it's bad because you get
> people who think they are just going to ream you out for whatever is bother-
> ing them. "How dare you do this! How dare you look at my child the wrong
> way in school! How dare you ask these questions!" The priest has much less
> unquestioned authority now.

A 56-year-old diocesan priest:

> We're certainly not on a pedestal, as when we were first ordained. But do
> they see us differently? I know a lot of people would answer *yes,* but I would
> say *no.* As I reflect back, they've always wanted that person of holiness and
> that person of prayer. It took me a while to understand that. I think now they
> believe they have a role in forming the priest and helping the priest grow.
> And maybe that's what they didn't think they had before. The lay people
> now see that they have that role. I'm not sure that, thirty years ago, someone
> would say, "Father, I think for your own growth, this is something you might
> look at." Well, they don't say it that way, but I think they have a perspective
> that they are very instrumental in your growth—I mean the ones that are
> really trying to live a Christian life.

The loneliness of priestly life was a topic many priests wanted to talk about.

A 37-year-old diocesan priest:

> The priestly lifestyle is a negative, because diocesan priests do not live in
> community. So often we will be negligent one with the other. It depends on

the rectory you live in and on whom you live with. Sometimes you live with people you just can't stand, and you're just thrown together. Sometimes you live with people who are completely indifferent to each other. It's like "So long as you hold up your end of the bargain on the schedule, you say your Masses and hear your confessions, fine. We don't have any problem." But we don't talk, we don't relate, we don't pray together. And sometimes it can feel like rectory living is like waiting for your next debut in church. You sit and you wait until you have something else you need to do. Someone said, "We don't really seem to have a life." And there are enormous temptations for how to get a life. You can become the hobby priest. This is in the licit area—the hobby priest who has all these hobbies. You can have the priest who liked to be a collector, and collect things. We have a fairly disposable income, which is not something a lot of people talk about—but we do. We are paid. And we have a certain amount of time that is disposable, more so than most people. And human nature being what human nature is, you can very often get yourself into hobbies, you can get yourself into trouble. You live alone, basically, even when you're living with others. To some extent you're living alone. You're not obligated to prayer hours or prayer time, aside from your Masses and confessions. So there is very little support network there.

A 64-year-old diocesan priest:

I think it is a big mistake to have our priests live in isolation. I want to advocate the Augustinian rule, where we live in community. Maybe three priests, and then travel out to the parish. I think when you're in a house, living with the associate is sometimes a blessing and sometimes a source of tension. But just living with another priest is another level of openness and trust. I would go for regional houses, a central house here for the clergy in the area where you could get a good meal and use the library. We need to live together. I think a lot of the sexual misbehavior is fostered by isolation.

A 64-year-old diocesan priest:

I know that having priests living alone is not good. It has its moments, but if you're cooking for yourself, you're going to shortcut the cooking. And it's not going to taste as good either. It always tastes better when people are over. So I would say, something has to be done to be sure that priests stay in communion with people two or three times a week and not go it alone every night. Because what they'll do is—one or two things: they won't eat or they'll eat out. And that's part of their living style. It will kick back to bad health later—high blood pressure, cholesterol, bad stomach, the whole works. It all builds up as time goes on.

You need to invite people in. Once in a while, go out to a layperson's home. But don't go to the same ones all the time. The priest needs to maintain a social life. Food. People. Get people together and nourish yourself that way.

Some priests are pretty good at mixing with people; they're always mixing. I'd say, just watch out for the loners, because they are the ones who'll leave the priesthood! And also they are the ones who least contribute to the diocese. People don't see them.

It's easy to come home, and you've got a television set. And a TV meal, which you stick into the microwave. And you sit there and watch your program. And you call that living! It's not. But you can get into that, into the habit.

Personal Future

What do these priests think today about their choice to enter the priesthood and their future as priests? Table 2.6 shows responses to four such questions. The first concerns a realistic possibility—that the worsening priest shortage might force priests to restrict their work to sacramental and liturgical duties. Would the men be satisfied, or dissatisfied, if this happened? Forty-four percent said they would be very or somewhat satisfied, and 43% said they would be very or somewhat dissatisfied. The attitudes are split about half and half. Sacramental ministry, as we have seen, is very fulfilling to most priests, but if that is all a priest does with his time, it precludes building human relationships with laity, and that is another fulfilling part of the priesthood.

Table 2.6
Four Questions about the Priesthood (In percents)

	All	Diocesan	Religious
In the future if you would be asked to restrict your work to sacramental and liturgical duties, would you be satisfied or dissatisfied?			
Very or somewhat satisfied	44	50	35
Neither satisfied nor dissatisfied	10	9	10
Very or somewhat dissatisfied	43	38	52
I don't know	3	3	3
Which of the following statements most clearly reflects your feeling about your future in the priesthood?			
I will definitely not leave	79	78	81
I probably will not leave	16	17	15
I am uncertain about my future	4	4	4
I probably will leave	1	1	1
I have definitely decided to leave	0	0	0

	All	**Diocesan**	**Religious**
If celibacy for priests became optional, do you think you would ever get married?			
Certainly yes	4	5	2
Probably yes	8	10	5
Uncertain	12	13	9
Probably no	29	31	26
Certainly no	47	41	58
If you had your choice again, would you enter the priesthood?			
Definitely yes	67	68	66
Probably yes	21	19	24
Uncertain	8	9	6
Probably not	3	3	4
Definitely not	1	1	0

The diocesan and religious priests did not feel the same way about this. Many more of the diocesan priests (50%) would be satisfied than the religious (35%). Also, older priests would be a bit more satisfied than younger ones. The question had been asked in 1985 as well as 2001, and the level of satisfaction rose during those sixteen years.

The priests were also asked if they expected to remain in the priesthood in the future, or if they thought they might leave. Very few thought they would leave. Only 1% said they "probably will leave," and another 4% said they are "uncertain." All the rest do not expect to leave. There were no differences between diocesan and religious priests. Older priests were even less likely than others to think they might leave. This question was asked in 1970, 1985, 1993, and 2001, and the number saying "I will definitely not leave" rose from 59% to 79% during this time. The level of unrest among priests has subsided.

If celibacy for priests became optional, do these priests think they would ever get married? Not many. Four percent said "certainly yes," and another 8% said "probably yes." The rest said no. Diocesan priests were much more likely than religious to say that they would certainly or probably get married (15% vs. 7%). There were no noteworthy differences by age. The trend since 1970 was gradually downward, with 18% in 1970 saying they would certainly or probably get married, compared with 12% in 2001.

Finally, if these men had their choice again, would they enter the priesthood? The vast majority said yes. Only 4% said they definitely or probably would not. Diocesan and religious priests agreed, and the age groups agreed—except that more among the oldest group said yes. When this question was asked in 1970, 78% said they would definitely or probably make the same choice for the priesthood, compared with 88% in 2001. Satisfaction with the priesthood has risen.

Sources of Support

All priests need personal support if they are to persevere in their work confidently and energetically. Do they receive much support? The questionnaire asked about this, and the details are in table A.4 in the appendix. The findings are clear: Priests receive their strongest support from their families, non-priest friends, and staff members where they minister. They receive less support from fellow priests, their bishops, their presbyteral councils, leaders of their institutes (if religious), and the Vatican. For religious priests, support from leaders of their institutes and from local religious communities was ranked next highest, while for diocesan priests the next-highest support was from parishioners and fellow priests. For all, the *least* support cited was that from the Vatican and from national organizations.

The age groups differed concerning only two of these sources of support. Concerning support from the Vatican, the 46–55- and 56–65-year-olds gave much lower ratings than the others, while the 35-and-under group gave the highest rating. On "the National Conference of Catholic Bishops," the pattern of age group differences was similar, but less extreme, with the youngest and oldest groups giving the highest ratings. In sum, the 46–55- and 56–65-year-old priests are unique in feeling much less support from the Vatican and the National Conference of Catholic Bishops than other priests feel.

In our interviews, we also asked the priests how they feel they find the strongest support. Most talked about family and friends.

Father Jack, age 49, spoke about support from his family:

> The primary support system for me is my family. That's just beyond telling. My family and I all get along very well; I have one brother and four sisters. We're very close, we can call each other for anything and yet we don't get in each other's business. We're very supportive. They are the rockbed of my support system.

Family is an essential support for a 40-year-old diocesan priest:

> My family is probably one of the strongest supports for me. If I have a problem, I would probably go to them first and say, "Does this make sense? What do you think?" I'm blessed with two sisters, and my mother and father are still alive. They give me good insights on things. If I need help, I can turn to them. Probably they are the first ones I turn to. My strongest support comes from my family.

Thirty-seven-year-old Father Hank told about support from his family:

> They're not local, which is a whole different aspect of modern priesthood.
> The detachment of the individual priest from his family because of the dis-
> tance creates a whole different set of dynamics and needs. When you live on
> your own long enough, you begin to realize that whatever the dysfunctions
> in your own family may be, these are people with whom you have this easy
> relationship that always turns your lock, as it were. It just fits in a way; there
> is a comfort that just isn't with anyone else, or that you have to sit and ex-
> plain. There is no awkwardness there. The known: it's the known; it's the fa-
> miliar; it's the people you grew up with. That level of familiarity I think can
> reduce the stress. If you're around people like that a little bit more, it can re-
> duce your own personal stress level because you are understood. Without
> speaking, you are understood. Whereas when you're only dealing with your
> friends, trying to draw support only from your friends, it's a lot more work
> and there are a lot more interpersonal confusions.

A 36-year-old diocesan priest benefits from a unique friendship:

> I have wonderful non-priest friends. One of my closest friends is a woman
> who is very involved in the life of her parish. We met during my pastoral
> years. She is like my sister, but my sister in a different way. I can be honest
> about things with her. She is my friend, in the sense that I can say things to
> her that I can't say to my family. And she's not in my parish. She was in my
> pastoral year parish twelve years ago, so we've been friends for twelve years.

Friends are especially important to a 32-year-old diocesan priest:

> I have to say I have an awesome network of non-priest friends. Those would
> include religious. I have some young ladies, they are in their twenties, who
> are in religious life. They have been a wonderful source of prayer support for
> me. We don't get to see each other because they live out of state or just be-
> cause of ministry. We exchange e-mails and letters; just to know that you
> have people out there that are praying for you that you don't come into regu-
> lar contact with, that you really begin to form these spiritual friendships with.
> And then, on a very practical level, this group of lay people, they're just fun.
> Good people who respect that I've got my life, they've got their life, but we
> have so much in common too, and that's kind of what we do, we celebrate.

Thirty-seven-year-old Father Mike described how his friends keep him
humble:

> Non-priest friends remind me that I'm not all that important or that good.
> They say, "Eh, you know, we knew you before. We knew who you were,
> washing dishes." Definitely a grounding, definitely a reminder of who I am,
> who I've been. How do you stay connected with them? I have a couple dif-
> ferent ways. This young adult group started at my parish, mostly young mar-

ried, once a month, and we go to each other's houses. I hosted them at Christmas. We just get together and talk. It's nice, because it keeps me connected with their lives, kids, family, job, all that kind of stuff.

A 59-year-old diocesan priest relies on his friends:

I don't have any family left, so I spent a family Thanksgiving with people who are my family. They love me. I was very sick this summer for two months with a lot of pain, a lot of problems, and they, and the people in this house, they loved me and looked out for me. I am a very blessed guy.

After family and friends, staff members were the next most important source of support.

A 32-year-old diocesan priest:

I think they support me, as far as they certainly respect the role that I have within the life of the parish. They realize that we are in this together. So I think there is a real sense of mutual support. And I think truthfully that's because I've made an effort. I really have made an effort to make that work, in the sense that, just because I'm wearing a collar doesn't mean that I deserve the day-to-day respect, but I think I've earned that because I show them respect. Even in our disagreements, I'll be the first to initiate a conversation that goes with that. So I think they respect that. I would say that the support is relatively moderate to strong, depending on the staff. But now I would say it is strong.

A 37-year-old diocesan priest told how he had worked hard to gain his staff's support:

The staff members have been very supportive. You know, you never want to follow saints [in your job]; you always want to follow sinners. It's always harder to follow saints. Harder for Cardinal George to come into Chicago, because he's following a saint. I followed a guy who was only here once a week for Mass, canceled all the groups, closed the finance council, canceled the parish council, and nobody could meet except on Sunday afternoons. The parish was a wreck. I come in, I show, and I'm a hero. And all I do is show up! The first year, I showed up at a school board meeting and people are saying, "What are you doing here?" It's the school board, right? Aren't I supposed to be here? They had a major fundraiser for the school, and everyone was supposed to have a table. So I said, "Where's my table?" "But pastors don't usually have a table." "What are you talking about? Give me a table!"

A 56-year-old diocesan priest:

Support from staff members is really high. Part of that is you're with a group of people who know me. I've been blessed here; most of the staff has been here twelve years with me. They know me. I know them. They can say to me, "David, I guess this isn't a day when we should ask you for anything, right?" And I can say, "Yeah, you're right." And we can laugh about that. They have a great respect for the priesthood, and I pray with them. I think that is an important thing too, to pray with them, to make them eucharistic-centered and prayer-centered.

The priests we interviewed had mixed feelings about the support that comes to them from other priests, from their bishops, and from the Vatican. The interviewees tended to have a few close priest friends but not a trusting relationship with most priests in the diocese or institute. Reactions to bishops and to the Vatican were mixed. Here are two statements about support or non-support from the Vatican.

First, a 36-year-old diocesan priest:

Yeah, I would definitely say that they're [the Vatican] supportive. It's another layer removed, so we don't have a whole lot of direct day-to-day connections with the Vatican. But as far as how the parish operates, what we teach, how we live, the practical norms of daily priestly life, they come to us from the instructions of the Holy Father in those congregations. Yeah, I do believe it is important to keep up on those instructions.

A 61-year-old diocesan priest was unsatisfied with Vatican leadership:

Instead of a pastoral church, which the Second Vatican Council is trying to make it, it's still a "do this and don't do that" church, unfortunately. It's not leading us; it's not training us. Even last night, at the RCIA class I was teaching, some of the people grew up Catholic and then left the church for a long time and are now coming back. Some of the people said, "When we were growing up in grade school, Sister told us to put JMJ [for Jesus, Mary, and Joseph] at the top of our paper. We didn't know what those letters stood for, but Sister told us, 'You've got to put JMJ at the top of the paper if you want me to read it.'" They had no idea what it meant. So often the Church says, "Do this" without an explanation, a dialogue, without a dialogue.

The picture of today's priesthood revealed in this chapter differs markedly from what one would have seen in the 1970s. Priests today are happier, less likely to want to leave the priesthood, and less likely to want to marry if celibacy became optional. They are older on average and more likely to be ordained at a later age. They find their greatest joy in the sacramental and liturgical aspects of their ministry and in the preaching of the Word.

At the same time, the dramatic decrease in the number of priests has changed the kinds of problems priests today must face. Today's priests are much more apt than their counterparts thirty years ago to feel overworked and to feel pressured by unrealistic demands from lay people. They are also facing the possibility that their duties may become limited to sacramental and liturgical responsibilities—something only 50% of diocesan and 35% of religious priests want to happen. In the next chapter we look at changes in ecclesiology, a topic that affects priests' ministries in many ways.

Chapter 3

The Shifting Emphasis in Ecclesiology

> Why is it I want to get into this line of work? What is so special about being a priest that I couldn't do if I just remained a faithful member of the laity?
>
> *—A young priest in a focus group*

The Second Vatican Council introduced an eminently new ecclesiology and numerous new institutional structures. As we discussed in Chapter 2, it moved the Church toward greater lay involvement, greater respect for lay ministries, and more democratic structures at the parish, diocesan, and national levels. While these new teachings were welcomed by many priests, they were not welcomed by all. Most older priests in the 1960s resisted the new ecclesiology, preferring instead to maintain their earlier priestly roles. Later, in the 1980s and 1990s, many newly ordained priests abandoned the ecclesiological focus of the postconciliar years in hopes of forging a new priesthood based on pre-Vatican II traditions.

Our surveys of priests included a dozen measures to help us plot these changes over the decades. Our questionnaire asked priests if they agreed or disagreed with seventeen statements, many of which had been asked repeatedly since 1970. The statements covered four topics: status of the priest, eligibility for the priesthood, lay ministers, and decision making in the Church.

Status of the Priest

Seven statements were about the status of the priest. (The responses are summarized in table 3.1.) A very strong majority of priests believe ordination confers on them a distinct new status. Seventy-seven percent agreed with statement 1: "Ordination confers on the priest a new status or a permanent character which makes him essentially different from the laity within the Church." Diocesan priests (83%) were more apt to feel this way than religious priests (64%). The opposite viewpoint is found in statement 2, saying that there is no ontological difference between the priest and the laity; 23% agreed with this statement, religious priests (29%) more so than diocesan (19%). In sum, about three-fourths of all priests hold to a high theology of ordination, and diocesan priests hold this view more than religious.

Table 3.1
Seven Statements about Priestly Status
(Percent agreeing strongly or somewhat)

	All	Diocesan	Religious
1. Ordination confers on the priest a new status or a permanent character which makes him essentially different from the laity within the Church.	77	83	64
2. There is no ontological difference between the priest and the laity, since all share in the common priesthood of Christ given at baptism; the difference is mainly one of assigned duties in the Church.	23	19	29
3. The idea that the priest is a man set apart is a barrier to the full realization of true Christian community.	26	25	29
4. I feel that I am most a priest when I am saying Mass (presiding at Eucharist) and hearing confessions.	73	77	63
5. What is lacking today is that closeness among priests which used to be present.	55	60	45
6. It is urgent that priests achieve greater status as competent professionals in the eyes of the Catholic community.	67	65	71
7. Priests today need to be more involved with broad social and moral issues beyond the parish level.	74	71	80

Statement 3, saying that the idea of the priest as a "man set apart" is a hindrance to Christian community, voices an objection to the high theology of ordination that was often heard in the wake of Vatican II. In 2001, only 26% agreed with the statement, consistent with the other responses regarding a high theology of ordination.

In what roles do priests feel their priestly identity most strongly? Statement 4 measured this by stating a viewpoint found in all recent research on priestly identity, namely, that priests feel it most strongly in sacramental ministry, worship, and preaching. Diocesan priests agreed overwhelmingly (77%), and religious priests by a clear majority (63%). These specific roles are the situations in which priests feel most authentic as priests and most fulfilled in their work, as we saw in Chapter 2. Sacramental and worship leadership roles are exclusive to priests and closed to non-priests. They are public roles in which the unique character of the priesthood is most visible and central.

Statement 6 voices a concern we sometimes have heard, that priests should become more like other professionals in our society, that is, more distinct, more competent in their defined areas, more credentialed, and higher in status in society generally. Priestly voices are divided on whether the priesthood should develop more fully into a profession, but in our 2001 survey, a clear majority (67%) agreed with the statement.

Do priests today believe that they should be more involved with broad social and moral issues beyond the parish level? Statement 7 found very strong agreement. The vast majority (74%) of priests said yes.

Patterns of responses to these seven statements were not consistent across the age groups. Age differences were clearly evident on statements 1 and 6. Regarding whether ordination confers a new and different status on priests (statement 1), the younger priests agreed more often than did the older men; the 56–65-year-old group was the least likely to agree. On statement 6, saying that priests need to achieve greater status as competent professionals, the younger priests were less likely to agree, the 35-and-under group least of all. This tells us that the youngest priests are not very concerned about professionalization of the priesthood; their priorities lie elsewhere.

Eligibility for the Priesthood

Who should be eligible for the priesthood? Should any of the centuries-old rules on this be re-evaluated? Three statements in table 3.2 touched on this. First, a solid majority (72%) agreed with statement 1 that the policy of welcoming Episcopalian priests, whether married or single, should be continued. A slimmer majority (52%) favored inviting resigned Catholic priests back into service, regardless of whether they are married or single (statement 2). A similar slim majority (56%) agreed that celibacy for diocesan priests should be made optional (statement 3).

Table 3.2
Three Statements about Eligibility for the Priesthood
(Percent agreeing strongly or somewhat)

	All	Diocesan	Religious
1. The Catholic Church in the U.S. should continue to welcome Episcopalian priests who want to become active Roman Catholic priests, whether they are married or single.	72	70	76
2. Priests who have resigned from the priesthood should be invited to reapply for permission to function as priests again, whether they are married or single.	52	51	54
3. Celibacy should be a matter of personal choice for diocesan priests.	56	53	60

Other recent surveys have shown that Catholic laypersons are even more inclined to make celibacy optional for diocesan priests. These surveys have found between 70 and 75% of laypersons agreeing with the idea. For example, a 1999 Gallup nationwide poll of Catholics found 71% in agreement with optional celibacy for priests (D'Antonio, et al., 2001: 109). (The same poll found 62% in favor of ordaining celibate women and 53% in favor of ordaining married women.)

The *Los Angeles Times* survey of priests found 69% in favor of the ordination of married men. This figure is higher than the 56% in our survey, but one must keep in mind the lower response rate in the *Times* survey, and probably 56% is closer to the true figure for all priests.

Returning to our own survey, on all three statements older priests agreed more than younger priests. Continuing to welcome married Episcopalian priests is a policy that older men were moderately more in favor of, and they were much more agreeable than younger priests concerning inviting back resigned priests and making celibacy optional. For example, the percentages in favor of inviting resigned priests back again, in the five age groups, were: ages 25–35, 23%; 36–45, 34%; 46–55, 53%; 56–65, 68%; and 66 or older, 50%. As we have seen repeatedly, those most committed to a post-Vatican II liberal ecclesiology were the 56–65-year-olds. A similar pattern appeared on attitudes about optional celibacy.

Lay Ministers

Priests' attitudes toward lay ministers are especially important today due to the rapid increase in professional lay ministers serving in parishes. A survey by Murnion and DeLambo in 1997 found a 35% increase in professional lay ministers doing parish work during the preceding five years (Murnion and DeLambo, 1999). At the time of the survey, an estimated twenty-nine thousand lay ministers were working in parishes, compared with twenty-seven thousand priests. Without doubt, professional lay ministers are one solution to the problem of fewer active priests being available in the future.

What do priests think about the growth in lay ministers? Two questionnaire statements are in table 3.3. On statement 1 they agree overwhelmingly that "the Catholic Church needs to move faster in empowering lay persons in ministry" (73%) and on statement 2 they again agreed overwhelmingly that "parish life would be aided by an increase in full-time professional ecclesial lay ministers" (72%). On both statements, religious priests agree more than diocesan.

Table 3.3
Two Statements about Lay Ministers
(Percent agreeing strongly or somewhat)

	All	Diocesan	Religious
1. The Catholic Church needs to move faster in empowering lay persons in ministry.	73	70	79
2. Parish life would be aided by an increase in full-time professional ecclesial lay ministers.	72	71	75

Age groups differed in their attitudes; the older priests were much more in favor of empowering lay ministers than the young ones. For example, on statement 1, saying that the Church needs to move faster in empowering lay ministers, the percentage agreeing in the five age groups (from youngest to oldest) were: 54%, 65%, 75%, 86%, and 69%. On statement 2, saying that parish life would be aided by more lay ministers, the percentages agreeing were 49%, 65%, 80%, 81%, and 68%. The older priests are much more favorable toward a further growth in lay ministers than the younger ones. The percent in favor rises with age, except for the oldest group (66 or older), which is less favorable than the 46–55 and 56–65-

years-old age groups. This is a pattern similar to other age differences we have seen. Most important is that the young priests today have different ideas about the nature of the Church, and about half of them are unenthusiastic about lay ministers.

Decision Making in the Church

Are priests today satisfied with the way decisions are made in the Church, or are they hoping for changes? Five statements on decision making are shown in table 3.4. On statement 1, saying that priests' attitudes can never have an effect in the present institutional church structures, 33% agreed; more diocesan than religious priests agreed (36% versus 27%). This finding indicates that the level of alienation from the hierarchical church felt by priests is not very high, but it is a bit higher among diocesan than among religious priests. The next two statements, 2 and 3, say that the presbyteral councils and other organizations of priests need to be improved if priests' viewpoints are to be heard, and a slim majority of priests agreed with both.

Table 3.4
Five Statements about Decision Making in the Church
(Percent agreeing strongly or somewhat)

	All	Diocesan	Religious
1. Priests' attitudes on church issues can never have an effect in our present institutional church structures.	33	36	27
2. Priest members of presbyteral councils need more influence if the councils are to be effective in enhancing priestly ministry.	60	64	52
3. More effective organizations of priests are needed to serve the needs of the priesthood today.	53	53	53
4. I think it would be a good idea if Christian communities such as parishes were to choose their own priest from among available ordained priests.	23	23	24
5. I think it would be a good idea if the priests in a diocese were to choose their own bishop.	47	45	51

The final two statements in the table touch on sensitive topics: who should choose priests for specific parishes and who should choose bishops for dioceses. Only 23% agreed that parishes should be able to choose their own priests from among available ordained priests, while 47% agreed that priests in a diocese should be allowed to choose their own bishop.

Age differences on the five statements about decision making were small, with one important exception: there were large differences on statement 5, that priests should be able to choose their own bishop. The agreement in the five age groups (from youngest to oldest) was 22%, 38%, 45%, 62%, and 44%. As we have seen repeatedly, the 56–65-years-old group was the most democratic, while the 25–35-years-old group was the most hierarchical.

Trends in Attitudes, 1970 to 2001

Because nine of the statements in tables 3.1 to 3.4 were asked in 1970, 1985, 1993, and 2001, we were able to gauge trends over time. The overall changes in agreement over these three decades were surprisingly small. (See table A.5 in the appendix.) The only notable trends were (1) a drop in the view that parishes should be permitted to choose their own priests (from 31% in 1970 to 23% in 2001), and (2) a similar drop in agreement with the statement that the idea of the priest as a "man set apart" weakens community (a drop from 33% to 26%). But even these trends are modest.

Looking at *overall* trends tells us little, but important lessons are learned when we look at how the specific *age groups* changed over the years. Figures 3.1, 3.2, 3.3, and 3.4 depict important age differences in each of the four surveys. We chose these four from the statements in table 3.1 because they depict the most dramatic age trends over the years 1970 to 2001. It is important that all four are statements about *priestly status*—a new priestly status derived from ordination, whether the idea of a "man set apart" is a barrier to community, whether resigned priests should be invited back, and whether celibacy for diocesan priests should be optional. The status of the priest—including his authority and his unique role in the parish—is a topic on which priests have changed dramatically over three decades. It appears to be a major topic dividing old and young today.

Each of the graphs contains four lines, each representing one of the four surveys. The lines connect the percentages agreeing in the five age groups, and the more slanting the line in any survey, the more disagreement there was among the age groups. All four graphs show that the recent younger priests are different from younger priests in earlier surveys; they have more often voiced attitudes supporting the cultic model that had prevailed prior to the Vatican Council II.

Figure 3.1
Ordination confers on the priest a new status or a permanent
character which makes him essentially different from the laity
(Percent who agree strongly or somewhat)

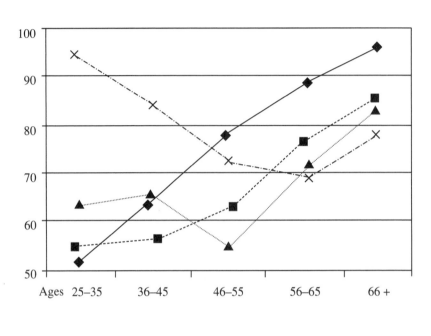

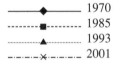

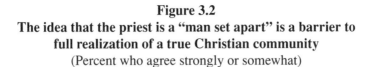

Figure 3.2
**The idea that the priest is a "man set apart" is a barrier to
full realization of a true Christian community**
(Percent who agree strongly or somewhat)

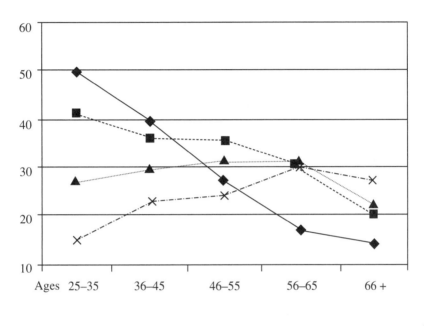

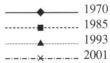

Figure 3.3
Priests who have resigned from the priesthood should be invited to reapply for permission to function as priests again, whether they are married or single
(Percent who agree strongly or somewhat)

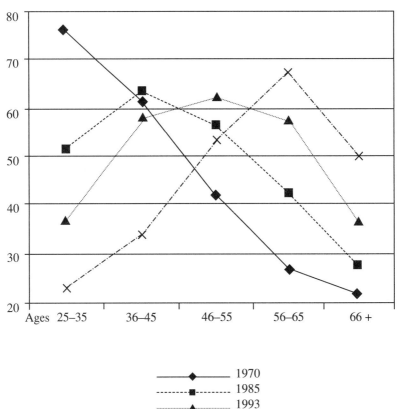

- 1970
- 1985
- 1993
- 2001

Figure 3.4
Celibacy should be a matter of personal choice for diocesan priests
(Percent who agree strongly or somewhat)

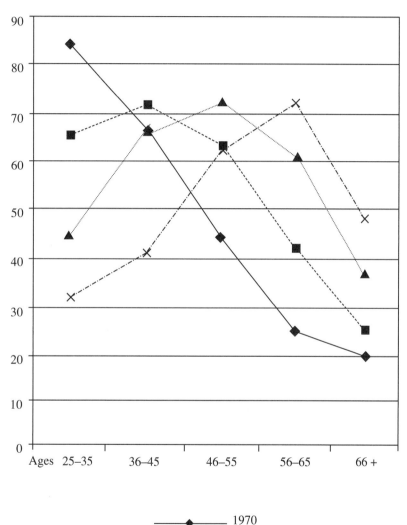

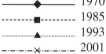

♦ 1970
■ 1985
▲ 1993
✕ 2001

Figure 3.1 graphs the responses to statement 1 in table 3.1, saying that ordination confers on the priest a new status different from the laity. The solid line connects the dots from the 1970 survey, and it tells us that in 1970 the oldest priests strongly agreed with the statement (95% did so), while the young priests (35 or younger) had mixed attitudes (52% agreed). This is a gigantic age difference, greater than we find in most sociological surveys. The young priests and the old priests were really divided on this topic.

Turning to the 1985 survey, shown with the line of dashes, the middle-aged and old priests continued their same attitudes. Their line simply moved to the right since its 1970 position, due to the passage of time, while the youngest category of priests voiced increased agreement, shown by the dashed line *crossing over* the solid line at the lower left.

In the 1993 survey, indicated by the dotted line, older priests again changed little but the youngest two age groups (25–35 and 36–45) were similar to each other in their attitudes. The 2001 survey depicted a continuation of the trend toward a high theology of ordination among the young, but it is more than that—it portrays a great *acceleration of change*, so that the trend from 1993 to 2001 is the fastest of all.

Figure 3.2 graphs change on another measure of the theology of priesthood—statement 3 in table 3.1, saying that the idea of the priest as a "man set apart" damages Christian community. Again the solid line showing the 1970 responses is steep and straight, with the young priests agreeing the most of all. It is virtually the opposite of the solid line in figure 3.1. The 1985 and 1993 lines are less steep due to a drop in agreement among young priests. The 2001 line is *reversed* in direction, telling us that the youngest priests in 2001 had an attitude on this issue similar to the attitude of the oldest priests in 1970. The earlier pre-Vatican II attitude is returning.

Figures 3.3 and 3.4, showing the responses to statements 2 and 3 in table 3.2, are similar to each other. In both cases the 1970 line was straight and steep, followed by inverted U-shaped lines in 1985 and 1993 and a line in 2001 which is nearly straight in the opposite direction of 1970—that is, straight except for a downturn in the oldest age group. These figures have a pattern similar to that in figure 3.2: after 1970 each new generation of young priests was more conservative than the last (moving downward in the figures) with each survey and maintained their same attitudes as they grew older. But the youngest priests in recent years came into the presbyterate with a much different theology of the priesthood, and in 2001 the line became nearly the opposite of what it was in 1970. In both figures 3.3 and 3.4 we can predict that the line in the next survey of priests we hope to do in this series (scheduled for the year 2009) will be straight again, but in the opposite direction.

Figures 3.1 through 3.4 have a common pattern, that of a pig traveling through a python: the curves rise when the pig (the ordination classes of the late 1960s and 1970s) arrives, then they fall again later. The "post-Vatican II" attitudes of the late 1960s and 1970s are not held by the later ordination classes. Rather, those classes held theologies of the priesthood similar to the prevalent views before the council. The figures help us answer another question: When did the new type of priest first appear? They started to appear prior to 1985, since in the 1985 survey they were already visible.

The *Los Angeles Times* survey of priests agrees with us in finding a sharp difference between younger and older priests on several issues. The news story summarizes:

> Clerics under age 41 expressed more allegiance to the clerical hierarchy, less dissent against traditional church teachings, and more certainty about the sinfulness of homosexuality, abortion, artificial birth control, and other moral issues than did their elders, the poll found. Those attitudes place the younger priests at odds with many priests who were shaped by the liberal reforms of the Second Vatican Council in the 1960s and who tend to support further changes in the church—including women priests, optional celibacy, more lay empowerment, and the direct election of bishops. . . . The poll found that younger priests who came of age after Vatican II and during John Paul's papacy were the most positive toward him, with 79% ranking him outstanding. That compared with 60% of the Vatican II-generation priests and 64% of the pre-Vatican II priests 60 years of age and older. (*Los Angeles Times*, 21 October 2002, sec. A)

In sum, views of the essence of the priesthood have undergone two shifts. The first occurred at the time of Vatican II—from the older model of priest as administrator of the sacraments and teacher of the faith, to a new model of priest as spiritual and social leader of the community. This change was accompanied by the council's new theology of the church as the "people of God." The young priests in 1970 were strongly in favor of the new model. The second shift, which began in the early 1980s, continues today and seems to be reversing the first, although not everyone agrees on this point. The question remains open: Is the current attitude shift a return to older forms, or is it something altogether new? We will pursue this question in chapter 4, which reviews how younger and older priests differ in their understanding of the priesthood.

Chapter 4

The New Priests

I think people want guidelines in their lives. I try to offer them guidelines. It's like the speed limit. People want to know what the speed limit is. It doesn't mean you always drive the speed limit, it doesn't mean you're a bad person if you don't always follow the limit. But at least you know the parameters. Without the parameters, people are drifting.

—A 37-year-old diocesan priest

The research is clear: a new type of priest has arrived. A process of change began in the early 1980s and picked up steam through the 1990s. Not only do our surveys indicate this, but everyone we interviewed said the same: they are different from priests ordained in the 1960s and 1970s.

Younger priests view the Second Vatican Council as merely part of a broad historical process. They take a longer perspective on the tradition and express a fascination with older liturgical forms and symbols—such as the ringing of bells at Mass and the priestly vestments (such as the birettas and cassocks), both of which were rejected after Vatican II. Priestly identity for these priests means having a unique and sacred position in the Church, clearly different from (though in principle not better than) the positions of lay people. Clarity about Catholic identity is also important to them, so they reject attitudes that strike them as too Protestant. Being solidly Catholic means following papal authority faithfully and unquestioningly.

Most of today's older priests were ordained in an era after the Council when the rigid hierarchical authority of the Church was in disfavor. As discussed in earlier chapters, lay people were welcomed to the "priesthood of all believers," and the importance of personal conscience in moral decision-making was given emphasis rather than obedience to the word of the priest. Priests began to see themselves as being among the faithful, having a unique role but with an emphasis on servant-leadership rather than on clerical authority. Today's older priests therefore see their long efforts to

involve all Catholics in the ministry being eroded by the renewed emphasis, coming from the younger priestly generation, on making the priest
once again a "man set apart."

In this chapter we will present three examples of the new priests and
three of the older priests as they reflected on the changes they have seen.
We quote them at length so the reader can get a clear sense of their viewpoints. We selected these priests out of our collection of interviews, preferring men who talked plainly and who were broadly representative of the
others; anyone who struck us as unusual or extreme we did not include. We
begin with young priests, all of whom were ordained in 1997 or later.

Young Priests

Father Matt: Reevaluating Tradition

Father Matt is thirty-two years old. He was ordained four years ago in
an eastern diocese. He enjoyed talking about his experiences in both a college seminary and in a diocesan seminary. In seminary he got to know
seminarians and faculty who felt disappointed that some of the anticipated
changes following Vatican II had never been realized. This was a source of
division in the seminary, and certain issues sparked controversy:

> Celibacy was a big one. I think for the guys *that* was a very real issue. And I
> think, liturgy. That was an issue: the way that the liturgy is celebrated, specif-
> ically the Eucharist. There was definitely one school of thought that we have
> a long way to go, using a common quote, "The vision of Vatican II isn't fully
> recognized in the life of the liturgy." On the other hand, there was a school of
> thought with a lot of resistance to the liturgical expression that we have in our
> Church today. The interpretation from that side was that there is a lot of abuse
> of liturgical norms in parishes now. One issue was overuse of Latin versus no
> Latin at all. Taking the principal orations during the prayer, one side said,
> "Capture the *spirit* of the prayer and use all the inclusive language that you
> can for the prayer" or "Do whatever doesn't offend the people that are
> there"—versus: "Are we really free to change the language of the prayers?
> Do we do that, as a church? If a new Sacramentary comes out, when it does,
> *then* you're free to follow whatever the prayer says."

> Also the idea of the standing and the kneeling—where are the consistencies
> in the practice? On the one hand, we have a bishop who's clearly trying to
> honor the total vision of the Church liturgically. At the same time, that may
> not be honored specifically within the life of a community. So guys pick up
> on all this inconsistency. There is a virtue in the middle there, between being
> overly preoccupied with just rubrics for the sake of rubrics, but at the same
> time being free to follow in the spirit of the Church, and being free to think,

as a future priest, to do that as the Church is *today*, not to be preoccupied with a future or a nostalgia of a past that we really don't have. So we need to live in the present moment with this, and that is a very powerful spiritual lesson that we can learn.

Father Matt feels a bedrock satisfaction about his ministry in the parish:

> Even the most challenging day, and even the crappiest day, there is blessing in it. They can be long, but there is always something you walk away with at the end of the day like, kind of in awe. Maybe it's not hitting you right that day, when you're really tired, but reflecting on it, all of a sudden you realize, "This is a great life!" and how many lives you get to be part of, just in a single day. It's the most amazing thing. I'll even use the word *sacred*. It's the most sacred experience that I think a human could experience, just being on that journey with so many people. Even the one who comes through the door and doesn't have very nice things to say about the fact that you did this or that, they don't agree with something you said in the homily, or you changed something in the church and they're just squawking about something. But even in those encounters, that's part of the day. That day might be more of the crappy kind, but at the same time there is something to that. I think also, the people that I've worked with are very enthused about the parish. I'm talking about parishioners involved in the different organizations. They're very enthused about the life of the parish. This is their parish, and they take great pride in it.

Matt believes that the most crucial role of the priest in today's Church is that of spiritual leader:

> I think, flowing right out of the whole image of Holy Order, I want to be a presence in the midst of the community—first of all a teacher, teaching the love of God in practical ways: How does all this make sense in the individual's life? To be present in that. And of course that comes through the preaching and the liturgical leadership. There is a spectrum of ecclesiologies regarding the role of the priests or theologies of the priesthood, but I do believe the priest is that one person who stands ordained in the midst of the community, and there is a special grace there. That comes out fully in the celebration of the Eucharist, but it can't stop there. It has to be in the day-to-day things. That is how I see my role there. Let me tell you what it *isn't*— what I don't want to be. Part of that is being the taskmaster. I have a hard time with pastors who have beautiful administrative skills and stress that. I don't want to be the accountant; I don't want to worry about the temporal aspects of a parish, the day-to-day operations.
>
> I think my ideas flow from a given ecclesiology. I see, for example, a pastor as one who is the ringleader, the one who gets a little fire stirred around. I've seen beautiful examples where they energize other people around them.

They are taking ownership in their own ways for a common project. Again, I think it goes back to that image of the Holy Order; it's bringing order in the name of one common vision. I think specifically in the parish, that does flow out of an ecclesiology—the idea that we're in it together. We are working in it together. There isn't an us-and-them mentality. It's kind of bringing that all into one and providing that leadership. What is not helpful is the renegade or the maverick, often used to describe a priest who might be doing his own thing. . . . The priest is a bridge between looking at the local church and the vision of the wider church; What are we doing in *our* specific community, in *our* parish?

There are sometimes clashes between Father Matt's point of view and the views of the older priests:

I think some of the priests in the '70s, they really anticipated ongoing change. Maybe the temptation was that many of them may have hoped for a church that isn't realized even today. In that, it was very different from my experience. I just think the temptation for our group is that we have to be challenged not to become stagnant. You still have to be open to a church which is always moving, and a church which is always rocking with the Spirit. And I think that can be hard for this generation. Certainly that is a temptation for me personally, because my temptation would be, "Can we just sit still for a little while, just to catch our breath?"

And I think there is a perception of younger clergy being more conservative. Part of that is maybe because of the whole idea of "Let's sink our teeth into some of the tradition that doesn't seem to really have been there and not be connected emotionally with some of that stuff back in the 1960s or '70s." We're looking at tradition as "This might be a good thing." And yet, sometimes that can offend a lot of people.

Can I give you an example? There are some things I really see a value to. For example, the ringing of bells at consecration. I know this is a huge theological thing. But in such a fast-paced, chaotic, destructive time today, for many churches there is nothing awe-inspiring about the liturgy at all. It's just kind of a plain canvas, and when you daydream, there is nothing to center on except on the immodestly dressed individual ahead of you or the formation of bricks on the wall. So, I think we're over-stimulated in our society, sometimes. The way I would approach that is, I would be a big advocate of restoring the bells, using those at points throughout the liturgy to kind of bring our attention. But yet, this is something I hear people in their fifties and sixties always talking about, "Oh, we're not going back to the old church; we're not going back to a time where we are told to salivate at the ringing of the bells!" I know all the history of that, but I don't have the baggage that somebody in another generation might have.

Another thing, I'm very open to having a conversation about whether the priest faces the people or whether we're all in the same position. I think there is value in both. And yet, you bring that topic up to people in their fifties and sixties and they say, "Oh my God, that is pre-Vatican!" Well, that doesn't resonate with me, as far as whether it is pre-Vatican or post-Vatican. I just look at it as, "There is a value to both." Are we open to keep that conversation going? My viewpoint would be labeled conservative by some. Why is Father ———, a 55-year-old, bent out of shape if I bring this up? As opposed to, Why am I bent out of shape if he's not even willing to listen? *Then* you begin to understand. Maybe that's why historically, they say seventy to seventy-five years are needed for the dust to settle after every major council, just to pull the people out of there and let a new generation take over. Seventy-five years afterward there isn't all that baggage that goes with it.

I think what is really exciting in my generation—it's kind of fun to see—is almost a sense of rediscovering some of the stuff that got buried. That "spirit of Vatican II" that older priests talk about, I just sense that there is a group of 50- and 60-year-olds—maybe because they were so connected to it—this was like their battle cry and they were in the trenches when this all began. And the way that they carry some disappointments over things that they failed to see—maybe things that they are still hoping will happen—and some of the things that they feel have been accomplishments in the life of the Church: I see that there is a huge chasm there, between that generation and some of the younger men, contemporaries of mine in the priesthood. I really don't get emotionally charged over Vatican II. I see it as a great, very significant, very worthwhile, very spirit-driven event in the life of the Church, but being born in 1969, I don't have the same feelings. But I do see places where the attitudes are changing. With a lot of my contemporaries, both in religious life and priesthood, there doesn't seem to be that drive of everything needing to be in the name of Vatican II. Rather, "Let's look at what's good for the life of the Church. Let's identify where we are at. Let's work together on this." I think the concern or the preoccupation would be, on our part, not so many external things happening, but maybe a spiritual renewal, one that I don't think really caught on in the last thirty years. I would just like to see some stability within the life of the Church, and I think that is a reflection shared by many of my contemporaries.

Father Matt has experienced division among priests on issues having to do with the Church:

Yes, I see divisions. Some of the theological divisions are: the role of the pastor, the role of the priest as far as being the administrator, the identity of the priest—going back to the priest's freedom to marry, and Who is qualified? I use that word "qualified," because there is a theology that we have a right to claim priesthood, and there is a theology that it is a calling—discerned through the life of the whole Church. And that leads to a bunch of different interpretations. I also think, too, the spirituality of a priest. And rectory life. And the things that I think are expected of priests, and their responsibilities of daily life and ministry. All those things, I think, flow out of different theologies.

Father Vincent: A Happy Religious Priest in a Parish

Vincent is a 32-year-old religious priest, ordained one year ago, now serving as associate pastor in a large parish in the Northeast. Before his theology he taught high school for three years. He talked about the hot issues in his seminary:

> I think the big questions right now are all on ecclesiology. It's what it's all coming down to. And it's from that perspective, at least in my experience, that I think are the really big questions right now. People are doing the rest of theology out of their ecclesiology—that first decision about how do you understand the Church. My generation in ordained ministry is one that certainly has gotten a lot of press as people try to figure out, What is going on with this group? Has some pendulum swung back? People in my generation are often accused of being neo-conservative, neo-traditionalist, things like that. And we caught some of that in seminary. There was almost an antagonism between the faculty and some members of my class.
>
> Some of the people in my generation, by the time we got to theology, were wondering about the distinctiveness of ordained ministry. In other words, Why on earth are we doing this? The distinction between ordained ministry and lay ministry was often not accented enough for some people, and that created some major tensions. People heard the desire for a more specific examination of ordained ministry as a denigration of lay ministry, as clericalism, as all the worst of that neo-conservative movement. On the other side, the response to that was dismissive, the typical left blurring all distinctions, and all the other stuff that would go with that. That was a big area of discussion during my three years there. It was a conversation within the ——— community, between the religious faculty and religious students. It was less so with the lay students.

Father Vincent is happy in his work, and he enjoys the "steep learning curve" of the first year in a parish. He is one of three priests, and he is younger than the others by twenty-five years, so anything to do with youth and young adults is delegated to him. He talked about the difference between his generation of priests and the generation before him:

> I've encountered many different positions on how ordained ministry plays out, from the most minimal to, let's say, the most clerical, and everything in between. There is probably a generation gap between my generation and some of the people who were in charge of our formation, who would be more minimal than my generation. So I guess that would be the main shift. And there is probably a *simpatico* between my generation and the generation prior to the older priests. I've thought for a long time that this group of guys got caught in the changes. I think that they're the guys who were trained under the old system, and they hit Vatican II and the world changed.

The world changed and the Church changed. And those were the guys whose ordination classes suffered the mass exodus. I call them the "lost generation," and there are a lot of walking wounded guys in that generation. I think they would be the ones with whom my generation would most often butt heads in terms of the priestly identity issue.

Father Vincent is concerned about priests' attitudes about the hierarchy in Rome:

I think it's a generational thing. People will say things flippantly, things about the hierarchy in Rome that they wouldn't say about their worst enemy in the world. My generation would react very strongly to that criticism, and probably not always realize that much of those things they hear, or at least what's behind them, is being motivated by love of an institution that these people have committed themselves to. I react very strongly to people who I think are bad-mouthing. And it's not even necessarily that I disagree with the critique. It's probably more about *tone*. And there is also something about loyalty, certainly publicly. Yeah, we can critique, but what's the tone? You're ordained to be a public minister, a representative. You have a certain obligation to at least put the game face on.

Vincent is one of the most contented priests we interviewed, and it is partly due to the strong identity he receives from his religious order. He admires many of the older priests with whom he works, and he is careful about ecclesiological viewpoints which might cause division. He affirms what his order is doing.

Father Dennis: A Priest Really is Different

Dennis, age thirty, was ordained four years ago and now serves as an associate in a parish in the Midwest. The interviewer asked him about the motivations felt by many of the young priests today:

I think I could probably speak as a representative for 75 percent of newly ordained priests in saying that one of the biggest issues is ecclesiology. By that, I mean that the men of the same generation as I am, in terms of when we were ordained, have all lived under the pontificate of Pope John Paul II. So obviously, he and his theology of the Church have formed us. And I see a big difference. The younger priests are not coming out of any of the issues or the baggage that were present in the '60s and '70s. You know, there were such sweeping changes not only in the Church but also in the world, and they kind of all dovetailed—certainly the Second Vatican Council and the changes liturgically that it brought in. Also you had the Vietnam War and a kind of spirit of rebellion, a sexual revolution—and all of these things which all converged at one moment—which created a lot of unrest and I think maybe robbed some people of foundations. And because of the changes that were sweeping at the time, I think people assumed that "Whatever changes we want will kind of rule the day." So, "We want married priests," and there was maybe an idea that it was going to happen. And when it didn't, I think people were hurt. And they said, "We want contraception to be not immoral." Well, that didn't happen, and again people were hurt. I think a number of things like that left people feeling, "Gosh, with all the other things that happened, why didn't these changes happen? I think they should." It maybe left them with a sense of uncertainty, or maybe being upset with the institutional church over all those kind of things.

Now you have a new generation of priests trained under John Paul II. We don't have any of those issues. Those were not issues that we went through. So there's a sense of "Gosh, if the Church teaches it, I accept it!" There isn't that sweeping sense of rebellion. People always say we are more quote unquote "conservative." I'm not a big fan of the conservative or liberal labeling. I think the Church is supposed to be Catholic! And so I think younger priests are coming from the mindset of "If the Church teaches it, I want to be faithful to it. I trust the Church." I think some of the trust level of older priests isn't there, a level which *is* there with younger priests. That creates a tension, when maybe a pastor says, "Well, we don't need to be doing ———— or we don't need to teach ————," and the younger priest is saying, "But Father, this is important!"—those type of issues. So I see *that*, ecclesiologically, as an issue. That dovetails into the issue of ontology, that the Church *clearly* teaches that an ontological change occurs at ordination. It's very clear.

I think some of those priests ordained in the 1960s and 70s saw priesthood as maybe more of a functional thing. It's looser in its foundation. It's "Priesthood is what I've been called to do, but I'm not essentially different from a layperson." Now, a young priest comes along and says—and I think this is the key— it's "We are not better, but we *are* different!" We've given up a wife and family because we believe *radically* that something occurs in priesthood." If you really *believe* that there is something that happens to you at ordination—and obviously there is all your seminary preparation—one needs to respond differently. We have to get out of the secular mindset. We have to strive for holiness. And I think some priests would see that as being clericalistic, kind of like we're being apologetic, because we're saying there's something different. But I think they've misunderstood the priesthood. There is certainly no need to apologize. Lay people have a profound vocation within the Church, as well as I do, but they're very different. So I think some young guys are maybe unapologetically Catholic.

It is disheartening for young priests to see older priests not following the rules—in liturgy, in parish leadership, in church teachings. And even more so if the older men are not committed to their work and are just going through the motions, or are not keeping their vows of chastity.

Young Priests: Summary

These three priests speak for the majority. The young-versus-old fencing match today is fought over just a few theological topics, while there is agreement on the rest. The young differ in three general ways from their predecessors.

The main difference is clearly ecclesiology. The young men hold a different view of the Church and the value of changes in the Church than the older men. They are not interested in the issues of the post-Vatican years or in any effort to realize "the spirit of Vatican II." As we have seen, they take pride in having a longer view which is open to adopting practices even from the Middle Ages. Unlike their elders, they don't see why some pre-Vatican II practices were bad and couldn't be reintroduced today. They are not pushing for changes in the Church but would rather have a breathing space of stability after the chaos of the last three decades.

Second, a specific issue felt with urgency by these priests is the theology of the priesthood. The young men hold to a sacramental and cultic theology of the priest. They reject a theology defining priesthood as merely a matter of function in church life. They insist that the priest is distinct from the laity, and that emphatically includes ontological as well as institutional distinctiveness. The priest-lay distinction of the pre-Vatican II era needs to be reconsidered and probably reinstated. The new priests are less enthusiastic than their elders about lay ministers and the possibility of working with lay ministers as equals.

The life of a priest is symbolic of spiritual things, and a priest must be mindful of this every minute of his life. A priest is an icon and even, in one person's words, "a mystical presence." This is one of the most important roles of a priest, not to be sidelined in favor of unending activity or doing good works. The priest must keep a strong prayer life to sustain him in his special role, and this requires nourishment from the breviary and from confession.

The third area of tussle is liturgy. Several voiced the desire to add beauty and transcendence to the liturgy through special vestments, Latin prayers, and chalices. They are open to reintroducing kneelers and bells, not just for the sake of innovation but to restore a sense of sacredness and mystery to the Eucharist. Now the liturgy is too plain, too Protestant. Older priests who disagree are seen by the young as unduly captive to their own specific issues from the 1960s and 1970s, issues which are no longer pressing. The young priests are not interested in the 60s or the 70s, but rather in the long sweep of Catholic spirituality. They ask: Who could object to that?

Older Priests

Father Donald: The New Church after Vatican II

Father Donald, age 58, was ordained thirty-one years ago in a western diocese. He spent part of his career working for Catholic Charities and part as a pastor. He talked about his own experience in college seminary and the theologate in the 1960s:

> I entered college seminary in 1961 after graduating from high school. It was before the Second Vatican Council, so it was a very regimented, structured environment. Really a total culture shock for me, going in for the first time and being regulated by bells, lights going off automatically at night, wearing a cassock twenty-four hours a day (except when you're sleeping), and following a real strict regimen of waking up, prayer, food, study, recreation—again structured. The day kind of ran in a cycle like that, almost like monastic life, I would imagine. The first year I was there was strictly a year of Latin, because I hadn't had any Latin in high school and wasn't familiar with it. That really was, in many ways, a good year for me because I didn't have to deal with the full academic schedule, and the professor was a very good person. There were about forty of us in that class at the time.
>
> I continued on for four years, completing that with a bachelor's degree. There was some loosening of structure during those years subsequent to the Second Vatican Council, but pretty small. We still wore the cassock, even wore birettas for a time, although that ended sometime during those four years. I enjoyed the classmates. It was such a close environment, you really got to know people, you knew their strengths, you knew their weaknesses. Probably the most heartbreaking moments were the departure of people you knew and liked and had become friends with. Some, you knew why they left, others just left suddenly and you never did really find out the story from them or anyone else as to exactly what happened.
>
> I don't recall the divisions then that I hear about today among priests. I think there was always some division between younger and older clergy. But in the seminary there weren't a lot of theological discussions—or there were theological discussions but they weren't left-wing right-wing kinds of things.

Father Donald sees differences among priests in the diocese today:

> There are differences in ecclesiology and theology. Fundamentally there is probably agreement, but differences as far as celebrating the Eucharist and a more traditional approach to ecclesiology. It's curious to me, because most of these traditional folks nowadays have no idea what it was like in the '50s, or '60s for that matter. And yet they hearken back to something they've never experienced and I'm not sure that that was the best way to be, either.

Donald takes pride in his collaborative style of leadership:

> The title [of pastor] is probably more important to other people than it is to me. I'm not the kind of person that is going to exercise authority over people because I'm the pastor and say, "I'm the pastor; I decide." I learned that there are pros and cons to the consensual way of doing things, trying to come to some kind of consensus with whoever it is that you need to work with to get something done in ministry. While that can be laborious and painful, at least while people come to a consensus about something, everyone has kind of bought in, rather than just directing or dictating what people are going to do. I think you accomplish more. So I would prefer that method of operating.

> I don't have to live with any clericalism here in our parish—where the priests think they are different, or apart, or better than anyone else. I think as a pastor, particularly the support staff looks to you to give the direction. Sometimes I find that difficult because there are other people on staff that are as capable as I am. But I'm blessed in that I don't have people playing out the role, in terms of "I'm a priest and you're whatever." That hasn't been a problem here.

He described his view of the correct role and highest priorities for a priest today:

> I really think that our role, and maybe my one overriding goal in life and in ministry, is to try and provide as many opportunities as possible for people to become involved. We really do share this as a staff, that we want to give and involve as many people, to give them some kind of experience of what church is about and what participating in church is about. It's a real inspiration to me, the goodness of people, the genuine goodness of people inspired by the Gospel and the Eucharist and guided by the Holy Spirit. So that is pretty much fundamentally where I come from. I do feel very supported in this parish and very encouraged by the people. As much as we try to let them know that we appreciate them and the work they do here and their involvement, they let us know too that we're appreciated and they're glad for it. So it is kind of a nice compliment, and that gives you some motivation, too.

For Father Donald some church positions have proven difficult to incorporate into parish life:

> I myself have concerns, and have since the time I was ordained, about some of the moral pronouncements of the Pope—*Humanae Vitae* I've always found very difficult. And interacting with people, I've found that most people today don't even deal with the issue. They just do what they do and they form their own conscience. In earlier times, I know people struggled much more with that and had a lot of questions about it, and I've never been sure that I understand it myself completely. I personally don't have any issue with the Church's position on abortion; I think it's the right place to be and where we should be.

On professional lay ministers and deacons, I see within the people that I associate with a great respect for them and others in the Church. To me, fundamentally, if a person is doing their job, doing their ministry and doing it well, why would I have any problem with that? Even if it's the custodian, all I want the guy to do is clean the place. If he can't do that, then we have a problem. Outside of that, I don't have any trouble with sharing ministry or people doing ministry. In the people I associate with, I don't see any attitudinal change except for the better in terms of involving professional paid staff in the parish and being willing to work with them.

The return to pre-Vatican II attitudes and clothing by some priests is difficult for Father Donald to understand:

From a historical view, there's always been some differences and divisions, although I think they are more pronounced today. Certainly with Vatican II and living through that, some priests just found it very hard to adjust to that and other priests didn't. It was obviously a time of real change and turmoil, reflected in all kinds of ways, not the least of which was a lot of priests leaving the ministry. But I think today, sometimes I feel like I lived in a time warp, growing up in the '60s and living through that, and all the turmoil and change that took place there—having lived through that kind of change, and even in the seminary, trying to adapt to the Vatican Council and some of the decisions that were made there. There are still some divisions among priests. Some are just fundamentally conservative in all ways, just what you see: people in more traditional kind of garb, be it cassock and capes and things like that. I just have no understanding for that. The day I left the seminary was the day I got rid of that cassock, and I never went back. Maybe because I wore it so much, I suppose I had some kind of resentment toward it. But I do think there are some divisions in there. There seems to be a wanting to go back to an earlier time by some priests. Not necessarily just younger ones, but middle aged ones too, who feel that we had something there. Maybe priests had a place there, a status there, maybe the Church did. But the fact is, it's gone. Whatever you wear and however you try to hearken back, you can't recapture the past.

Father Tony: Ministry is Broad

Father Tony, age 50, is provincial of an international religious order, living in the Midwest. He was ordained in 1977 and has spent most of his ministry in parishes. He talked about his change in attitude toward lay ministry in recent years:

I think one of the most profound convictions that I've come to is that lay ministry is not a result of a shortage of priests or ordained ministers. The validity of lay ministry comes from baptism itself and that in entering into a relationship with laypersons in ministry, it's respecting their call as a result of baptism rather than some practical necessity like the shortage of ordained ministers. To me, that is a very challenging thing. And I know that that has been a struggle for the Church. To me, that's a very important conviction I've come to, and that's something that forms the basis of our efforts in our congregation to reach out and welcome the associates.

Father Tony described his attitude toward the correct role of the priest in today's Church:

> For me as a priest, probably one of the most important things I do is try and preach effectively. Before I was ordained, I thought that would be the thing I would least enjoy. But now people seem to find benefit in what I say. I think, as a priest *that* is really at the heart of it. Celebrating the sacraments in a meaningful way, as a presider and as one who brings forth the gifts of the other members of the worshiping community, that's also very important. Be the person in the community who names God and who calls the community to a sense of God in its midst. That is, really calling people to explicate what it is in their own experience. Is the priest ontologically distinct? I guess we say that ordination imposes a character upon the individual, so I guess I would have to say that. My church model is really the cyclical model, rather than the hierarchical model. And I see a priest as being in the midst of the people of God. The more fundamental ontological change, I think, is the result of baptism. We priests are still baptized persons, and our relationship is to others who are baptized in the community, even though the role is distinct.

He has observed changes in priestly attitudes in recent years, including greater resistance to administrative responsibilities and more acceptance of church authority:

> I think one of the changes I've seen is, I hear a lot of priests say, "I want to be a priest, but I don't want to be an administrator." There is a certain movement away from that responsibility and a wanting to do what is pretty priestly in terms of preaching the Word, celebrating the sacraments, counseling, supporting people. Part of it may be a function of the aging of the clergy, that after a certain while you don't want to deal with all of the complaints and the criticism. And often people observe that some of the younger priests entering religious life are more conservative. I think at times it creates a certain tension between those of us who are the products of the renewal of the council and now some of the younger members of the community who see things differently, whose allegiance is much more to the authority of the Church and the integrity of the doctrines as they see them. Those are the two principal changes: the sense of not wanting to deal with the negative aspects of administration, and some of the tensions according to theological positions—mainly ecclesiology—and the understanding of hierarchy, understanding of the exercise of authority.

Father Tony sees some moral and ecclesiological issues as areas of dis-agreement:

> Well, certainly the role of the papacy. The way authority is exercised, more
> of a hierarchical rather than an inclusive model. The role of Mary at times is
> much more critical for some people than for others. Moral teachings—the
> rigidity to adherence to teachings prohibiting abortion and birth control.
> Those seem to be the burning issues that I hear about.
>
> About the moral teachings of the Church, the most obvious thing I can say is
> I think there is more concern among some of the younger priests and reli-
> gious, but mostly priests, with adherence to church positions, orthodoxy, and
> maybe a movement away from some of this ease of working with laity on a
> par. Those are interesting trends. I don't know where they are going to go,
> and I hope they don't lead to hardened, inflexible positions. I believe that in
> the Catholic Church, as has often been said, the word "Catholic" means *uni-
> versal*. There should be a certain ability to include rather than to exclude, to
> bless rather than to vilify, different positions. And I am hoping that some of
> these tangents that I'm beginning to see don't become so inflexible in the fu-
> ture that we're going to go back to "it's either this or that" in terms of some
> teachings and styles of ministry. I'm a little worried about that, because we
> don't know what it's going to evolve into.
>
> I see, among some of our young priests, a movement away from this sense of
> the validity of lay ministry being in baptism and seeing it more as an exten-
> sion of the priest's role or the bishop's role—the hierarchical or ordained
> ministry—and less of an ease in working with lay persons as equals, as part-
> ners in ministry. There is a certain separation and a certain tendency toward
> off-putting words and behavior: "I'm the priest and you're the lay person."
> It's like going back to the expert versus the learner, or the empowered versus
> the unempowered. I see it in our community. The ecclesiology is different;
> the understanding of the way ministry is to be exercised is different. And I
> think, from what I've heard and observed, it's also happening in dioceses.

Father Vic: Need for More Flexibility, Less Rigidity

Father Vic is fifty-eight years old, a parish pastor for two years and a
former vicar of priests in his southern diocese. He was ordained in the late
1960s. He reflected on how priests have changed over time:

> One of the striking things, of course, is the difference between the young
> and the old. But not all of the young, and not all of the old, either. I've been
> struck by how a number of years ago I was getting together with a group of
> older pastors. They were fairly conservative, traditional men, and I was
> struck by how they all found their associates very traditional, more so than
> they were themselves. I think, probably, what bothered them most was the
> rigidity—not the conservatism or traditionalism—but a sense that some of

the younger men are trying to come in and help the older men do things better. They come in as teacher rather than as learner, some of them. Others, that's not the case. Certainly some of them want to correct what the older priest has been doing.

They're coming from a very legalistic mentality, a very rigid mentality as well, and also, frequently, a lack of pastoral sensitivity. Anyone coming into a parish needs to be pretty flexible in dealing with people, in that you have to be accepting of where people are at and then you work with them. You try to move them from where they are. To come in and think that people are going to listen to you immediately just because you're a priest is unrealistic for the most part, and some of the younger men feel that way. And they run into conflict with people, and therefore people are not open to them, and therefore they don't change the people. Now there are others that are different. But what many of them can do easily is galvanize more right-wing people in a parish to the detriment of the parish at large. It can be divisive. And if I had a right-wing associate here, that could create major problems for me, because what I'm trying to do is bring the parish to the center so that everyone is welcome. But sometimes the most traditional right-wing priests will create major problems. I've watched it around the diocese.

Father Vic sees the laity as basically unchanged over the years:

The people that I'm experiencing here in the parish are no different than the ones I experienced years ago. There is not a difference. You get people who are left of center, people who are right of center, and those people who are just trying to live their lives and do the best they can.

He sees conflicts among laity over liturgical issues:

Like, we have a communion rail here and people kneel for communion. Some people told me, as soon as I arrived, that that was why they came here—which is basically telling me that if I changed it, they would be leaving. Now, some would be on the other side of that too. One person I know doesn't come here because of communion kneeling. So you have people on both sides. The liturgical issue is certainly one of the ones here that has been striking. The liturgy is the most obvious thing. I just started silence in the Mass after the readings, and I got no negative feedback on that. . . . I haven't done anything radical.

Father Vic talked about the increasing involvement of lay ministers in the diocese:

The priests that I've found have the most difficulty are the newly ordained, who come into a parish and have nothing that they can kind of grab hold of other than a general sense of being a priest. When I was ordained, I immediately was in charge of the CCD program, the religious education program in the parish, the youth program, and things like that. Now you have lay people being responsible for those things, so when a person comes in and has no responsibility, that can be difficult.

Today you have some pastors, men who are not clerical, who don't want a clerical associate because it creates more problems than it's worth. It's easier to be alone than it is to have someone that's going to create conflict within the parish and galvanize the parish on a particular side of the issue. I think, too, that the people help the priests mellow out a little and not take themselves too seriously. They help some of them—not necessarily all of them. The people are pretty honest at times with priests, and that can be helpful. Probably the more affluent the parish, the more vocal the people would be. I'm thinking of [a very affluent parish nearby] versus this parish here. You get much more feedback over there from the people, when they don't like something, than you do here. So a lot of it depends on where you are, where the people are, as to how much feedback you get.

We have to train the people and the priests for more and more lay ministry, and help the people realize that they can come to a lay man or woman on staff for spiritual direction, and they don't have to come to a priest. That is a huge learning. That is so important. And it will take a while—that is the hard part. The priest doesn't have to do everything, there will be somebody else that can do things. This parish has now gotten used to Eucharistic ministers bringing communion to the sick, which has been good.

Father Vic is concerned about rigidity, especially among younger priests:

Rigidity to me is the biggest difficulty. It reflects itself in pastoral practice, whether it be a moral issue or whether it be an ecclesiological issue. It's the same underlying matter of how flexible can you be or should you be. I find that the more rigid ones in this diocese are younger men. That doesn't mean that the older ones haven't been rigid, but maybe they've been in pastoral ministry long enough to be softened a little. See, any weakness a priest has, like rigidity, it is magnified when there are fewer priests. It can't be lost. It can't be hidden. It becomes much more obvious. That's an enormous factor.

He talked about the main concerns he has heard from younger priests:

Well, I think they worry for the Church, most of them. They think the older guys are maybe a little too flexible and aren't holding the people to their understanding of what the Church is designed to be. I vividly remember a young associate going into a parish where the pastor was about seventy, and he was a fairly traditional pastor. The young guy wanted to correct the man's liturgical style. And the older man was horrified that someone would feel that it needed to be corrected, when to him there was nothing inappropriate. So that's where the rub is all the time.

Father Vic has not experienced major divisions or fault lines in the presbyterate in his diocese:

> I don't think there is enormous division in this diocese. There are challenges
> for some of the young guys adjusting and the older guys working with them
> in parishes. Those are challenges. There are some very fine young men out
> there that are not rigid and are wonderfully pastoral men, and there are oth-
> ers who are having a tough, tough time because they are so inflexible. But I
> don't see us having any major diocesan problems.

He thinks half of the young priests will encounter conflicts in the parishes:

> Certainly half will find it very difficult to be priests. That is my guess. They
> will certainly run into conflicts with the priest that they live with and with
> the deacons. Well, let's say about half of them.

Older Priests: Summary

We saw several times in these interviews a conception of three historical
eras in ecclesiology. The first was pre-Vatican II, illustrated by the "tri-
umphant" church of the 1950s. The second began at the close of the council and lasted about twenty years. It was a time of rapid change and a
feeling of expectation among priests. At the same time it was a time of be-
wilderment for those priests not caught up in the post-council enthusiasm.
The third era began in the early 1980s and continues until today. It is a time
of reaching back into church tradition and maintaining distance from the
post-council reforms. By the middle 1980s the Vatican II era was over and
a new stage of ecclesiological conservatism had begun.

This periodization of post-council history is convincing to us. The older
men whose interviews were excerpted here are products of the second era,
and it is understandable that they are turned off by priests representing the
third era. Many of these older men probably hoped in their hearts that the
innovations of the post-council years would be permanent gains in the history of the Church. But for the most part it did not happen. These post-
Vatican II priests now find that they represent only one short period in
Catholic history, a period whose influence has already waned; it lasted
only twenty years. No wonder these priests find it hard to appreciate the
younger ones.

We have seen repeated calls for flexibility and repeated condemnations
of rigidity. All the older priests agree: you need to be flexible, collaborative, and open if you want to have any impact in today's parish. They stress
that being flexible doesn't mean weakness or a tendency to sell out the
Gospel. On the contrary, it is the only possible way to convey God's will
and God's way of life to today's diverse and outspoken laity.

We have also seen from the older priests a conception of the priest's role as a community leader and coordinator, a person who calls forth the gifts of the faithful to serve the parish and the total society. The older priests did not talk about ontological differences between priests and laity, but spoke repeatedly of the ministry of all the baptized and the need that it be done collaboratively. Their vision of the priesthood has been largely eclipsed among recent seminary graduates.

Given that a seismic shift has occurred in ecclesiological viewpoints, the question now is, what does it mean for the priesthood and for the Church? We turn to this question in the chapters below.

Chapter 5

Issues and Needs Felt by Priests

Sometimes I'm just too tired—because the needs are too great. And because sometimes the expectations of others are bigger than I can handle at the moment. Because personally, I'm not feeling that I can handle my own expectations, let alone theirs.

—A 36-year-old diocesan priest

In chapter 4 we saw how older and younger priests have developed different views on ecclesiology, the priesthood, and liturgy. In this chapter we look at specific issues important to priests. After reviewing our survey results on two questions concerning such issues, we voice the viewpoints and feelings of priests through interview and focus group excerpts.

Survey Results on Issues and Needs

Issues Priests Want Openly Discussed

During the preparation of the 1993 and 2001 surveys we identified topics about which priests told us they wanted more open discussion. We wanted to list them in the survey to get a more precise measure of priests' need for more open discussion, due to the frustration of some priests who felt intimidated in bringing up their concerns. We collected twenty-four topics, all of them practical, rubber-hits-the-road-type concerns. Table 5.1 shows the percentage responding "very important to me" to the ten topics rated highest. Besides "very important to me," four other possible responses were listed in the questionnaire: "somewhat important to me," "not important to me," "I don't want it discussed," and "don't know." (For the list of all twenty-four topics see table A.6 in the appendix.)

Table 5.1
Importance of Open Discussion: Top Ten Issues (In percents)

	All	Diocesan	Religious
Numerous issues relating to the priesthood are being discussed today. How important to you would open discussion be in the following areas? (Percent saying "very important to me")			
1. The image and esteem of the priesthood today.	62	64	58
2. Psychosexual maturity of priests.	51	46	59
3. Support for living the celibate life.	49	47	53
4. Sharing ministry with laity.	47	46	49
5. Problems of overwork.	43	43	43
6. The policy of mandatory celibacy.	42	42	42
7. Problems of sexual misconduct by priests.	42	38	48
8. The process of selecting bishops.	41	41	42
9. Multiculturalism and race relations.	39	34	49
10. Problems of rectory or community living.	32	32	32

The top ten topics are arranged in the table according to the number of priests who rated them as very important. In first place—most pressing of all—was "the image and esteem of the priesthood today." Among diocesan priests this was far ahead of their second ranked topic, which was "support for living the celibate life." Among religious priests, by contrast, it was virtually tied with the second ranked topic, "psychosexual maturity of priests." These results suggest to us that diocesan priests sorely want the image and esteem of the priesthood analyzed and debated in open discussion. (Bear in mind that the survey was done in 2001, prior to the recent pedophilia crisis.)

The ten topics in table 5.1 give national Catholic leadership an agenda for discussions that would truly serve the needs of priests. Put simply, priests' top concerns are the esteem of the priesthood today, sexual maturity of priests, celibacy, sharing ministry with laity, overwork, sexual misconduct by priests, selection of bishops, and multiculturalism.

Diocesan and religious priests are different in important ways. When we look at all twenty-four topics, four are of greater concern to diocesan than to religious priests (using a ten-point difference rule): "sharing ministry with deacons," "quality of representation as a priest nationally," "policies on living arrangements," and "clarification and standardization of salaries." Three are of greater concern to religious than to diocesan priests: "psychosexual maturity of priests," "problems of sexual misconduct by priests," and "multiculturalism and race relations."

It is worth noting as well which topics received the most "I don't want it discussed" responses. This response was given by more than 5% of the priests on four items. The highest percentage choosing it was on "ordination of women"—22%. Second highest was on "the admission of self-declared homosexuals to the priesthood"—12%. Third was on "the policy of mandatory celibacy"—7%. Fourth was on "differences in sexual orientation of priests"—6%. Apparently these topics feel threatening to some priests today. It could possibly be that a portion of the priests fear they will lose something precious to them if there is an open discussion.

All of these topics pertain to gender, sexual orientation, and celibacy. *Which* priests don't want them discussed? The diocesan priests were a bit more averse to discussions than the religious. More important, the age groups differed. The priests 46 to 65 years old were less opposed to discussion of these topics than the younger men (45 or younger) and the oldest (66 or older). For example, concerning the ordination of women, the percentage who did not want the topic discussed were: priests 25–35 years old, 29%; 36–45, 33%; 46–55, 14%; 56–65, 13%; and 66 or older, 27%. Similarly, on the topic of the admission of self-declared homosexuals to the priesthood, the proportion opposed to discussion in the five age groups were 18%, 16%, 7%, 8%, and 15%.

These patterns among the age groups reflect what we have seen repeatedly in the survey: the priests in their fifties and sixties are more open to reassessing the definitions of priestly life than are the youngest and oldest priests.

Concerning their choice of topics they *do* want openly discussed, age differences were also fairly large. The young, more than the old, found issues concerning finances and living situations to be very important to them (specifically, "problems of rectory or community living," "policies on living arrangements," and "clarification and standardization of salaries"). The older priests more often wanted discussion on: "the problem of mandatory celibacy," "the process of selecting bishops," "ordination of women," "problems of sexual misconduct by priests," and "sharing ministry with laity."

In sum: the younger priests want more discussion of their work conditions, and the older priests want more discussion of central church rules and disciplines, including celibacy, the ordination of women, and the process of selecting bishops.

The questions listed in table 5.1 were asked in 1993 and 2001, and there was little change in the responses. The most noteworthy changes were an increased importance of "problems of overwork" for diocesan priests (up from 31% to 43% saying this was very important), and an increased importance of "sharing ministry with deacons" (again for diocesan priests up from 25% to 34%).

How Can Priests Be Helped in Their Ministry?

Our second method to assess the needs felt by priests was to ask them, "Would any of the following help you in your ministry as a priest?" and to list eleven opportunities or possible improvements in church life. The responses are shown in table 5.2, listed in order of their perceived helpfulness.

Table 5.2
Helpfulness of Eleven Possible Opportunities (In percents)

	All	Diocesan	Religious
Would any of the following help you in your ministry as a priest? (Percent saying "very helpful")			
1. More opportunity for my personal spiritual development.	63	66	58
2. Greater feeling of fraternity among priests.	56	59	51
3. More opportunity for training in strengthening the prophetic role of the priesthood.	37	37	38
4. The opportunity for greater participation in decision-making in my diocese or religious institute.	33	31	35
5. More opportunity for training in specific leadership skills, for example, conflict management and communications.	28	29	27
6. More opportunity for training in personal skills such as time management and stress management.	28	30	24
7. More opportunity to discuss theological and pastoral issues in a public forum.	24	22	29
8. More opportunity for training in specific organizational skills, for example, budgeting, investing, and insurance.	22	25	17

	All	Diocesan	Religious
9. More opportunity for training in multicultural leadership.	20	19	24
10. More opportunity to share my concerns with priests in other regions or ecclesiastical provinces.	16	16	17
11. The opportunity to be free from involvement in diocesan or religious institute affairs, so I can concentrate on my own ministry.	13	13	12

Although table 5.2 lists numerous opportunities for training or discussion, the top two were more closely related to personal life than to leadership skills. Most important was "more opportunity for my personal spiritual development" and second most important was "greater feeling of fraternity among priests." These two ranked far ahead of everything else. The various opportunities for training—in multicultural leadership, in organizational skills, in personal skills such as time management, or in leadership skills such as conflict management, were rated as being less helpful. On these questions, diocesan and religious priests gave very similar responses.

We wrote this series of questions in hopes of eliciting feedback from priests to national Catholic leaders about how their needs might be better met. The preeminence of the top two responses in table 5.2 suggests that priests want more help with their personal lives, a finding having implications for issues of work expectations, living situations, and isolation.

Two of the eleven were rated as more helpful by older priests than by younger ones, namely: more opportunity for participation in decision-making and more opportunity to discuss theological and pastoral issues in a public forum. One of the eleven was rated higher by young priests: more opportunity for my personal spiritual development.

Feelings of Priests on Central Priesthood Issues

The Image and Role of the Priesthood

What is the main task of the priest today? Is it being an example or icon, providing spiritual leadership, conveying church teachings, leading a community, managing an organization, pushing for social betterment, or what?

How have priests changed in their answers to this question over the past thirty years? And how has the image of priests changed in the broader society? These topics were central to all our interviews and focus groups. The viewpoints of the priests were diverse, making summarizing risky. However, they did, once again, tend to fall into a pattern divided by age. To communicate them as clearly as we can, we again present interview excerpts in two categories: older priests and younger priests.

We begin with older priests. A midwestern focus group we conducted contained a group of men in their fifties, sixties, and seventies.

Priest #1:

> There has been a breakdown in the fraternity that we once had, when we were very much at home with one another and could stop in and visit. And other priests would stop what they were doing to accommodate and greet their fellow priests. I've noticed a breakdown in that fraternity.

Priest #2:

> One of the realities that has changed for a lot of us is using more of the collegial approach, and not seeing ourselves as that the priest has all the answers and that the people come to us. We are the facilitator and enabler of the people, allowing them to do the ministry.

Priest #3:

> I didn't always think of myself as old. But what I see now about the men who are being ordained at present—I wonder if we are members of the same church! I'm surprised at their liturgical conservatism. I'm surprised at their uncomfortableness in working with women. I'm surprised at their retreat to practices that were gone before I was ordained. So for me, one of the obstacles of the present time is that I'm amazed at the number of priests who are younger who are suspicious and look askance at their older brother priests, as if we are the unfaithful ones and they are the ones who are the keeper of the keys.

Priest #4:

> One of my fears about the new conservatism is not so much the conservatism itself, but whether some of the priests are going back to some of the older symbols. What really freed me was the Vatican Council, because of its whole image of the priesthood as servant-leader. It was "I come not to lead but to serve"—and not a status thing. And my fear is that some of those symbols that are being used and some of the things that are being done are emphasizing more the status of the priest and wanting to be sure that there is a clear distance between the priest and the people, and that "We're in a special kind of realm up here" rather than "We are servants."

Priest #5:

> I would echo that to some extent. I was a priest in those early days, and it seemed like the term *aggiornamento*—the updating and the renewal—there was this tremendous excitement about becoming more relevant to the world and to do things to make the Church very much a part of the world situation. There was a great sense of activism. And I experienced a lot of attention to going outside the church into the community, whether it was in social justice kinds of issues or working with poverty people, and to put less emphasis on the other kinds of really "churchy" things. We were out to be very much involved in the community. But I think a lot of that has changed. Now there is a lot more attention to serving the Church and being very aware of our identity as church people and as priests working for the good of the Church, and much more attention to those kinds of clerical issues. In the early days, we didn't focus a lot on clerical issues at all, but now there is much more attention on clerical issues.

Older priests from different regions expressed similar feelings. A 64-year-old diocesan priest described his image of the priest:

> I'm an instrument, a servant, a servant-leader. Jesus on the donkey—I'm the donkey. I'm carrying Him in, in His presence. You don't get puffed up. It's a service role. The bishop who ordained my class to the diaconate did so in a very quiet ceremony—no big fanfare; parents weren't there; it was in the seminary chapel. At the end he gave the world's shortest sermon, which I remember till today. He said, "Congratulations. Remember, you're not ordained for your own sweet selves." And he was absolutely right, and we should remember that. And that was the end of it. You're not ordained for your own sweet selves. And we should reflect on it. I think that is our role. We have to humbly accept and serve, and I believe that God does nourish us in His word and sacraments.

An older diocesan priest in a focus group in the West:

> I was schooled between '72 and '80 on the east coast, and the attitude about what a priest is was less clerical than it is today. It was much more a social worker, teacher, and preacher, and less the figure that just runs around in a collar and cassock.

Another older priest in the group:

> When I was a young priest right after Vatican II, really loving everything new about the Church, and seeing some of the older priests having a lot of difficulty with the changes, there was a real sense of who was ready for change and who wasn't. And I remember a sense of dividing up the clergy of those that were going for things new and those that were holding back. But I

remember, after five or six years that seemed to disappear. I can recall real-
izing that at a retreat after I'd been ordained five or six years, and there was
this wide range of people present. It seemed like we were no longer talking
about who was liberal, for example, and who was conservative. That didn't
seem to be there, in my experience, until about 1993. I can remember the
very moment when that division came to my attention again. I was taking a
walk with Father ———, and we were talking about all the things that were
going to happen with the new bishop coming and everything, and I mentioned one person. And he said, "I don't think he's got a chance. He's a liberal." And I had not heard anybody use "liberal" or "conservative" for many,
many years. I think that did come back.

Another 64-year-old diocesan priest, who has given retreats in numerous places, talked to us about the new priests:

I think one of the big things right now is that they try to get back to orthodoxy. It's not that we're not orthodox now. *They think* we're not orthodox.
That's the thing that is sort of mystifying. It's this idea that it's got to be
black and white again, and to get things done in "this way." I'm all for keeping the core of the truth alive! But today it's definitely different than right
after Vatican II, when we had a lot more theologians writing much more
freely and taking ideas and exploring them and not worrying about looking
over their shoulder, worried about being called to Rome because of what
they did. They are holding back.

He gave his views about the effect of the new priests on the Church:

What I think is, as the newly ordained go out there, one of two things is going
to happen. Either they're going to do like some of them have done, minister for
four or five years and then say, "I never saw ministry as being this way," and
they're going to get out, because they saw it as a black or white thing—they
were going to lead the people back to the true religion and they thought that
Vatican II was a disgrace. And they'll find that, "Gee, I can't do it" and just
turn off on it. Or, they're going to come out of seminary with a lot of ideas and
then the people will reform them. That is, as they go out, the people will just
say, "No, it's not that way, or this way, at all." People speak out now. They're
not going to put up with a dictator or something like that. They'll just tell him.
If he doesn't care what they think, they won't care about him. It's a two-way
faucet! If you want to live a miserable life, that's the way to do it.

Younger priests tended to have different emphases. Father Bruce, a 37-
year-old diocesan priest, described in an interview how the recently ordained men view the priesthood:

The newly ordained tend to be more traditional. They tend to be more ecclesiologically sound, ecclesiologically traditional. By and large, they're not

grinding any axes. But they also have greater instability, I would say, because of the changes in our society and because of the decay of the family in the '60s and '70s when I was coming up. I think you see those personality problems come out later in the priesthood. So there is a certain instability among individuals, which unfortunately is then seen as the reason they are traditional. The fact is, the generation before mine threw everything out the window and my generation knew nothing of it. We didn't have anything to throw. Latin was nonexistent in 1972 when I was coming up on First Holy Communion. We never did any of that. There were some traditional forms, but we didn't know the preconciliar church. And then, the further we got, the more we realized how we had been deprived. And yes, the instability of the '60s and '70s did lead my generation to seek out the stability of the more traditional forms. But it's not really just a crutch; it's in order to embrace the entirety of the Church, instead of rejecting everything that preceded the council. My group said, "No. We liked the Church then; we like the Church now; we liked the Church for two thousand years."

Father Bruce noted several things that distinguish younger priests and older ones:

Chalices, and interest in the transcendent liturgy, the cultic liturgy—titles too. A lot of the older priests will say, "Oh, just call me Bill." But that doesn't happen in this diocese much. The younger priests will tend to say, "Just call me Father." I used to think that that was important when I was younger, but now I couldn't care less, by and large, unless it's a parishioner, and then you need the distance. Our life is much more symbolic than other people's lives, in the sense that everything we do, everything we have, everything we wear, every way we present ourselves at liturgy and in the street is symbolic of something else.

A 36-year-old diocesan priest criticized some of his elders for calling undue attention to themselves in their liturgies:

I find it difficult, in terms of liturgical style, to see priests who really feel the need to express themselves and make the liturgy kind of their own, rather than submit themselves to the liturgy of the Church. You follow the liturgy in the books and it's absolutely beautiful, and I've found that if I'm faithful to that, it comes through in my own experience and in the experience of many of my peers. They've had a lot of people come up to them and say, "You know, Father, we have no doubt we've been to Mass when you've celebrated," which tells me that there have been times when they've gone to another Mass and wondered if anything Catholic happened. So I think it's the style whereby one humbles himself to what the Church asks him to do in terms of liturgy, rather than try to stand apart from that or put his own stamp on it.

A 42-year-old priest criticized some of the older men for not wearing the collar:

> Some of them are just too secular. Some are ashamed to dress like this, with a collar. My experience, in the short time I've been here, is that it has helped me so many times to wear a collar. It has gotten me into places, like into a crashed car where a woman would not let anyone else in until she saw the collar, and I could get in and comfort her until help was given to her. There is no place I don't go here in this town without this collar—unless I'm jogging or playing basketball.

In an interview another 36-year-old diocesan priest described the newly ordained:

> I would say, almost without a doubt, that those ordained now are probably (I hate to use the term) much more "company men": "This is what we were ordained to do; this is how they told us they want us to do it; this is what is coming out of Rome; therefore, this is what we're going to do when we go out there"—as opposed to my personal impression of those who were not strict, those ordained in the '70s and '60s. With them it's more, "This is what the Church has told us they want us to do and what we're ordained for, but the Church is growing and changing and we need to grow and change with it. We can be pioneers in this respect; thirty percent of the churches in Europe are doing this and I think this is the way the Church is going, so we're going to make those changes here." Yeah, and sometimes they're right. Look at altar girls. Change came and they were right, and the practice became the practice for the diocese. I think there are very few parishes that still have only altar boys; I could probably count them on one hand. With those priests with whom I hang out, if it had not been approved by Rome, we wouldn't have done it. I would have said, "I'm sorry, it's out of my hands. If you want altar girls, write to Rome, write to the bishop. It has nothing to do with me." And take the example of taking kneelers out of the church. Different bishops say different things. That's why it's a lot easier to just say, "This is what I'm told to do. This is what I'm going to do."

A young priest in a focus group:

> A thing that struck me: the common experience that I think we all have of the awesome reality of the Second Vatican Council. As someone who was ordained just three years ago, my seminary training was thoroughly infused with the documents of the Second Vatican Council, as I'm sure all of ours was. The difference is, as someone who did most of my growing up in the 1980s, I never experienced the immediate post-Vatican culture and all of the things that went with that. And so, while I consider myself a priest thoroughly infused with the documents of the Second Vatican Council, I find as

I encounter other priests, and even the people to a lesser extent, I encounter labels that I don't even relate to. I'm "the young conservative priest." I'm "trying to take the Church back to the 1950s." But I don't even know what the Church of the 1950s was like. We would be told things in the seminary, like "Don't wear cassocks"—just a small example—"because if you wear a cassock, you're making a political statement to older priests that you are a young archconservative." We never even saw it in those terms. We see the cassock as a nice thing to wear, something like a Roman collar that shows some priestly identity. And we can't even relate to why in the 1960s the cassocks were thrown out the door and burned. So the challenge has just been to be labeled in a certain way that you don't necessarily feel you deserve.

Conveying the Church's Moral Teachings

The problem of the priest's correct role in teaching the Church's position on sexuality, marriage, and gender issues was repeatedly raised by priests in our interviews and focus groups. The men tended to divide into two schools of thought. One called on the priesthood and the Church to be clearer, more direct, and more countercultural in its teachings. The other said that to have maximal impact on laity today the priest needs to be a *mediator* between church teachings and present-day cultural reality. Following are examples of each viewpoint.

First, a 66-year-old religious priest:

> There is this big silence about teaching the Church's moral position. I think that they need to develop a new vocabulary, a new way of handling some of these issues. Not to give in. Not to say that homosexual activity is right. No. Absolutely not. Or not to say that living together before marriage, which they are implying now is just another way of passage and we have to minister to them where they are. I really don't agree with that. I say that we don't have to agree, but we can always be friends and try to minister to them. We don't have to call that right. We have to call that what it is, as wrong, as directly against the sixth commandment. So on the morality thing, I find that we're not finding the right vocabulary yet.

A young priest in a focus group:

> In this world of ours where married life, family life, sexual morality—where all these things are in crisis, what better can we do than to give our people this beautiful gift of the Church's moral teachings? And who on earth are we as priests to dissent from those, especially as public ministers, to suggest that it's okay to pick and choose on those moral issues or to affirm our people who have decided to dissent on moral issues? Who are we as priests to do that in this Church of Jesus Christ, not the church of me?

The second viewpoint asserted that the priest has a role as a mediator between the Church's moral teachings and the realities of individuals' lives. It was voiced by priests of all ages. A focus group in the Midwest contained several middle-age and older priests.

Priest #1:

> Here I am, ordained by the Church, and hoping to bring God's joy and good news into people's lives. And yet, at the same time, especially when I do home visits and see what the people are going through, especially in terms of moral decisions, it's very difficult. For example, some people that I have been in contact with recently, they have many children, their sex life has real values, that's what they talk about in terms of enhancing their life. And when it comes to moral issues of whether or not they could use contraception or any means to not have children, this is something I am still struggling with in terms of my ministry with them and also in the sacrament of reconciliation. How do I bring the sacrament that is meaningful to them and at the same time respect their life conditions? I've been asking many people, and I haven't been able to find an answer. That is still frustrating.

An older priest in the group:

> In my own personal ministry, my attitude towards Rome is a little bit of "I don't know how I am supposed to represent this official larger church and yet deal with my folks pastorally in their concerns." One of the things that occurs to me is, like, marriage preparation. We've got the teachings of the Church from Rome. And yet I've got well over half, if not three-quarters, of the people coming to me living together and cohabitating. Now how am I supposed to handle that? Should I shake my finger at them? I'm involved in a ministry in the diocese with parents of gays and lesbians. And yet Rome says I'm supposed to be kind of wagging my finger at their children and saying "Shape up or ship out" [sigh]. I've become, even on that very personal pastoral level, alienated, in a sense, from that authoritarian stance that I see there.

Priest #2:

> I've felt that it fits the priesthood. If we're acting in the person of Christ, where was Christ? He was in that middle position, mediating. You know, where "Here's the teachings, and here's the people," and you're in the middle trying to draw them together. That's kind of been my vision of it. So, even though the people are not where the teachings are, I don't think they're supposed to be where the teachings are. I'm not there either.

Priest #3:

> I think, if you walk into the priesthood thinking, "Now I'm the one who'll be making pronouncements, and no backtalk, please," then you're going to find

yourself between a rock and a hard place. [All laugh.] But if you're willing to be in conversation or in dialogue, and I think that is where we should be, it removes a lot of that stress. Then we are acting as mediator or translator, trying to put it into everyday language or imagery so they get it. Like, "Oh, now I get it! I can't quite live that ideal, but now I understand it!"

A 36-year-old diocesan priest:

My role is to try and translate, to make the teachings accessible but also to recognize that there are certain areas where Rome can spout all it wants. Like birth control. I don't necessarily agree with the position on birth control. I understand it and I respect it, but to be honest with you, when you've got a woman who has three children, had several miscarriages, is in a position economically where she can't afford children, and who wants to enjoy that part of her relationship with her spouse and not worry—because it's going to give them strength considering the challenges that they face today and it's one of the areas that gives them the greatest harmony, where that intimacy can fill their lives with something that it's lacking in other areas—they can't be worried if, at that moment, that she's in ovulation. I would say the ideal is wonderful, and I agree with the ideal in theory, but when it comes down to the practical and it comes to people's lives, I can't condemn somebody because they're using birth control. I have to make a pastoral decision, and it may not be in agreement with what the Church teaches. I will always tell a person what the Church teaches, but when it comes down to it, I'm not going to condemn them. I can't do it with my heart.

Sharing Ministry With Laity

Our numerous discussions of collaboration with lay ministers tended to drift to the issue of status and role in ministry. The priests emphasized that pastors need to feel secure in their own role and identity if they are to work with lay ministers successfully. This was discussed in a focus group.

Priest #1:

I had an experience once, just a few years ago, I was looking for someone like a DCE [director of Christian education]. And the young man I interviewed, I remember making a comment to someone on the staff: "This man is more qualified than I am. He ought to be pastor." I guess what I'm saying is that they can be very threatening to the clergy, especially as they become more qualified and have master's degrees or Ph.Ds, especially if they have specialized in a certain area. So I think it is important that the priest has to be confident and strong in who he is and what he's doing. Also, I'm in a parish that can afford some professional lay ministers and pay them just salaries, but other places don't have that grace and those resources. So it can take a lot of time on the pastor's part.

Priest #2:

> I guess it saddens me when I see some priests, when they are confronted with competent professional lay ministers, they tend to become more authoritarian and defensive. Partly because, I think, of some feelings of inadequacy. Rather than being able to appreciate the gift they have and being able to say to themselves, "Hey, maybe I need some more training, if I'm feeling inadequate."

Priest #3:

> I've really seen the role of the pastor as an enabler. I really was trained by the lay people in my first parish. So many gifted people were committed to ministry! It was my task to enable them to use their gifts and maybe discover their gifts. In spite of some of the difficulties, I'm very optimistic. The thing that worries me is the thing that some of you have brought up, that we all don't have the same vision. You can have a parish where the pastor has enabled people to use and to see their gifts, and trained them, and then if you have a pastoral change there can be a real reversion. And that is a difficulty that we're going to face more and more.

A middle-aged priest in another focus group:

> About professional lay ministers, I feel that in our diocese there is real clarity for the need for lay ministers and the importance of them, but I see a shift in the Church as a whole, I don't know about just our diocese, that maybe there is a little more reticence about lay ministers. And I think that comes from the idea of clericalism, the question of what a priest is and the relationship to lay ministries. So I do think there's a change of attitude. I think the attitude now is, "We need the priests more than the lay ministers."

A 36-year-old diocesan priest:

> The Church has been very careful about what the roles are. I've seen cases where the lay ministers haven't been allowed to do enough, and I've also seen cases where they've been allowed to do too much. Got to be careful. We have to make sure the laity don't become clericalized and the clergy don't become laicized.

One or two priests mentioned that forceful women on a parish staff can be frightening.

A 61-year-old diocesan priest with experience in diocesan leadership experience:

> I think it depends on the female. I know from listening to the comments of some of the priests talking about some of the pastoral associates or youth ministers who are women, some of their comments are very negative because these are very, I guess what they call "strong women," people who

make their opinions known. And I have worked, in one situation, with one of these women—very respectful, very helpful, very knowledgeable, knew what to do. But I know that the general opinion of most of the priests that I talked to about her is very negative because they see her as a strong, opinionated woman. I worked with her. I thought she was wonderful: she was taking care of things; people related to her well; they were very comfortable with her ministry in the parish. And her ministry in the parish was marvelous. But the pastor, in effect, let her go. She realized she couldn't minister there. He was just overly threatened by the fact that she was so popular.

Help in Personal Spiritual Development

For all priests, but especially the younger ones, the opportunity for personal spiritual development was viewed as essential for carrying out their priestly ministry. What would this entail? In interviews and focus groups we asked priests what had been helpful to them in their spiritual lives.

A 36-year-old diocesan priest relies on self-discipline and on specific devotions:

> It comes down to—especially as a diocesan priest—your own faithfulness, being your own schedule-maker and disciplinarian, making sure that I'm faithful to each hour of the Divine Office, having a Holy Hour every day (sometimes I do, sometimes I don't— sometimes it's fifteen minutes; sometimes it's an hour and a half). I need to develop more consistency with that. I've struggled with that as long as I've been a priest. You want to be faithful to all those staples of the spiritual life—the Office, having a Holy Hour, preferably before the Blessed Sacrament, being sure you prepare adequately for Mass, being sure you give a good thanksgiving after Mass and say Mass reverently. The rosary—I've become more convinced of its effectiveness. That is one of the things where people say you should do it. But in my case, the only way I became convinced of the rosary was praying it for certain intentions and seeing that those prayers were answered, so I really became convinced of the effectiveness of it and pray that a lot more often. That has become a more or less daily discipline. So I'm still struggling to instill spiritual disciplines and I think the more those become ingrained, the better you are as a priest, the more you have that to fall back on.

A 36-year-old priest has found having a spiritual director helpful:

> A priest friend of mine once challenged me—he was my spiritual director for a while. He said, "I want you to do a rosary every day for the rest of your life, and if you get home at three o'clock in the morning and you haven't said your rosary, stay up till four o'clock in the morning saying it, and the next day you won't forget." So I have been true to that. I'm meeting with the spiritual

director, and regular confession keeps me honest. There are some things I admit I'm failing on. I wish I did my Holy Hour more faithfully, and I don't. I always have the excuse of "there is too much to do." And our church is constantly being used, all the time, with all the groups that go through there. There is no time to go over there when it's quiet and no one's going to be in there.

For 42-year-old Father Stephen, both a spiritual director and the fraternity of other priests are necessary:

I would say spiritual direction is very important, that it be done regularly, like once a month minimum. I have a spiritual director and go to him as a support system. Number two, good fraternal relations with brother priests in the rectory and the diocese is very important as a support system. And obviously, it goes without saying, a regular private prayer life. But even when you have that which will help you hang on, if you don't have a good spiritual director in priestly relations, it's difficult.

Having close priest friends was often mentioned as important for spiritual life.

A 37-year-old priest relies on personal discipline and a network of priest friends:

My resources are personal discipline including certain *sine qua nons:* like the Divine Office and a network of priest friends—we talk about the spiritual life; we talk about God and things—frequent confession, and very much a sense of the priesthood and a sense that we are not just sacramental dispensers, but we are meant to be spiritual leaders. We are meant to be able to point the way to God, and to live as icons of the Lord in the world.

Thirty-two-year-old Father Eric describes his support system, which includes priest friends and a supportive prayer group:

I belong to a prayer group that consists of both priests and lay people, mostly in their twenties and thirties. They are wonderful people. They come from all walks of life and the spectrum of careers, from blue-collar to executive level. We usually get together once a month, a Saturday night of prayer and reflection and venting and giggles and everything else that goes with that. But that means a lot to me, because they've been a good support as far as seeing where they are at and having an honest conversation, bringing that to prayer. I get to distance myself. These are not parishioners, so this is a place where I find refuge to just be with spiritual friends. And then I think another fundamental tool—and this has been essential—the idea of a spiritual director, having that once-a-month check-in to hold you accountable. Sometimes there is nothing, not a topic to discuss in spiritual direction, but the fact that you're coming in and checking in to see How are things going?,

Where are my blind spots?, if there is a topic, things like that. Where is God in this experience? In that regard, that has been a very powerful tool.

As this chapter has shown, priests feel a need for greater clarity and support in several areas of their lives. They need more clarity about their own role over against those of the laity and lay ministers; they need help dealing with moral questions in the realm of sexuality; and they need help with their own spiritual lives. When laity change and social norms defining what is moral and immoral change as well, priests are unavoidably affected. Priests need help to regain self-confidence and a clear sense of their identity. In chapter six we look at length into one topic causing unease among some priests—the question of homosexual subcultures.

Chapter 6

The Question of Homosexual Subcultures

Are there more homosexuals in the seminary today, proportionately, than there were thirty years ago? I don't think so. But if you have only eight guys in the seminary and three are homosexual, they are more visible and the culture is more obvious.

—A 59-year-old religious priest

Recently the discussion of homosexuality in the priesthood has been more open, and at the same time more opinionated, than ever. For this reason we included two questions in the 2001 survey asking about homosexual[1] subcultures. Donald Cozzens, in his widely read and controversial book, *The Changing Face of the Priesthood* (2000), argues that the most dangerous effect homosexual seminarians and priests can have on the priesthood is when a distinct homosexual subculture develops in a seminary, diocese, or religious province. The term "subculture" can have a variety of meanings, but Cozzens uses the term in a strict sociological sense—a group of persons who interact continually with each other and seldom with outsiders, and who develop shared experiences, understandings, and meanings. Though Cozzens describes in his book a type of homosexual subculture that he believes is destructive to priestly life, it is important to note that subcultures, in general, can serve as an important source of support and integration for people who find themselves at odds with or outside of the dominant culture. They often arise naturally. A child of immigrant Irish-Catholic parents raised in Boston would share norms, values, and experiences of that subculture, providing a clear identity in the midst of a larger non-Catholic or non-immigrant society. Other subcultures

---

[1] We use the term homosexual to refer to sexual orientation, not sexual activity. We use the terms homosexual and gay interchangeably. We encountered some uses of "gay" as implying sexual activity, but that is not our meaning here.

develop as people discover that society is unable or unwilling to address their needs. People who don't feel accepted find others like themselves and form what has sometimes been called a "contraculture," specifically designed to challenge society's limits.

In seminaries, as in other settings, supportive groups will arise naturally among those who have common interests, views and lifestyles. It is only when these views begin to confront or even undermine the prevailing seminary culture (i.e., become contracultures) that conflicts arise. McDonough and Bianchi, in their recent study of Jesuits, describe this division among self-identified homosexual Jesuits:

> Homosexual Jesuits are divided about advancing gay subculture within the Society. One position favors assimilation in what is taken to be a nonhostile, mostly nonsexualized environment. A second option favors the assertive cultivation of a queer lifestyle among gay Jesuits. (p. 101)

James Martin in his article "The Church and the Homosexual Priest" (2000) agrees with Cozzens that the emergence of a homosexual subculture in the priesthood is a challenge to the Church today. Homosexual men struggle for acceptance within themselves and within the larger society, Martin says, and this desire for acceptance may cause them to prefer the company of other homosexual men. In time, supportive networks may develop which, consciously or unconsciously, exclude heterosexuals. A heterosexual priest, feeling excluded, may resent this but hesitate to express his concerns for fear of being labeled "homophobic." Seminary president Gerald Coleman says these subcultures are unhealthy:

> We must avoid at all costs a "homosexualized" climate in seminary formation programs where cliques develop among homosexual students, cliques which set them apart as different from all other students. These types of cliques are unhealthy in any context, and create unacceptable problems in seminaries and in the priesthood itself. (2002:21)

But a 30-year-old gay former Jesuit sees the issue from another perspective:

> For the most part it really didn't matter if a Jesuit was gay or straight. Everyone was expected to live the same way, celibate. But there were some differences between the two groups. . . . The gay Jesuits, being a minority in the overall society at large, tended to seek one another out for support as a group in the Society of Jesus. Straight Jesuits were much less likely to network. . . . Oftentimes gay Jesuits were persecuted by religious superiors and by members of their community, but they had their network of friends to rely upon in hard times. . . . We had to actually live in the same house with homophobes; we couldn't "go home" and get away from them. This is why the

gay networking was so essential to our survival. Once early on in my formation, our provincial gave a speech where he condemned the fact that gay
Jesuits would network with one another, but it just forced us to strengthen our
ties to one another and keep things even more to ourselves. (McDonough and
Bianchi, pp. 105–6)

Clearly subcultures vary in their intent and in their ability to enhance or
undermine the larger culture.

Cozzens believes that a gay subculture exists today among the priests in
most of the larger U.S. dioceses (p. 100) and that a similar situation exists
in many seminaries. McDonough and Bianchi believe that a gay counter-
culture among Jesuits is not only on the increase but is helping to maintain
a sense of being set apart from the rest of society.

The problem that may arise when a gay subculture is strong in a seminary is that the subculture can undermine the self-confidence of straight
seminarians and force some of them away. Stated differently, seminaries
develop various subcultures, and a kind of "tipping point" phenomenon
comes into play—one in which a dominant heterosexual subculture will
threaten the gays and drive some of them away, just as a dominant homosexual subculture will drive some of the heterosexuals away. Cozzens explains:

> Inevitably, gay men form gay circles of friends and associates. While not nec-
> essarily exclusive by intention, these gay subgroups exercise an influence
> upon the straight men who find themselves either working with or living in
> close proximity to homosexual men. . . . Straight men in environments
> populated by significant numbers of gays experience a sense of destabiliza-
> tion. They wrestle with a certain self-doubt, a feeling that they don't fit in. On
> both psychic and spiritual levels, they are not "at home." (2000, p. 109)

Martin agrees. It is the homosexual *subculture*, in Cozzens' and Martin's estimation, that is the number-one problem arising from the number
of priests who are homosexual—and not their sexual orientation as such.
Therefore we decided to try to get an estimate of how widespread the subcultures are perceived to be. Our two questions, asked for the first time in
2001, are shown in figure 6.1. (The data are in table A.7 in the appendix.)
In our priest focus groups we discovered that the concept of subculture was
sometimes vague and misunderstood. To help clarify the concept we
defined the term in the survey questionnaire. This section of the survey
began, "There has been talk about homosexual subcultures in seminaries,
dioceses, and religious institutes today. A 'subculture' refers to a definite
group of persons which has its own preferential friendships, social gatherings, and vocabulary."

Figure 6.1
Is there a homosexual subculture in your
diocese or religious community? (In percents)

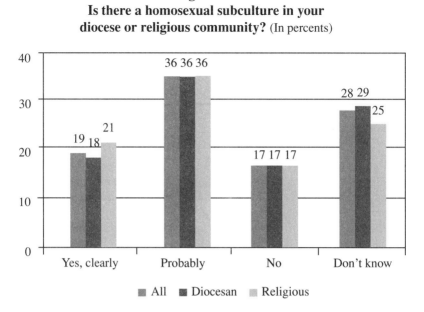

Figure 6.2
Percent saying there was clearly a homosexual subculture
in diocese or religious institute (By age group)

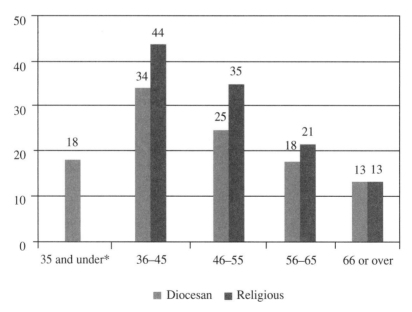

*The sample for religious priests in the 25–35 age group is too small to report.

First we asked if there is a homosexual subculture in the respondent's diocese or religious institute. Nineteen percent said "yes, clearly," and another 36% said "probably but not clearly." Diocesan and religious priests made similar reports. The younger priests were more apt to respond "yes" or "probably," though the pattern was uneven. Figure 6.2 shows a steady decrease in propensity to identify a homosexual subculture as the age of priests increases. (Our sample of religious priests had too few persons 35 or younger to report.)

The younger and middle age priests are more aware of homosexual subcultures than the older men. In fact, a larger percentage of the older priests answered "don't know" to the question. But, contrary to the trend, only 18% of the youngest diocesan group said there was clearly a homosexual subculture in their diocese.

What about seminary life? The second question asked about the presence of a homosexual subculture in the seminary (or seminaries) that the priest attended, at the time he was there (see figure 6.3). Overall, 15% said "yes, clearly," and another 26% said "probably but not clearly." Diocesan and religious priests made similar estimates, but responses varied greatly by age. The younger the priest, the more likely he was to report a homosexual subculture in his seminary. Figure 6.4 shows how great the differences were. Among the youngest priests (combined diocesan and religious, age 35 or younger), 45% said there was clearly a homosexual subculture in the seminary they attended. By contrast, only 8% of those 56-65, and only 3% of those 66 or older, recalled a clear homosexual subculture in their seminaries. (Diocesan and religious priests again showed similar age patterns.) These findings raise important questions. Did this difference between young and old occur because more homosexual subcultures actually exist in seminaries today, or merely because they are more visible or more openly discussed? Or perhaps are the younger priests more aware of homosexuality because of its acceptance in the larger society? This survey does not provide us with the information we need to answer these questions.

The *Los Angeles Times* survey asked the very same question about homosexual subcultures that we used in 2001. (Their research team adopted our question but changed the response categories.) Regarding the presence of a homosexual subculture in the priests' diocese or religious order, 17% of the respondents in their survey said "definitely yes" and 27% said "probably yes," while 52% said no. When asked if such a subculture existed at the seminary they attended, 12% said "definitely yes" and 14% said "probably yes," while 71% said no. But of the priests who were ordained in the last 20 years, 53% said "yes"—much higher than the 26% overall. These figures are lower than we found in our survey, and the discrepancy is probably due to the lower response rate of the *Times* survey.

102

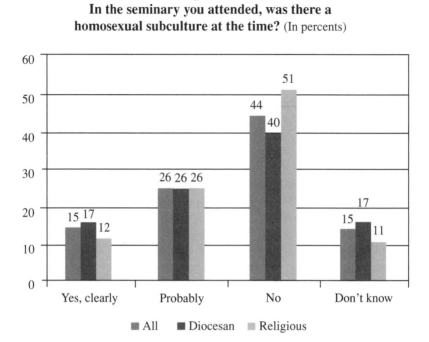

Figure 6.3
In the seminary you attended, was there a
homosexual subculture at the time? (In percents)

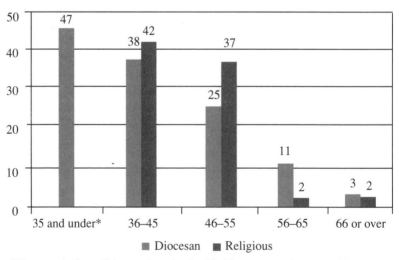

Figure 6.4
Percent saying there was clearly a homosexual
subculture in the seminary they attended (By age group)

*The sample for religious priests in the 25–35 age group is too small to report.

The *Times* survey also asked priests about their own homosexual or heterosexual orientation. A direct question such as this has never been asked in a survey of priests, and we wonder how accurate or honest the responses are. But in any event, 9% of the priests said that they were homosexual and 6% said "somewhere in between, but more on the homosexual side." Five percent placed themselves "completely in the middle" between heterosexuality and homosexuality, while 67% identified themselves as exclusively heterosexual, 8% referred to themselves as "mostly" heterosexual, and 5% declined to answer the question. These reports of the numbers of priests with a homosexual orientation are lower than estimates made by earlier researchers, whose figures range from 25% to 50%, and due to the low response of the *Times* survey we believe its estimates of homosexual priests are lower than reality.

Priests' Observations about Homosexual Subcultures

The priests we interviewed were more able to identify with confidence the presence or absence of a homosexual subculture in their seminaries than in their dioceses. Some recalled a blatant and disturbing subculture, while others were clear that there was no homosexual subculture at all or that, if there was, they were unaware of it. Priests who clearly identified such a subculture tended to say it had negative effects. In one focus group, three priests talked about the obvious homosexual subculture in their seminaries and its effects on them.

Priest #1:

> Indeed there was [a homosexual subculture] when I first went to seminary in 1982. There was a very strong subculture, one that actually shocked me. It was something! I thought it had some negative effects. It created a certain kind of an atmosphere and a certain kind of irreverence. That for me was a problem. I just didn't expect that.

Priest #2:

> My first negative experience was that certain of the seminarians were kind of predators to other people in the seminary community. It made me angry when some people's minds were played with, and they decided to leave seminary. But that's the main concern I had about that. There was an incident, and so the seminary decided to clean house. Basically I experienced it in a negative way, because we were in preparation for celibacy, and some people did not care. I had a problem with that.

Priest #3 addressed the broader issue of priestly sexuality:

> It had a negative effect on me, in the sense that it categorized everyone because of the subculture, a subculture which may or may not have been the

majority, in this case the minority. It categorized everyone, in that if you want to be a priest, you have to be sexual! And that's not true across the board. I don't think the issue of homosexuality was a problem. I think the issue was how the authorities dealt with it—how the issues of priesthood, the issues of masculinity, the issues of spirituality, and the issues of celibacy were brought to bear on that particular issue and from that particular perspective. Clearly there were heterosexuals there who were also taking the celibacy issue—and all of that—just as lightly, and had little things on the side as well. It wasn't just homosexuals.

A 37-year-old diocesan priest emphasized the difference between those in the subculture and those with simply a homosexual orientation:

It was extremely corrosive. It was a corrosive element to the nth degree. It was a backbiting, unpleasant, vicious group. It was not solely those who had homosexual orientation. That's the wrong way to look at it. There were many who had that orientation but were perfectly fine and reasonable human beings and weren't really shoving your face in it. Just somehow you knew, or you sensed it, or they told you in confidence or something. But other than that, they were pious, good, hardworking guys who just were getting on with it. But there was a homosexual lifestyle subculture, which, when I first entered the seminary, ran the seminary practically— thoroughly tolerated by the faculty, in fact in some instances supported by it and promoted.

Some younger priests were also conscious of individuals who were homosexual but not part of a clear homosexual subculture. Father Eric, age 32 and ordained in 1998, described his experience:

I have to honestly say that if what you mean by "subculture" is a group defined as such, I didn't experience that. Now if you're talking about individuals who struggled with their sexuality, that is a different question and I think I saw that. But I haven't seen evidence of a subculture. I know that others claim to observe that through some of the material that has been in the media, but that isn't my experience in the eleven years of formation that I was in.

Father Charles, a 32-year-old priest, found groups of gays in the seminary to be inclusive:

There were certainly scholastics who were gay, people who were out to me. And sometimes they would socialize together, but there was never anything like an all-gay small community or an all-gay faith sharing group or an all-gay liturgy group. And I never encountered anybody who sought that. And those are the things that I would identify as a subculture, an exclusive socialization. Did guys who were gay socialize together? Yes, I think they did, but not to the exclusion of anybody else. And sometimes I think that socialization is probably very helpful in terms of getting the affective support that people needed for themselves and their ability to do ministry as a gay man in our culture.

A 40-year-old religious priest saw homosexuality as the main *culture* rather than the subculture of his seminary, but could see no harmful effects:

> I don't know if it was a subculture; it seemed everyone was a homosexual. But most people forget that people with homosexual orientation are oppressed people, and there needs to be support given when they're with their own. I had somebody here, a young guy in the parish in his mid-twenties, say he was interested in priesthood, but now because of the whole pedophilia thing and the association with homosexuality, he's just really thinking twice. I challenged him by saying, "If you think you're going to go through life without meeting anyone who is ill or anyone who is different, you're going to have a very difficult life." We have to really be healthy in our own selves that we can allow the fact that there are going to be people who are different.

Older priests ordained in the 1960s and 1970s typically were unaware of any homosexual subcultures in their seminary experiences. One older priest ordained in 1968 described the strict moral code imposed by his seminary:

> It was a very rigid sexual-moral code for everybody, all the time. In my day, there was a lot of stuff about particular friendships. I must be honest: I was well through the place before I figured out what the heck that was about. So there were certain pieces of this that you were just stupid about. No regrets, that's just the way it was. And the other was: If this was my room and somebody walked over the threshold, we were both expelled immediately without any conversation. It was over—so lots of structure around boundaries, very structured. And there is a certain ease with that, this is how you do it.

The priests had more difficulty identifying homosexual subcultures in their dioceses or religious orders than in their seminaries. In seminaries, men preparing for the priesthood are thrust into a communal setting that few will experience once they become priests. Once out in the parish, priests naturally become less aware of and less affected by whatever homosexual subcultures may exist among priests. The men we interviewed were more concerned that both heterosexual and homosexual priests live a healthy lifestyle, free from the potential destructiveness caused by any exclusive subgroup.

The Effects of a Homosexual Subculture on the Church

Fifty-year-old Father Angelo, a religious priest ordained in 1977, talked about the potentially negative effects of a dominant homosexual subculture:

> As religious and as priests we are called to integrate sexuality into our lives and not to make it the defining characteristic of who we are. It's one aspect

of who we are; it's an important one, obviously. So I think integration is the goal for which we strive. I think one of the effects can be, if there is a certain perception that a diocese or a community is accepting a preponderance of gay men, then those who are not may not feel comfortable. Just anecdotally, somebody said, "That religious community accepts only gay men." Well then, others who are not homosexually oriented could say, "I'm not going to consider them, even if I'm attracted to their ideals or ministries." I think *that* perception is out there. Either if you're gay, you can't apply; or if you're not gay, you won't be welcome. That's a real effect.

Father Rick, age 59, expressed his concern about the effects of homosexuality on the Church:

I'm concerned about the Church, with its mission, and that the Lord be known and that we enjoy this thing and let's go on with it. And since most of us are heterosexual, there is a relational issue here. Why are we not attracting heterosexual men? Secondly, and I think much, much more importantly, How do we integrate women into being leaders in this church in a very healthy way?

A 36-year-old priest asked for a closer look at sex in our culture:

I think automatically there is a sense in this diocese, in the Church, and in our culture, that to be gay automatically means you're promiscuous. When you think about it, the average straight person sleeps with how many partners before they marry someone or they're committed to somebody? (if they ever commit to somebody). So before homosexual persons are condemned for being promiscuous, I think we have to look at straight culture. Because that's an acceptable thing: to be straight and sleep around, as a part of that culture. Rather than just saying, "Because you're gay or because you're straight, this is why you're choosing to sleep around," you should be looking at the issue itself. What is the human hunger that makes us look for someone? And why are we trying to fill that human hunger with the sexual act and not looking for the things that would really fill the center of our being?

Father Craig, age 36, is concerned with sexual promiscuity in the priesthood:

I guess what I'm coming right down to saying is: If anyone is advertising his homosexuality, they aren't necessarily people I hang out with, probably because we don't move in the same circles. And I don't want to say that it's not having an effect, because anybody who is having sex with anybody, whether it's a man, woman, child, is going to have an effect on all of us eventually. I've probably had more problems with guys that were having sex with women than guys that were having a homosexual relationship; if that's what was going on, that more directly affected me. They tend to be more open about it, probably because it's more accepted. A friend of mine had a retired priest living with him, had his girlfriend over there, "just my secretary"—but it wasn't just his secretary.

The Effects of Changing Cultural Attitudes

In a recent international study on the acceptance of homosexuality, Americans were more likely than the Italians, French or British to say that homosexuality is wrong (Fetto, 2002). Despite our prudishness from an international perspective, Americans are changing our attitudes. Acceptance of homosexuality is rising. A Gallup poll asked adults across the United States whether they thought homosexual relations between consenting adults should be legal. In 1977, 43% agreed that the relationship should be legal, in 1989, 47% and in 1999, 50%. The General Social Survey has polled adults repeatedly since the 1970s about their attitudes toward sexual relations between two adults of the same sex, and from the early 1970s through 1991 the percent of adults saying that same-sex relationships are "always wrong" hovered around 72% to 75%. In 1993 that percentage dropped to 66% and by 1996 it had arrived at a new low of 59%. Those finding same-sex relationships "not wrong at all" jumped to 29% in 2000, whereas before 1993 it had never risen above 16%. Gallup polls also asked if homosexuality should be an "acceptable alternative lifestyle." In 1982, 34% found it to be acceptable, and by 1996 that percentage had risen to forty-four.

These data show that homosexuality has become more acceptable to Americans. The barriers to the gay lifestyle are diminishing. In Catholic circles as well, the past decade has witnessed more openness in discussions of homosexuality, including homosexual priests. In *The New York Times* Laurie Goodstein writes: "Catholic publications from the liberal Jesuit magazine *America* to official diocesan newspapers are calling for an examination of homosexuality in the priesthood." (19 April 2002)

Since priests are drawn from men living in today's culture, the norms established in American society are likely to influence, at least in subtle ways, priests' attitudes. How will the Church help priests reconcile these cultural changes with unchanging church teachings?

The Effects of Church Teachings

While promoting acceptance of homosexuals "with respect, compassion, and sensitivity," church teaching about homosexuality is at a distance from present-day attitudes. According to the 1993 *Catechism of the Catholic Church*, "homosexual acts are intrinsically disordered" and "contrary to natural law." Even a homosexual orientation is viewed by the Vatican as an "objective disorder." A 1986 Vatican pastoral letter to bishops states, "Although the particular inclination of the homosexual person is not a sin, it is a more or less strong tendency ordered toward an intrinsic moral evil; and thus the inclination itself must be seen as an objective disorder."

The recent pedophilia crisis in the Church has further threatened the security of homosexual American priests. Homosexuality and celibacy are both connected with pedophilia in the minds of many people, even though no valid scientific evidence shows a connection. Adding to the confusion are recent statements made by Vatican spokesman Joaquin Navarro-Valls who told the *New York Times* that "people with these inclinations [homosexuality] just cannot be ordained." (3 March 2002)

In an interview, a 40-year-old religious priest complained about the Church's message to homosexual priests:

> If the priest is celibate, and he's doing what he's supposed to do, and he's ministering, and he's doing well, what's the problem? What's starting to come out now, with the plan to go to the seminaries scrutinizing people—I didn't know homosexuality was something that would exclude you from seminary. We're telling them, the orientation itself isn't sinful, the *activity* is, the product of it. So we sentence them to a life of celibacy anyway. And when they do want to be celibate and come to priesthood, we still tell them no. So it seems like they can't win *anywhere*.

A Healthy Celibacy

We asked priests in interviews and focus groups what they would recommend to bishops about the number of homosexual priests. The men were more concerned with the healthy integration of sexuality and celibacy for all priests than with how many priests are homosexual. For most, it did not matter whether a priest is homosexual or heterosexual as long as he keeps his vows of celibacy, but some cautioned that problems could arise if the priesthood comes to be perceived as a homosexual profession.

The priests we talked with made a distinction between those with a homosexual orientation and those who display their homosexuality.

Father Don, age 36:

> I know that there are some people who feel that when they're with the boys [other gay men] they can let their hair hang out, and in some ways that subculture then makes itself present. But then I know other guys who are gay but are just themselves. I accept them for who they are and I know that they are gay.

A 37-year-old diocesan priest focused on the need for celibacy:

> It's not a big deal so long as you understand that these guys have to live celibately like everyone else. There needs to be some sense of training for them

like everything else. I think one of the reasons so many gay men come in, in a good sense, is that they've sensed the need for God more, the pointlessness of gay relationships, and they sense the need for a greater dependence on God or need for God. And so they are drawn to try to give themselves completely to this. The problem is they get in, and they find out that, well, there is nothing in the lifestyle that is going to help them be celibate—and they wind up losing it.

A 49-year-old diocesan priest placed responsibility on the individual priest:

> My bottom line on this is: Yeah, it's fine to ordain a homosexual person. But I think that they have the moral responsibility, just as a heterosexual or a bisexual, to live by what the Church claims in its priests, and that is that you're going to live celibately and chastely. I think homosexual priests who come out publicly and make a big deal about it, especially from the pulpit, I think that is professional malpractice. I think that is a personal thing, which needs to be dealt with in private. I think belonging to homosexual clubs and frequenting homosexual bars is inappropriate for priests. So all those things have to be taken into consideration. Though I think that a homosexual person has the right as a priest to come out publicly and say they're homosexual, but you do that in a professional way. You don't do it inappropriately from the pulpit, and get in the media and flaunt the fact that you're having an affair with somebody. The same rules apply whether you're heterosexual or homosexual: You're supposed to live chastely and celibately, bottom line.

Father Angelo, a 50-year-old priest, stressed the need for maturity and healthy integration:

> In general I think we need to screen candidates better; we need to make sure that they're mature, that they are people who are growing toward the integration of the human, the sexual, the intellectual, the spiritual, the physical. All of those aspects of personality which make well-rounded persons and ministers, I think they are very important.

Forty-year-old Father Paul recommended support for living the celibate life:

> You know, you can talk to someone till you're blue in the face, but maybe we're not helping them. What we need to do is to help people to embrace celibacy, instead of making it a word that we have to live. I find in my own life, if I embrace my celibacy as a part of who I am and not something that I have to do, then it's not a chore. It's something I do naturally because it's part of who I am. Yes, I have to pray every day for that. Every time I say my prayers, that's part of my prayer: "Help me embrace it; help me to make it a part of who I am so I can live it out." But maybe that's what we need to help guys do: to embrace our celibacy instead of forcing it on us. Do I believe that we should

have a celibate clergy? Yes, I do. Because it keeps us more faith-filled to the
people that we serve, more available. And I feel that to be very, very important.

Most priests feel that the real issue concerning homosexuality is the
healthy integration of sexuality into priests' lives. The priests' recommendations are built upon the expectation of a continuing celibate priesthood.
But many in the Church today believe that celibacy should become optional for priests, as a way to overcome the priest shortage. A potential
problem looms on the horizon: if celibacy became optional, homosexuals
would, by church doctrine, be excluded from optional celibacy; only heterosexual men would be free to marry. It would be perceived as being un-
fair. Would homosexual priests resent the companionship experienced by
married priests but unavailable to them?

To sum up: Most priests recommend a healthy integration of sexual orientation—whether it be heterosexual or homosexual—into the total celibate life of the priest. Sexual issues, including homosexual issues, need to
be consciously addressed from within the larger community if priests are
to successfully embrace the celibate life. Without this acceptance from the
larger community, subcultures are more likely to arise because of priests'
need to resolve these issues.

For those we interviewed, homosexual subcultures pose few problems in
dioceses. Although many priests recognize the existence of homosexual
subcultures in their dioceses, they do not express concerns about divisions
or disruptions in their dioceses. Some have questioned whether the failure
of younger priests to attend diocesan meetings is related to the issue of homosexual subcultures, but we have no evidence to substantiate this concern.

Most problems with homosexual subcultures occur in the seminary.
Some priests expressed concerns about promiscuity, a predatory attitude
toward young seminarians, and an unwillingness to acknowledge or address these issues on the part of seminary faculty. Others found that gay
seminarians socialized together in ways that were supportive but did not
exclude heterosexual priests. These two differing perceptions emphasize
the wide range of possibilities among homosexual subcultures: They can
provide essential and non-threatening support for men who find themselves outside the cultural norm, but they can also develop into "contracultures" that devastate the harmony of the seminary community. Distinctions
need to be made between helpful and supportive subcultures and those that
are destructive. If healthy and supportive subcultures are to be encouraged,
an honest evaluation of how each develops would be in order.

Several other issues about homosexuality and homosexual subcultures
remain to be addressed:

1. Should homosexual priests "come out" about their sexual orientation? If so, to whom and under what conditions?

2. In light of a changing societal attitude toward homosexuality, should the Church reassess its own attitudes? James Alison (2001), for example, encourages us to discover that gay people "are not defective heterosexuals, but just are that way."

3. How has the way seminaries address sexuality influenced the current crisis of pedophilia, if at all?

4. Are fewer heterosexuals being attracted to the priesthood? If so, why? Does it matter?

These and other questions form an essential agenda for the Church in the twenty-first century.

Chapter 7

Understanding the Changes

Priests and lay people each have a different part to play. Priests belong in the sanctuary and people belong in the pews. Faithful and committed Christians, who understand the ecclesiology of the Church, would have no trouble with that.

—A 37-year-old diocesan priest

Our survey and interview findings corroborate one another in presenting a clear picture of change in the priesthood. They show that the priesthood has seen two basic transitions since midcentury: first a barrage of innovations in the 1960s largely resulting from the Second Vatican Council—including reorientations in ecclesiology, liturgy, and seminary training—and then a second transition beginning in the 1980s and continuing until today. The direction of the second transition is open to interpretation. Many older priests see it as a return to the cultic model of the priesthood dominant in the 1940s and 1950s, whereas many of the newly ordained see it as an innovative blending of pre-Vatican II and post-Vatican II elements into a new vision of the priesthood. Whatever it is named and wherever it is headed, the second transition is a fact and an important one for the Church's future.

The polarization today can be depicted in the following diagram. The left column is the view of priests adhering to the cultic model of the priesthood, while the right column represents elements of the servant-leader model. These five polarities are the ones we found most clearly in the survey, interviews, and focus groups. The language the older and younger priests use to describe themselves and each other helps us understand each position. Older priests referred to themselves as servants, servant leaders, instruments, facilitators, enablers, pastoral leaders, and liberals. Younger priests called the older priests liberals, leftist fringe, secularized, anti-establishment, a "lost generation," and priests with a social work model. Younger priests described themselves as traditional, conservative, establishment, "unapologetically Catholic," and "ecclesiologically sound."

Older priests referred to the young men as inflexible, divisive, liturgically conservative, institutional, hierarchical, and believers in a cultic priesthood. We heard these broad-brush labels and stereotypes again and again—although not everyone used them or accepted them.

CULTIC MODEL	AREAS OF DIFFERENCE	SERVANT-LEADER MODEL
"man set apart"	*Ontological Status of the Priest*	pastoral leader
values strict hierarchy	*Attitude Toward the Church Magisterium*	values flexible structure
follows established rules	*Liturgy and Devotions*	allows creativity
defends "orthodoxy"	*Theological Perspective*	allows for theological differences
essential to the priesthood	*Attitude Toward Celibacy*	optional for the priesthood

At the same time we found many areas of *agreement*: all agreed on their love for God's people, desire to serve God's people, love for the Catholic Church, desire for personal fulfillment, and acceptance of celibate homosexual priests. In other words, not everything is polarized. The polarization today mainly concerns ecclesiology, the theology of the priesthood, and the liturgy.

In the rest of this chapter we will consider two questions: Why did the second transition occur in the 1980s and 1990s? What does it mean for the Church?

Why Did the Transition Occur?

Of the numerous explanations we have heard, the most common is that the type of man being ordained has changed. Without doubt this is true. Research shows that the men being ordained today, compared with earlier decades, are older, more likely to be foreign-born, and better educated prior to entering seminary. In the 2002 ordination class, the average age at ordination was 36.7 years, 32 percent were born outside the United States, and 27 percent had an advanced college degree (beyond a bachelor's degree). Even in the four short years since 1998, the average age of ordinands has risen approximately one year (Hoge, 2002b). If we look at trends over three decades, we find a sharp decrease in numbers of seminarians, a great increase in age, an increase in the percent born overseas, and more education prior to seminary. For instance, the average age of ordination in 1970 was 27, while today it is about 36. In 1970, of all the priests age 35 or younger, 9% were born overseas, while among the ordinands in 2002 it was 32%.

Do these trends help us understand why a transition in ecclesiology would take place between the early 1980s and today? We must ask, first, Is there evidence that older seminary students tend to be different from the "standard" student (that is, the vast majority ordained at 26 or 27) of the 1950s and l960s? We know of two studies comparing younger and older seminary students. One, a large survey of seminarians in 1985 done by Eugene Hemrick and Dean Hoge, found that the older men were different in five respects. First, they had had fewer years of Catholic higher education than the younger men. Second, more of them had served in the military. Third, they had had more experience before seminary in practical parish life. Fourth, they included more converts to Catholicism. And fifth, they were more certain about their vocational decision (Hemrick and Hoge, 1985).

The second study, done by the same researchers two years later, looked again at young-versus-old differences. It found that older seminarians were more in favor of including lay persons in the seminary program and held more favorable opinions of their seminary experience (1987, p. 45). But these were the only two differences; on numerous other measures the younger and older seminarians were the same. We must conclude that the older and younger seminarians were not different on ecclesiology, and the increase in older seminarians is not an important explanation of the transition in ecclesiological views.[1]

Another possible explanation may be that seminarians who had attended high school seminary and/or college seminary would differ from those who had entered seminary only for the theologate. This could be a factor, since few of today's seminarians had attended high school or college seminary. However, again, past research on this has shown that the differences are small. The former college seminarians were more certain about their desire to become priests and their perseverance rate in seminary was higher, but otherwise the researchers found no differences.

[1] The 1986 survey of seminarians (published in 1987) looked at their visions of priesthood and found a clear polarization between an "institutional model," which stressed upholding the Church's traditions, collaborating with the bishop, and performing liturgical rites which are exclusive to the priesthood, and a "communal model," emphasizing active involvement in social issues such as poverty, racism, sexism, and pro-life; being a moderator who coordinates many ministries in the Church; and empowering lay ministers. These models are the same ones we are calling the "cultic" and "servant-leader" models. The polarization is the same one discussed in chapter 3 above. In the 1986 survey the diocesan seminarians were much more devoted to the institutional model than were the religious seminarians.

Yet again, perhaps the generational difference is explained by the increased percent of diocesan ordinands and the decreased percent of religious ordinands. Research shows, however, that this can't be a strong factor, since the trend toward more diocesan priests has been a small one—in 2001 and 2002, 21% of the ordinands were religious priests, compared with 26% in 1985. Nevertheless, it is important to note that recently ordained diocesan and religious priests differ from one another in their views. The clearest evidence for this is in attitudes of priests who had been ordained for only one to five years, discovered in a survey in 2000. Table 7.1 shows six statements from that survey indicative of support for the cultic versus the servant-leader model. The average difference in agreement between diocesan and religious priests was a strong 26 points in the six items. All of the differences work in the same direction—that the diocesan priests were much closer to the cultic model of the priesthood. Our own interviews with numerous priests assure us that this pattern is indeed real and not simply a side-effect of the research process.

Table 7.1

**Comparison of Attitudes of Diocesan and Religious Priests
Ordained Five Years or Less, 2000 Survey**

(Percent who agree strongly or moderately with each statement)

	Diocesan	Religious
1. Ordination confers on the priest a new status which makes him essentially different from the laity.	75	52
2. A priest must see himself as a "man set apart" by God.	69	40
3. It is essential to make the distinction between priests and laity more important in the Church.	43	24
4. Catholic laity need to be better educated to respect the authority of the priest's word.	36	16
5. Celibacy should be an option for diocesan priests.	29	64
6. The Catholic Church should allow women greater participation in all ministries.	45	75

Source: Hoge (2001).

The question remains, *Why* are the newly ordained diocesan priests more inclined to the cultic model than are the religious priests? We don't know, but it is a question which needs to be answered, since it might help us understand the larger question of why the transition to a more cultic model is occurring. For whatever reason, the newly ordained *diocesan* priests are leading the transition to a more cultic model.

The Reduced Number of Seminarians

Can we learn anything helpful from the long-term drop in the number of men entering seminary to become priests? From 1970 to 2001 the number fell an amazing 47%. This is undoubtedly a clue. Does it help us understand any trends in the motivations and spiritualities of the men who *do* come? For example, Do the seminarians today come from a more restricted range of homes or parishes than was true in 1970? If it turned out that the seminarians today are coming only from very traditional Catholic first-generation or second-generation immigrant families, that would be important for our understanding. The theory is promising, given the undeniable changes in Catholic family and community life in the decades after World War II. But we lack detailed information and must label this theory as plausible but not yet proven.[2]

A related theory, which we have often heard, is that the percentage of seminarians who are homosexual has risen in the last few decades, and this accounts for a change in ecclesiology among the ordinands. But no one knows for sure if the homosexual percentage has actually risen or if, on the other hand, the recent discussions about homosexual seminarians are only a result of greater *openness* in discussing the situation. And no one knows if gay seminarians or gay priests are different in their feelings about priesthood, ecclesiology, or liturgy. (We have heard speculation that gay priests tend to be more talented in music and the arts, but we lack reliable information.) These are serious gaps in knowledge.

Reflections of Broader Catholic Trends?

Many persons told us that the new conservatism among Catholic seminarians simply reflects a trend toward conservatism in American Catholicism.

---

[2] The shifting ethnic composition of seminarians is a possible explanation for changes in ordinands. Our surveys did not ask about ethnic identity. But Father Ken Rudwick, a faculty member at St. John's Seminary, Camarillo, California, told us that ethnicity is important. He reported that Asian ordinands are quite closed to working collaboratively with women. They tend to see women as separate, not suitable for entering into working relationships. Also Asian ordinands are disproportionately closed to any discussions about changes in the priesthood, for example, changes in mandatory celibacy or the ordination of women. Future research needs to assess ethnic factors in priestly attitudes.

Is this true? To check, we reviewed the best research on trends in the Catholic population (see Davidson, et al., 1997; D'Antonio, et al. 2001). The research is unanimous: *There is no broad conservative trend among Catholics on beliefs in the areas of ecclesiology, priesthood, or liturgy.* On the contrary, recent decades have seen a gradual trend in the opposite direction.

Let us explain. A series of Gallup polls of American Catholics between 1987 and 1999 found a modest trend toward according less authority to church leaders on moral issues. That is, a growing number of Catholics are looking to their own consciences, rather than to the magisterium, as the locus of final moral authority. Young adults view things this way more than older persons (Davidson, 1997:85). Individualism and a distancing from church authority are also on the rise. For example, when a random sample of Catholics in 1995 were asked to agree or disagree with the statement, "It is important to obey church teachings even when one doesn't understand them," 38% of the adults 55 or older strongly agreed, compared with 24% of those ages 35–54, and only 11% of those age 34 or under (ibid., p. 127).

On topics related to the institutional church, the research found a gradual trend among Catholics toward desiring more democratic church structures and more lay participation in decision making. From 1987 to 1999, there was a slight increase in those desiring more democratic decision making at the parish level (from 60% to 66%) and at the level of the Vatican (an increase from 51% to 55%). Also, lay Catholics increasingly believe that they have the right to select the priests for their parishes; young Catholics have been the most apt to believe this (D'Antonio, 2001:120).

Support for a married priesthood has also gradually increased among the laity. In 1987, 63% were in favor, and in 1999 it was 71%. In all surveys, the younger Catholics were more in favor of this change than older Catholics.

In their analysis of polls, James Davidson and his associates looked for a "rebound" effect that some observers were talking about in the middle 1990s—the idea that young adult Catholics were rebounding to more conservative beliefs and attitudes about the Church, similar to pre-Vatican Catholics. They searched but could not find any rebound (Davidson, et al., 1997:134).

We conclude that the change in ecclesiology found among young priests has no counterpart among young adult laity. On the contrary, the young priests and young laity are heading in different directions on many issues. This should be a red flag: we are likely to see increasing priest-versus-laity differences in coming years.

Polarization in the Catholic Community

Even though the total Catholic laity is gradually moving in a more participatory and individualistic direction in its views of the Church (as seen in polls just discussed), it is still possible that increasing polarization among Catholics can help explain what is happening. Polls may show an *overall* shift in one or another direction, but that does not mean that *all* Catholics share those views. If a certain subpopulation of Catholics holds a traditional cultural view of the priesthood, and if it is especially this subpopulation that is supplying seminaries with students today, that would explain why seminarians and newly ordained priests are moving in a direction contrary to that of the laity in general.

This theory is difficult to test. All we could do to test it ourselves was to interview seminary faculty, researchers, and vocation personnel to see if they have evidence to support it. We found that there is consensus that seminarians today come disproportionately from conservative parishes. Sister Katarina Schuth, an expert on Catholic seminaries, told us that conservative parishes with conservative pastors promote vocations more than other parishes do, and in many cases serve as attractive models to young men. These parishes hold to a traditional model of the priesthood emphasizing the distinctive status and ministries of priests.

We also wondered if vocation directors have been changing their emphases or methods in the last two decades, since if so, this too would help us understand the changes in seminary students. The numerous interviews we had with vocations personnel, however, did not turn up any evidence of such a change.

Trends in Protestant Seminarians

Some insight might be gained by a comparison with Protestant seminarians. Have their views changed in the same way since, let us say, 1970? In several respects, Protestant seminarians are similar to Catholic seminarians. One large survey of seminarians was undertaken in the United States and Canada in the year 2000. Unfortunately for the sake of making comparisons, not all the students in the survey were Protestant, but 92% were, so some statements are possible. (We were unable to acquire data solely on the Protestants surveyed.) The average age of master's of divinity students in their third year of study was 35, an age similar to current Catholic seminarians. But Protestant seminarians were more varied: about one-fourth were enrolled part-time, and over one-third were women (Wheeler, 2001).

Openly gay and lesbian students are found today in the liberal and mainline Protestant seminaries, and commonly they organize into caucuses with the intent of influencing seminary life. For example, in 2000, at the Pacific School of Religion in Berkeley, California, it was reported that an estimated 15% to 30% of the students were gay, lesbian, bisexual, or transgendered (Lattin, 2000).

Have there been discernible trends in theology, piety, or ecclesiology in the Protestant seminaries? Not clearly. In an annual trend study conducted between 1995 and 2000, entering students were asked to identify themselves theologically as conservative, middle-of-the-road, or liberal. The five-year trend was a slight movement in the liberal direction (Lonsway, 2001:5), but this finding should be treated skeptically due to the difficulties of definition on which the measurement depends. A safe conclusion would be that little change occurred. Besides this five-year study, reliable research does not exist, and all we possess are observations by seminary leaders. These observations indicate little theological change in recent decades. Barbara Wheeler, President of Auburn Seminary and an authority on American seminaries, observed, "Something distinctive happened in the Catholic seminaries in the last couple of decades which didn't happen in the Protestant seminaries."[3] We need to keep in mind that the theology of the clergy (or priesthood), which is central in Catholic theology, is much less prominent in Protestant theology and less freighted as a topic for conflict.

One fact should be remembered about Protestants—that the conservative and evangelical Protestant seminaries have fared better in enrollment in the last three decades than the mainline and liberal seminaries. More students have sought admission to the former, and this is important for gauging cultural trends.

What does the recent history of Protestant seminaries tell us? In a nutshell—no basic theological shifts have occurred. But because evangelical seminaries have grown disproportionately in enrollment, we should conclude that Protestant seminaries, *taken as a package,* have moved to some degree in an evangelical and conservative direction.

A Search for Solid Rock

A sometimes-heard theory holds that seminarians in the 1980s and 1990s came to the priesthood after being disillusioned by today's relativistic "I'm okay, you're okay" American society. A society that lacks moral and religious definitions will not be spiritually sustaining to earnest people, who will hunger for solid rock on which to base their lives. Thus, the theory goes, many come to Catholic seminaries in search of stability and so-

---

[3] In an interview Dr. Wheeler noted that Catholic seminaries are unique in another way: that the Catholic community has seen a bifurcation in religious training in that seminaries are largely limited to students preparing for ministry, while students preparing for academic careers in theology or religious studies prefer to go to Catholic graduate schools. This separation of functions has not occurred in Protestant institutions, where the leading seminaries are the principal locus for training persons both for ministry and also for academic scholarship.

lidity, viewing the Catholic Church, with its two-thousand-year history and its theology of being the closest embodiment of God's truth, as the single best place to make a home. According to this theory, seminarians today gravitate to safe ground and orient their ministry around institutional authority, including faithful adherence to Vatican rules about liturgy, sexual morality, and catechetical teachings. We have no doubt that this theory contains some truth, but beyond that we cannot assess its strength.

A related theory is that while seminarians in the 1950s and 1960s came from supportive Catholic families and strong parishes, the seminarians today are not direct products of the Catholic community in the same way. Rather, as we know, seminarians today are older— usually with a history of working in a secular occupation which they found to be meaningless— and often without warm feelings about their parishes and religious education in childhood and youth. A higher proportion than in past years are recent converts to Catholicism. Thus, some seminarians today are not direct products of the Catholic cultural heritage but are "late entrants" who come to seminary with a sense of alienation from a wasteland world and a desire to hold to bedrock Catholic doctrine (Latcovich, 2002:2). Insofar as they are traditional in ecclesiology, it is not out of nostalgia for a past which had a pleasanter clericalism, but out of a longing for the time-tested, the true, and the authoritative in knowing God's will. Mark Latcovich, vice-rector of St. Mary Seminary in Wickliffe, Ohio, holds this view:

> Priests ordained in the '60s to late '70s might use the word "conservative" to describe this new breed of seminarians. I for one think the word is incorrect. These men are trying to find their way into church circles. Their personal sense of disconnection, disorientation, and crisis contributes to needing icons that offer stability, and models to draw direction and inspiration. Some of the Gen Xers' icons are seen by some as a retrenching to the past—by the amount of enthusiasm this generation of seminarians has for the catechism, papal authority, encyclicals, etc. I feel that they are grasping for the basics and want to realign their personal faith journeys to both the tradition and history of the Church. (2002:4)

Evidence for this theory comes mainly from seminary faculty who have interacted at length with their students and tried to explain how the recent students are different (for example, Marzheuser, 1999). James Garneau, a professor at the Pontifical College Josephinum, expresses the feelings of the "new generation" of priests:

> The new generation finds solace and direction in the prodigious writings of Pope John Paul II and in the recent documents of the Holy See. . . . While liberals tend to receive the documents with suspicion and perceive them as little more than vague guidelines to be interpreted for local circumstances,

the new generation usually finds authentic directives in them and receives them with joy. A conflict often ensues for the younger generation when their pastors, diocesan ordinaries, and curial staffs give the impression of seeking to circumvent teachings and legislation from the Holy See. In this conflict of obedience there is great struggle and tension. The younger clergy recognize that there must exist a hierarchy of loyalties, and this angers or frustrates many local authorities. The younger clergy, in attempting to observe all of the papal initiatives, draw the conclusion that their deepest commitments are largely being supported at the highest levels of the Church's hierarchy, and so they are willing to suffer the local consequences. (2002:8)

The Priesthood's Loss of Authority

Everyone who talked with us about the changes in priests invoked the priesthood's drop in public status as part of the explanation. The most common viewpoint is that being a priest is not high-status today, unlike in the 1950s or 1960s, and thus priests today feel psychological pressure to develop a strong and clear priestly identity which reassures the young priest that "it's all worth it" to sacrifice worldly things to be a priest. The clearer identity is also believed to shore up the public esteem for and influence of the priesthood. In this view, the 1970s mantra that a priest is "just like everyone else" only brought about malaise—and today's lack of public recognition—while a priest who is clearly "a man set apart" will receive proper esteem.

Historian Leslie Tentler, an expert on priests, emphasizes the importance of the loss of a supportive Catholic culture after the 1960s. She argues that priests today do not enjoy the backup of nuns in the schools to explain to children what a priest is and why he deserves deference and respect. They do not enjoy a consensus among lay Catholics that a priest, solely because he has been ordained, deserves special deference. Today, Tentler argues, a priest needs to earn his own respect from the laity, and this puts an unprecedented burden on him. To make the job easier, it is useful to point out to everyone his specialness and his distinct ontological status. The lower status of the priesthood today is felt by priests as a personal loss, giving rise to feelings that they need "to reclaim what is ours."

Tentler points out that priests ordained in the 1960s and 1970s were reacting against the background of the pre-Vatican II Catholic ghetto culture, with its compliance with priestly authority and its habit of putting priests on a pedestal. Priests of that era lost nothing by stepping down from the pedestal, taking off their cassocks, and in post-Vatican II fashion saying, "We're all in this together." But today the cultural situation is the opposite: no pedestal, little deference, less church authority, and an uneasy sense among young priests that in spite of the sacrifices they are making, they are not being given due respect. This theory is plausible, since according to all accounts the public esteem of the priesthood has dropped since the 1950s.

Does this theory apply broadly to large numbers of seminarians and priests today? It is difficult to know. From our research we believe it does explain the outlooks of *some* seminarians and priests.

The Result of Changes in Church Leadership

During the research we repeatedly heard a theory about the impact of church leadership, which, stated simply, is that the new type of priest seen today is the result of the papacy of John Paul II. Proponents of this argument point out that the predominant type of seminarian began shifting in the early 1980s, soon after John Paul II began his papacy in October 1978. They note that the bishops John Paul appointed were different from earlier appointees—the new bishops were, to a man, conservative in their ecclesiology and their theology of the priesthood. In effect, the theory argues that Pope John Paul produced a reaction to many of the innovations of the Second Vatican Council through his appointments, pronouncements, and actions, and this influenced the type of men entering seminary in the United States—or at least the type continuing on to ordination and priesthood.

The theory is bolstered by the historical fact that many priests loyal to the innovations of Vatican II resigned in the late 1960s and early 1970s (Greeley, 1972) and by the strong loyalty newly ordained priests today feel toward the Pope. Indeed, in our interviews we heard many new priests say repeatedly how inspiring they find the Pope to be and how much they want to be loyal to him—in contrast to the priests ordained several decades ago, who often maintained a distance from Pope John Paul II and his leadership.

Theories About Post-Council Effects

At least three priests we interviewed told us that Catholic historians who have studied councils have found that it takes seventy-five years for a council to take effect in the Church. We have been unable to find the source of this idea, but sociologist Joseph Fichter attributed something like it to Karl Rahner:

> Karl Rahner believes that "it will certainly be a long time before the Church which has been given the Second Vatican Council will be the Church of the Second Vatican Council, just as it took a number of generations after the close of the Council of Trent before she became the Church of the Reform of Trent." (Fichter, 1968:36)

Fichter, however, did not believe Rahner was correct about today, since the pace of twentieth-century change is far swifter than that of the sixteenth century. We have encountered many people who do and who use this time-delay premise to explain the changes in American priests since 1965. They said it was "natural" that the second decade would be different from the first decade after the Second Vatican Council. We cannot understand how this theory is supposed to work, and we have no evidence to support it.

What Does it Mean for the Church?

The task of assessing the impact of the ecclesiological transition is a risky one, since it requires a combination of research and speculation. Caution is needed. We will look first at research clarifying the impact on priests, then at the impact on parish life.

The Impact on Priests

In chapter 2 we reported that priests today are happier and more committed to their priesthood than was true in 1970, 1985, and 1993. These trends are unmistakable. The rise in morale since 1970 was mostly among young priests. We have noted that young priests in 1970 tended to be underutilized and often chafed under the requirement that they serve as associates for probably twenty years before being promoted to pastor (and under the practice that promotions were based solely on seniority). We also found that fewer priests today than in 1970 are seriously pondering whether they should leave the priesthood, and likewise that today more say that if they had everything to do over again, they would still become a priest. Is it possible that the transition in ecclesiology is associated with the higher morale and commitment among the young? To check, we looked at correlations in the 2001 survey data.

We found that in 2001, the priests who held a cultic model of the priesthood also had higher morale than the others. For making our tests, we looked at the non-retired priests only, and we divided them into old and young (56 or older versus 55 or younger). On every measure, the priests with a cultic ecclesiology reported more happiness, less inclination to leave the priesthood, and a higher percentage saying that if they had it to do over again, they would become priests again. The pattern was strongest among the young priests. For example, the priests were asked to agree or disagree with the statement, "There is no ontological difference between the priest and the laity, since all share in the common priesthood of Christ given at baptism; the difference is mainly one of assigned duties in the Church." Disagreement with this question is one measure of the cultic ecclesiology and rejection of the post-Vatican II mentality. Among the younger priests, out of all those who agreed, 25% said they were happy today; while out of all those who disagreed or were uncertain, 46% said they were happy. The older priests showed the same pattern—of those who agreed, 39% said they were very happy, compared with 50% of those who disagreed.

A second example is the statement, "Ordination confers on the priest a new status or a permanent character which makes him essentially different from the laity within the Church." Of the younger priests who agreed, 45% said they were very happy, while of the younger ones who disagreed, 28% said this. Among the older priests, of those who agreed, 48% said they were happy, while of those who disagreed, 45% said this.

The same pattern appeared when the priests reported whether they were thinking of leaving the priesthood: priests holding the cultic model of the priesthood were less often thinking of leaving. It appeared again on the question of whether a priest, if he had it to do over again, would still enter the priesthood.

Did these patterns also hold true in 1970? We checked the data and found that they did. In 1970 priests, both young and old, who held the cultic model of priesthood reported being happier than others and being less likely to leave the priesthood in the future. For example, take the statement, "Ordination confers on the priest a new status or a permanent character which makes him essentially different from the laity within the Church." Of the priests 45 or younger in 1970 who agreed, 47% said they would definitely not leave the priesthood, while of those who disagreed, 21% said they would definitely not leave. Among priests 46 or older, 87% of those who agreed said they would definitely not leave, compared with 60% of those who disagreed. Other measures of ecclesiology led to the same conclusion: Priests holding a conservative ecclesiology were happier and were more committed to remaining priests.

We have additional data from research on men who have already left the priesthood. Both in 1970 and in 2000, the men who had resigned from the priesthood told investigators that they held to a more servant-leader, participatory model of priesthood than the priests who have remained in service (Greeley, 1972; Hoge, 2002). These who had resigned from the priesthood favored more lay participation in parish leadership and less distinction between priests and laity. For example, in 2000, on the statement, "It is essential to make the distinction between priests and laity more important in the Church," 43% of the diocesan priests ordained in the previous five years agreed, and 24% of the religious priests ordained in the previous five years agreed, but only 8% of the men who had resigned agreed. Similarly, on the statement, "A priest must see himself as a 'man set apart' by God," 69% of the recently ordained diocesan priests agreed, as did 40% of the recently ordained religious priests, but only 28% of the resigned priests (Hoge, 2002:28).

Our data does not tell us *why*—both in 1970 and again in 2000—the servant-leader-type priests had lower morale and more thoughts of resigning. We can only guess. Our best guess is that possibly they felt a less distinctive priestly identity, providing them less self-affirmation and esteem. Maybe they also felt less support from their bishops and superiors in 1970 and again in 2000. Or even maybe the servant-leader model, which requires more collaboration with laity, is more stressful for priests. This topic deserves further study.

The Impact on Parishes

How about the impact on parishes? The question requires that we begin with a different angle of vision—we need to think first of the needs of parish life and then ask whether or not the new vision of the priesthood will serve those needs well. Is the new ecclesiology hopeful for producing revitalized parish life, or not? When we spoke with older priests committed to the servant leadership model, they tended to say *no*, but when we spoke with the young priests they assured us the answer was *yes*.

We have heard older priests argue that the older cultic model of the priesthood cannot succeed given the preferences of laity today—they are more educated, culturally sophisticated, accustomed to democratic organizations, and hesitant to accord absolute authority to any institutions no matter how ancient or hallowed. The older priests are especially fearful of young priests who take a high view of church authority and preach that Catholics need to follow church teachings even on unwelcome topics such as birth control: How can such priests lead their flocks today? They are also fearful that the new priests cannot work well with the rising cadre of professional lay ministers.

Can the new priests work well with lay ministers? In chapter three we saw that younger priests are a bit less accepting of lay ministers in parish life than are older priests. Our interviews and focus groups suggest that it is due to a fear, felt by some, that priest-lay cooperation may lead to fuzziness about the role and status of the priest or possibly to a loss of priestly control over parish life. We checked the 2001 data to see if the priests who were relatively more collaborative than others have higher (or lower) morale and if they are more (or less) inclined to leave the priesthood. We found that the younger priests (55 years old or younger) who are more in favor of expanded lay ministries do have lower morale; for older priests, however, there was no difference. Priests of all ages who favor greater lay ministry report more thoughts about resigning, and thus we may expect that the more collaborative priests will resign disproportionately more often. The lukewarm interest shown by some priests in working with lay ministers may be troublesome in the future, when lay ministers will be indispensable.

Ecclesiological Attitudes of Lay Ministers

We possess new research data on the viewpoints of lay ministers. During 2002, we commissioned two research studies, first a large survey of lay ministers, and second, a modest phone survey of lay ministers inquiring about their experiences with newly ordained priests.

We will report first on the large survey. We paid for a series of questions to be asked in a new phone survey of professional lay ministers working in parishes.[4] The lay ministers who responded were overwhelmingly female (81%), with an average age of 52. Eighty-six percent were salaried, and 14% were volunteers. Fifty-three percent had received some graduate or professional education beyond college, while at the other extreme 7% were high school graduates only. The most frequent area of ministry in parishes was religious education. For present purposes we looked only at lay ministers who were salaried (that is, not volunteers) and who were 65 years old or younger. This is the category of persons destined to have clout in parish leadership in years ahead.

We asked the lay ministers to respond to five statements about ecclesiology, the same statements to which the priests had responded earlier (see table 7.2). The first statement in the table, that "Ordination confers on the priest a new status or permanent character," expresses a view belonging to the cultic model of priesthood. It received fairly similar levels of acceptance among priests (77%) and lay ministers (69%). Priests differed markedly by age, but the lay ministers had similar attitudes regardless of their age.

The second statement, that resigned priests should be invited to reapply whether they are married or single, received a bit more agreement from the lay ministers (62%) than the priests (52%). Both the priests and the lay ministers varied sharply by age, with the older persons agreeing much more than the younger. Here is a finding we did not expect: that the youngest lay ministers resemble the youngest priests in that they more often espoused the

---

[4] The survey was carried out by CARA, the Center for Applied Research in the Apostolate, in March 2002. It was done by phone and included 795 lay ministers identified by phoning a random sample of parishes. The definition of lay minister was any staff member besides a priest, deacon, or seminarian working or volunteering for a parish at least 20 hours in a typical week, excluding secretaries, clerical workers, and school employees. Persons with multiple duties were included if part of their responsibilities were pastoral. It was determined that about 63% of parishes have one or more lay ministers by this definition, and of the parishes with at least one, the mean number was 2.9. Because the CARA definition of lay minister was broader than we wanted for present purposes, we limited our analysis to lay ministers who were paid (that is, not volunteers) and who were 65 years old or younger. This reduced the sample from 795 to 614.

cultic model of priesthood, in contrast to the older lay ministers and priests. Responses to the third statement, that celibacy should be optional for diocesan priests, showed the same pattern: the older priests and the older lay ministers agreed much more than the younger ones.

Table 7.2
Agreement with Five Statements about Priesthood and Parish Life
(Percent who agreed strongly or somewhat)

	All	35 or less	36–45	46–55	56–65	66 or more
				Ages		
Priesthood						
1. Ordination confers on the priest a new status or a permanent character which makes him essentially different from the laity within the Church.						
Priests	77	94	84	72	70	79
Lay Ministers	69	74	75	65	66	
2. Priests who have resigned from the priesthood should be invited to reapply for permission to function as priests again, whether they are married or single.						
Priests	52	23	34	53	68	50
Lay Ministers	62	37	55	65	78	
3. Celibacy should be a matter of personal choice for diocesan priests.						
Priests	56	33	41	64	73	48
Lay Ministers	59	22	52	64	77	
Church Governance						
4. I think it would be a good idea if Christian communities, such as parishes, were to choose their own priest from among available ordained priests.						
Priests	23	22	21	20	29	23
Lay Ministers	42	25	43	41	51	

	All	**Ages**				
		35 or less	**36–45**	**46–55**	**56–65**	**66 or more**
5. I think it would be a good idea if the priests in a diocese were to choose their own bishop.						
Priests	47	22	38	45	62	44
Lay Ministers	43	18	45	38	60	

The last two items in table 7.2 concern church governance. The fourth statement, saying that parishes should choose their own priest, received much more support from the lay ministers than from the priests (42% versus 23%). Age differences among the priests were small—most disagreed with the idea—but large among the lay ministers. Older lay ministers were relatively high in agreement, while younger lay ministers were low. The fifth statement, that bishops should be elected by priests, received similar agreement from priests and lay ministers, but again both categories of respondents showed strong differences by age. Older priests and older lay ministers were much more in agreement with the statement than their younger peers.

When we looked for patterns of attitude differences among specific categories of lay ministers, the results were mixed. Men and women held similar attitudes, as did those working full time (versus part time), those engaged in different ministry tasks (religious education, liturgy, administration), and those in different regions of the nation. But one breakdown was important: level of education. Lay ministers who had some graduate training (including a graduate degree) differed in their views from those who were less educated; they were closer to the servant leadership model of the priesthood (see figure 7.1).

To complicate matters, the level of education among lay ministers was closely associated with their age. The proportion with graduate training was 38% among the lay ministers 35 or younger, 36% among those 36–45, 57% among those 46–55, and 77% among those 56–65. The older lay ministers had much more education, and this raises the question of whether or not the differences among lay ministers in table 7.2 is really a product of education and not of age alone. We controlled for education while looking at age differences and found that both influences existed: both education level and age seemed to affect lay ministers' attitudes.

Do these responses from priests and lay ministers mean we should anticipate future tensions between the two groups? If we take as a rule of thumb that a difference of 25 points predicts future tension, we can anticipate tension on all five topics named in table 7.2. The main tensions will occur between older, more-educated lay ministers and younger priests. The lay ministers believe less than the young priests that ordination confers on the priest a new status; they are more in favor of inviting resigned priests back; they are more in favor of optional celibacy; they are more in favor of allowing laity to choose the priests for their parishes; and they are more in favor of having priests elect their bishops. All five issues are potential areas of tension. Related topics, not measured here, would probably be sources of similar tension as well.

Figure 7.1
Lay Ministers' Responses to Five Statements
in Table 7.2 by Educational Level
(Percent agreeing strongly or somewhat)

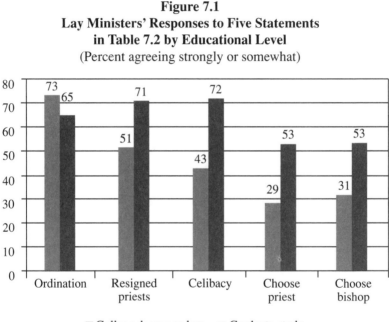

How about tensions between younger (also less-educated) lay ministers and older priests? We expect tensions to arise on the question of inviting resigned priests back, on optional celibacy, and on the idea that priests should elect their bishops, but they should be less severe than the tensions connected with older lay ministers.

The second research initiative was a telephone survey with eighteen lay ministers in different regions of the nation who had recently worked with newly ordained priests.[5] Nearly all (fifteen of them) were women, and most

[5] The telephone survey was carried out by Father Aniedi Okure, a graduate student at Catholic University, in May and June 2002. For details see Okure (2002).

were in their forties or fifties. Twelve have been serving as lay ministers for more than six years. In the interviews, these lay ministers voiced a somewhat negative evaluation, overall, of the newly ordained priests. They said that new priests tend to be clerical and rigid in their views. The new priests, they said, tend to exclude the laity, especially women, from decision making; they do not listen to laity with an open ear; and they feel they should have the last word on issues affecting the lives of parishioners. The lay ministers said, in effect, that most of the newly ordained priests would probably have been more comfortable in the pre-Vatican II church.

Not all of the comments were negative. The lay ministers said that the newly ordained priests bring some definite strengths. They are wiser in worldly affairs than many other priests; they have better than average management skills; and they reach out in a good professional manner to troubled kids. Recently ordained *religious-order* priests, moreover, tend to be relatively more conscious than average of social justice issues.

The lay minister interviewees guessed that in the future, if there are problems between lay ministers and recently ordained priests, it will be on issues of status, ministerial domain, and "turf" more than on creedal or theological issues. In our judgment, since the numbers of lay ministers are increasing year by year and the numbers of priests in parish life are decreasing, it is inevitable that future priests will feel encroached upon, and some may act defensively. The question will be, "Whose Church is this anyhow?"

To give the flavor of the lay ministers' accounts, we will present three of them here.

First, a lay minister in his mid-40s, who has worked with numerous priests in the last fifteen years:

> The new priests perceive themselves as clergy first and foremost. They are conscious of their status as priests. However, they are very service-oriented and they see the laity as partners. They are glad to have laity work alongside them. They are not as clerical as their immediate predecessors, that is, those ordained in the last ten years of the '80s. There is a wide acceptance of the trends of the Second Vatican Council among the new priests. There is an excellent degree of tolerance of the views of others—but with some notable exceptions. They focus on the hierarchical aspect of the Church and would rather not have the laity come too close to the altar.

A lay minister in the East described a young priest who has strong concerns about the altar and sanctuary:

> As far as he is concerned, there is an imaginary line between the sanctuary and the congregation that the laity, especially women, should not cross. Although some children are drawn to him, he does not think that children belong at the

altar. There was an incident where kids were to go up to the sanctuary to sing during a children's pageant. He decided against it, saying, "Children do not belong at the altar." He would not come down from the sanctuary during the kiss of peace at Mass to greet parishioners, as do the older priests, because in his mind a priest belongs in the sanctuary and should not mingle with parishioners during the celebration of the Holy Eucharist. He would also have forbidden the children to read at the Mass but for the intervention of the pastor. He [the younger priest] is very much a protocol man.

A midwestern lay minister who has worked in the parish for fifteen years talked about a priest ordained six years ago:

> He is very much a pre-Vatican Council priest. He feels that the bishop has allowed the older priests—whom he views as too liberal—an unlimited freedom for experimentation with Vatican II programs, especially in regard to the celebration of the Eucharist. Many of his peers behave in a similar way. There is a group of three newly ordained that meet regularly with him. I have heard them lament the selling out of the Church to liberal priests and the laity. They feel that the older priests have watered down priestly identity, making it unattractive.

> He is a good preacher. His preaching is generally theologically sound. However, he does not always relate his homilies to life situations. He follows liturgical rubrics faithfully. Due to his prior life experience, he has practical management skills. The parish was in debt when he arrived, and within a short time he pulled the parish out of debt, plus he augmented the enrollment in the parochial school.

The telephone survey provides us with a glimpse of lay ministers' evaluations of the new priests. We do not know if the eighteen phone respondents were typical or not, since they do not represent a random sample of lay ministers. Therefore we cannot claim that their (overall somewhat negative) evaluations are held generally. We need to be cautious.

Comparing Attitudes of Priests and Laity

We can reliably compare the attitudes of priests and laity on only two ecclesiological topics. The first we noted earlier, in chapter 3. On the statement, "Celibacy should be a matter of personal choice for diocesan priests," 56% of the priests agreed, compared with 71% of the laity in a 1999 Gallup poll. Whereas younger priests agreed less often than older priests, the reverse was true of laity, where younger persons agreed slightly *more* (see D'Antonio, et al. 2001:110).

The second comparison is on the statement "Ordination confers on the priest a new status or a permanent character which makes him essentially different from the laity within the Church." Of all the priests, 77% agreed, and of all the Catholic laity, 54% did so.[6] Whereas younger priests agreed more than older priests, the opposite is true of the laity, where younger persons agree *less* than their elders. (Among the laity, 46% of those 18–35 agreed, compared with 53% of those 36–45, 58% of those 46–55, and 60% of those 56 or older.) These two priest-lay comparisons have a common pattern: the laity insist less on celibacy and hold a lower theology of ordination than priests, and the young laity and young priests are moving in different directions. In the future, the gap can be expected to widen.

We may conclude, tentatively, that lay ministers are in an intermediate position between priests and laity in their views of the priesthood. It would follow that, if this is correct, any future tensions will probably pit priests against *laity* more than priests against lay ministers.

What are the implications of the new type of priest for the Church? They are mixed. The new ecclesiology gives new confidence and energy to the young priests, and it seems to be helping in the recruitment of seminarians. Whether it is hopeful for parish life is another question, since we found some notable differences in viewpoints between the priests and the laity—especially the younger laity. Catholics should prepare themselves for future tensions in parishes over roles, turf, and collaboration.

[6] The 2002 data were from the CARA Catholic Poll 2002, with 2,100 respondents. We thank CARA (the Center for Applied Research in the Apostolate) for giving us the results.

Chapter 8

Recommendations Made by the Priests

The first month I lived in the rectory I went down to get coffee in my pajamas at seven o'clock in the morning, and the curriculum secretary comes in early. She said, "Oh no, you're not dressed!" I said, "Well, I'm at home, it's seven in the morning!"

—A priest in a focus group

In every interview or focus group we asked the priests to make recommendations to seminaries and bishops, with the goal of improving future priestly life and ministry. The men gave us numerous thoughtful answers which they hoped would get a hearing, and we promised to do what we could to disseminate them. Here we present the seven suggestions and recommendations that were mentioned most often, first those to seminaries and then those to bishops.

Recommendations to Seminaries

Recommendation 1: More focus on seminarians' spiritual development, emphasizing the importance of prayer.

Foremost in the minds of most priests we talked with was the need for seminaries to guide them in their spiritual development. Over and above their concerns about practical daily tasks and responsibilities was their insistence that seminaries impress upon their students the importance of prayer and spiritual development in everyday life and train them how to pray.

A 32-year-old priest emphasized the importance of this matter in these words:

Looking back, the most important thing, without exception, is teaching the men how to pray. Teach them what it is, and I don't want to sound melodramatic, but teach them to learn how to die to themselves. I think we have to be, in the seminary, even more countercultural. Of course we have to be part of the world. That goes without saying, since we're working hand in hand on a daily basis with people that are in the world. . . . Maybe our witness is being that gentle, calming presence in the midst of chaos. And I've learned that that can only be done when you've got your own spiritual life together, when you've been given the tools to learn how to be contemplative, reflective.

A 42-year-old diocesan priest, ordained in 1999, offered a suggestion for structured prayer:

Perhaps the one thing that I might recommend would be for more of an emphasis on prayer, not that it wasn't there, but I would think more of an emphasis. Because from what I've witnessed from priests since I've been out here is that the priests that tend to fail—to burn out—tend to be priests who neglect their prayer. So perhaps a recommendation would be to have eucharistic adoration, if not once a week then at least more often to set aside time for that kind of prayer, to sit in front of the Lord and to pray. To sit quietly with the Lord. Many, many times out here in parishes I see priests so upset and so nervous about things. And I see a lot of those priests are ones who have forgotten their relationship with God, trying to do everything by themselves, forgetting that God has to be a part of it.

A 61-year-old diocesan priest, ordained in 1965, bemoaned his lack of early training in how to pray:

All the different forms of spirituality that I'm familiar with today, I never heard about any of those. It was just "learn to meditate." I don't think I was ever taught to meditate. It was embarrassing. After I got out of the seminary, somebody asked me to teach them to pray. Nobody ever taught me to pray. Well, they taught me how to say words. So spiritually I think there was a lot lacking in the seminary.

Another older priest, ordained in 1972:

I think I would like to have seen, personally, more courses on spirituality and prayer. Not that we didn't have some of those, but I guess part of that is, How do you make a person realize the importance of prayer and its connection to ministry before you're really involved in ministry? That is the eternal question. Lay people want to see priests who are in love with the Lord, have a passion for God, and they want guys to share that passion for God. And, in my mind, you're only going to get that passion as you see the need for prayer and ministry.

Recommendation 2: Provide practical preparation for parish life.

The men had some practical suggestions for seminaries, especially in preparing graduates for parish life. Their suggestions ranged from more preparation in liturgy and homiletics to more help in addressing marriage and family issues from the Church's point of view.

A 36-year-old diocesan priest described the difficulties of transition from the seminary to the parish:

> I think somehow there could be a little more preparation for what life is like in the parish when you first get there. I think for myself—and for a lot of guys—there was a real shock. It was a whole lot different than we thought it would be when you make the transition from the structured life of the seminary to the much more necessarily flexible life in parish work. . . . In the seminary, life was quite structured and you had the different things that you had to be there for: the classes, the times of prayer, and so forth. You come into the parish and, as a diocesan priest, you really have to provide that structure for yourself. . . . That was a hard transition: becoming my own schedule maker as a priest.

A 32-year-old diocesan priest:

> Practically speaking, I would say definitely more on family life, marriage, on pastoral approaches to dealing with annulment—since it is such a big part of our life today: To really see the components of healing that can be found through the annulment process. How to deal better with cohabiting couples. A lot of this is post-ordination; you can't fit it all in the seminary. But I think that the light bulb has to go on in the seminary, and tools need to be within arm's reach—in order for us when we get out there—to best deal with these.

A 68-year-old religious priest:

> In seminary we felt the need to make sure that we were inserted in the reality of the world, where people were living and people were making their bread and people were raising questions. We were being ordained to serve these people. So first and foremost I would say they need, as I see it, to make sure there is a real insertion in the world. And not just a dabbling, but a thorough insertion in the world and contact with lay persons.

Better liturgical preparation was repeatedly mentioned.

A 50-year-old religious priest:

> I would say good liturgical preparation. When you think about the fact that for most Catholics, their touch point to the Church is through the liturgy, and so seminarians need to have good liturgical training—which really accents the best in our tradition while also being open to new forms. Preaching: I think homiletics is very important. Those are some of the things that I would emphasize. And then also, you think of what Andrew Greeley has said: If

people find that they are nourished through the preaching that they hear, then they tend to feel quite satisfied about their Catholic life.

Recommendations to Bishops

Recommendation 3: Separate work space from living space.

The priests, both young and old, were clear that offices and living quarters must be separated. Priests are only human, they told us, and, even if you can live with being on call twenty-four hours a day, you need a place that is private, where you can count on a measure of peace and quiet.

At one time rectories housed only priests and a housekeeper, but with an increase in lay involvement and with fewer priests, rectories are being used simultaneously as church offices and priests' homes, a combination for which most rectories were not designed.

Father Don, a 36-year-old priest:

> Get the rectory away from the church buildings. Live away from the office. If this is not possible, the pastor has to strictly enforce privacy. In my first placement I walked downstairs in my pajamas early one morning and found five people from the parish at the kitchen table having breakfast. I was also once accosted by a Right to Life man right in my own kitchen early one morning. Either architecturally design the space for privacy *or* enforce some boundaries so that the living space can be protected.

Father Eric, age 32, explained some of the difficulties:

> Separate the rectory from the office. The model of the rectory worked in the past, but as soon as you started bringing in support staff, lay pastoral ministers, and religious, they have their own place to go to. We should have a capital campaign in the diocese and new rectories should be built . . . maybe it is a cluster rectory, where you're bringing in pastors to live together. Some guys may need to live on their own. I don't think that is the healthiest thing because it comes back to a sense of accountability. Get the residence out of the office environment. Again, it will be good for the people, ultimately, in the end. And ultimately I think resentments build up with the others. You get to go home; you don't have to live in this office. We're human. I don't think we have to be this machine that's on/off.

Forty-nine-year-old Father Jack thinks priests need "down time":

> Living above the store, so to speak, is very unhealthy. Our bishop does not believe in priests living in their own homes, and when guys do live on their own—somewhere else—if he finds out, he gets very upset. Part of it is, I

think, that he just has this old-fashioned theology that the priest needs to be available one hundred percent of the time. I don't agree with that. I think priests need "down time" and separate space. I think it is extremely unhealthy to live right in your rectory. I think we should be allowed to live in homes separate from the rectory office building itself, whether it is on the same grounds or down the street somewhere. It's a big issue today, especially in the context of overwork and everything, and the person needs a real place to go to relax and rest.

The need for privacy does not mean that priests do not want to be available to parishioners. One priest says he carries two beepers, which give him the freedom to have some private time and space while still being accessible.

A 36-year-old priest describes his ideal living situation:

> If I were going to have my ideal, I would definitely have my living arrangements on the church grounds. They would definitely be in some way attached to the offices, but a much more distinct and clear break would be made between those two realms. A lot more privacy, no one crosses over into my private space, etc. This is my house; this is where I live. If I want to have my dirty clothes thrown on the floor, so be it. If I want to go downstairs in my bathrobe at night to get a glass of milk, I could do it, and the entire parish doesn't have to know about it. I know some guys want to live completely off the grounds, but I wouldn't want to live that far away.

A 40-year-old religious priest spoke of the benefits of community life:

> We're very public people. Here we really had to insist upon, and we educated our people, that from 5:00 in the evening to 6:30, the friars are just not available. We have our meditation period from 5:00 to 5:45; we have our evening prayer and our dinner. We need *that much* each day. And so we communicated it to them. When I first arrived, we ate at this table [in the rectory], and we lived down here. We came in and had our coffee in the morning and the staff was walking right through. So we moved up. And in our life, there is a cloister. There is a section where we do not have outsiders come in unless there is permission. So just being able to create ourselves a space—we've finally been able to do it here. It's very important, where you can come down in shorts and a t-shirt and just relax and read the paper without the world walking through. And we're always supposed to be available. But we need to encourage private spaces and vacations and retreats. If you feel you need to go away for a couple days, you go and that's all right. We do that with one another; if things are tense we say that to one another, [laugh] "Maybe you need to take some time." But a lot of guys, because there aren't too many of us, don't feel that they have that freedom. They'll go a year with no vacation or retreat. It's bound to build up.

Recommendation 4: Combat loneliness by fostering priestly fraternity, especially in living situations.

Closely aligned with concern about living space is the issue of loneliness. Priests often live alone, especially today as the number of priests has diminished. The people they spend the most time with are not colleagues but those who look to them for leadership: parishioners, lay ministers, and staff. The image of priestly camaraderie that flourished in the 1950s and 1960s no longer matches reality today. There are fewer priests, the nature of the priesthood has changed, and even the broader culture has shifted away from recreational companionship in groups and toward more individual pursuits and pastimes.

Although some priests we interviewed believed the problem of loneliness needed to be solved by each priest, most recommended a systematic effort to strengthen priestly fraternity. An older priest in a focus group:

> We've lost fraternity among our clergy, so we don't feel comfortable just stopping in and visiting one another as we used to. So there is an aloofness and loneliness that comes. And as you get a little bit older, my age, a lot of the guys that I was friends with in the seminary are dead, and my close friends have all moved away or died. So you begin to be more or less by yourself as you get a little older. But among the young clergy, there is sometimes a lack in the seminary of closeness and a development of fraternity, and so when they go into the priesthood there is even more of that distance. You may not have as many friends as you should have. So you get out into a parish, and most of the people you're friends with are the lay people. And there is a difference between having friends among the lay people and friends among the priesthood, where you can really share yourself. And in recent years we have not had as many assemblies of clergy as we used to, where we would get together and have some social life together.

Specific suggestions for creating fraternity involved changes in living situations.

Father Craig, age 36:

> There tend to be clusters of parishes in the city. Could the guys live together? Then at least someone else is in the house. Then again, it's one of those things, Do you like those other guys? Do you want to get together with them? I wouldn't know exactly what my opinion would be.

A 32-year-old priest echoes this idea:

> One of the things that I think causes [loneliness] is isolation, where, certainly in an urban environment, there is no reason for priests to be living alone in a parish. Groups of guys should be living together. Not that every-

one has to have a sense of community or some kind of obligation to a group, but when you have a group, it seems to me, it is healthier living. My God, if nothing else, when you have someone who hasn't left his room in two days, when you're living with a couple of people, they would pick that up. And especially in an urban area, there is simply no reason for guys to be living alone.

A 64-year-old priest, ordained in 1968:

Priests have to live together—even though in a rural diocese it might be a fifteen-mile commute to work. Now they feel the effects of not being in communion with one another in a supportive way. But even that living together has to be structured so that it's supportive. You can live in isolation in the rectory too.

A 40-year-old friar described the friction between his community and the diocese:

In our own community, we had trouble because our charism is that we don't live on our own; we live in community. As our friaries decreased, we began to establish that our friars would live in one fraternity and go out each day to parishes surrounding it. And the bishop in the diocese did not like that, because he wanted a priest in every rectory, because I guess he thinks that if the people know there is a priest in their rectory, their church is active and alive. So our solution was to pull out of these parishes; we can't sacrifice who we are. And I think that is going to be a reality for dioceses as their guys age and the numbers decrease. I think they have to find other alternatives for these guys to get support with one another. It's okay to live in a group and go out. If there's no one living in a rectory, that's okay. But find other ways and means of them living with one another and getting some kind of support.

Recommendation 5: Provide clear guidelines for healthy limit-setting by priests.

Concerning the problem of overwork among priests, the recommendations given to us fell into two areas: the need for more hierarchical support and the need to expand parish staff. First of all, diocesan leadership needs to provide guidance and support for healthy limit-setting.

A 49-year-old priest sees the need for structural change:

They give us all these recommendations to balance your life, rest, and whatever else, but that's lip service. There's got to be a systemic, structural change, and I think only the bishops can initiate the discussion to look at what those changes need to be, whether it's in promoting laity or cutting back on duties or promoting vocations. They've got to deal with that openly. That would be the key thing that I would say about overwork. Too many priests are too dedicated, and they're going to overwork no matter what. They just don't have the ability to say no, because they're too willing to give. They see the work and they go do it.

A 40-year-old priest recognizes how difficult it is to take time for himself:

I think, as priests, we're almost called to be workaholics. You can be made to feel guilty if you don't work seventeen hours a day almost. You feel you should be in your office. If you're not, it's not so much that somebody else is looking at you saying, "Why aren't you in your office?" but it's that self-infliction, you know, "Why aren't you? You should be down in your office instead of working in your room or taking a half hour break," or something like that—or even taking that hour for a quiet hour for prayer. You want to do it, and yet people are going to think I'm not working because I'm up here praying and not in the office. Well, really it's nobody's business. But you kind of inflict that on yourself. So I think the recommendation needs to be made that we need to be able to say that it's okay to take time. It's okay to take care of yourself. If you want to go exercise, it's okay to take an hour off and get out of the rectory. It's okay to do some things for yourself.

A religious priest, age 40, suggested exploring alternatives:

Find ways for priests to not be overworked—other alternatives for ministry, maybe being more inclusive of others. I'm kind of torn, because I would like to see women in the priesthood; I'd like to see married folks in the priesthood. But as I work here with young people and help them with discernment, I don't think the problems of the priesthood will be solved if we just allow these other groups to take part in the ministry. . . . But maybe look at other alternatives: lay folks, religious, women religious—whatever it might be to take some of the responsibility away.

Recommendation 6: Increase financial and moral support for hiring lay staff.

The priests, both young and old, recognized the need to delegate to staff and laity, but they also felt a need to clarify expectations and a need for increased financial support.

A 37-year-old priest describes the role that money plays in being able to adjust the workload of priests:

The problem is that some of the structure is inherent. To change the workload of priests you have to be able to expand lay staff or other staff, and that takes money. So those with money are able to hire staff, and people without money have to do it all themselves. It's more of an issue of stewardship. They want to inspire Catholics to give more, to tithe; then they have more money to do more programs.

A priest in a focus group:

> We don't want bishops or leadership to be Big Daddy and take care of us.
> But I think we are asking for leadership that encourages us to take responsi-
> bility for our own health. I also would say we need leadership that says, "It's
> okay to look at alternative forms of staffing, running, and maintaining
> parochial life." Okay, John here [another priest] said he is going to hire a
> business manager. He's going to get flak for that from some parishioners or
> whatever. I think we as a local church are not at a place where we can say to
> the people, "Let's buck up with thirty thousand dollars a year to hire some-
> one to do what Father used to do." We are still re-imaging what Father is
> going to do in this church with fewer priests.

Another priest in a focus group emphasized the financial difficulties in a
poor parish:

> I would say, we need more paid staff for the poor parishes, and the diocese
> should commit itself to see that. Be the true church across the board and not
> just the church of the rich, of those who can afford it. Provide for paid staff
> for the poorer parishes.

A 64-year-old priest focused on the spiritual role of the priest:

> Figure out how we can govern our parishes, administrate our parishes, in
> ways that do not depend so highly on the pastors involved in all the adminis-
> trating. We're not plant managers. We're out to plant the Word of God, but
> we don't deny that we live in this very real world. We have to entrust to lay
> commissions, managers, or however we want to say it, the real fiscal man-
> agement of the Church.

Recommendation 7: Encourage prayer and the use of spiritual directors.

The priests offered two main recommendations for strengthening the spiritual life of priests: encourage priests to pray and to use spiritual directors.

A 40-year-old priest:

> If you love God and are spiritual in your prayer life and in seeking guidance,
> people see that. And they're attracted to that. And they know it because you
> will live that out in your life, not just by what you say but by what you *do*. I
> think that's important. So you've got to make sure that guys are spending
> time in prayer and that they are seeking spiritual guidance. And I think too
> many guys think once they're ordained, they don't need it anymore.

A 68-year-old religious priest emphasized prayer:

> I think it is so important to be a person of prayer, to know Jesus intimately,
> to love Him ardently, and to follow Him closely!—and to do this on a daily

basis in one's prayer. It spills over into the liturgy, the celebration of liturgy, eucharistic liturgy, and it spills over into apostolic work.

Several priests recommended that all priests have a spiritual director to encourage conscious effort to develop and nurture the spiritual life.

A 40-year-old diocesan priest stressed the necessity of spiritual direction in forming a solid prayer life:

> I think we need to encourage guys to find spiritual directors and do spiritual direction. Too many guys are out there that don't seek spiritual guidance. And I think if you're not grounded in spirituality, then your priesthood is fake. You have to have a strong spiritual life, because if you don't, you're up there blowing wind. Who should believe you?

A priest in a focus group:

> I think spiritual life doesn't just happen. A person needs to be proactive with it. And all the stuff that has been written about continuing formation, I was doing it before it was written down, because that's the way my seminary was in our formation, showing the importance of having an advisor and spiritual director— or both at the same time. I continue that in my priesthood, and that is part of my spiritual life. And I think that's why I'm still a priest to a certain extent, because I took a proactive approach, therefore I meet with a person. . . . But I think we could do a better job of making it known who are spiritual directors here, or who are older pastors who would be willing to be spiritual directors or spiritual mentors. I think it would be a good thing.

A 40-year-old religious priest:

> Make sure that men have a spiritual director: someone they can trust, someone they have a good relationship with who knows them well, and their sinfulness, and their giftedness, and is comfortable with them. I think that is the primary relationship. And, if it's not the same person, a confessor to keep you grounded. And education and fun social activities to get them together so they can find support in that. That is very important too, because they forget how to have fun, or that we're allowed to have it.

From the various suggestions made by priests in interviews and focus groups we gleaned the above seven recommendations. The priests' two main suggestions to seminaries were to increase the focus on prayer and spirituality and to prepare seminarians better for the practical aspects of parish life. They felt that the demands of ministry and the need to be a role model cannot be managed without a solid prayer life and a growing depth of spirituality—the groundwork for which had to be laid in seminary. Reliance on prayer did not blind them, though, to the practical realities of parish life.

Their suggestions to bishops were focused on the practical issues of daily life. Priests see a need to separate their work and living spaces, and to create living situations that encourage priestly fraternity and alleviate loneliness. As fewer priests serve a growing Catholic population, they are finding themselves with more to do than they can manage. They would like their bishops to help them adjust to the new realities.

Epilogue

Effects of the 2002 Sexual Misconduct Crisis

The research project upon which this book is based was envisioned early in 2000 and begun in the autumn. We mailed the priest survey in the spring of 2001, and we carried out the interviews and focus groups in late 2001 and early 2002. All of this was prior to the sexual misconduct crisis, which broke in February and March 2002 with revelations concerning priests' abuse of minors and bishops' failure to remove those priests from parishes. Much has changed since then.

As we write this in the autumn of 2002, we find ourselves in the midst of an upheaval in the American Catholic community the likes of which neither of us has personally experienced before. What effects will it have? When will it end? There is no doubt that *some things will change*. Here are the voices of two older priests talking candidly in a February 2002 focus group:

> I think we've been affected by not only the shortages in our numbers but also some of the moral crises that have affected our integrity. I think we wrestle with continuing to be credible while at times we are under a cloud of suspicion because of brothers who have been unfaithful to their vows and dishonest with their responsibilities. So I think that is a recurrent, painful predicament that we are experiencing much more now than any time in the last twenty-five years.

> Personally, I find myself battling depression when I see all the continuing negative news about priests with problems, even like this morning's paper. It affects me personally. I think it affects us all. This presbyterate is kind of under a general depression.

These views are widely felt. The *Los Angeles Times* survey of priests, done in July, August, and September 2002, asked, "What are the most important problems facing the Roman Catholic Church in the United States today?" The top four spontaneous replies were "shortage of priests" (25%), "problems with bishops and hierarchy" (20%), child abuse by clergy" (18%), and "restoring credibility to priests" (13%). Issues related to the sexual abuse crisis were the third and fourth most frequent.

147

The problem facing us authors is how to convey our pre-crisis research findings in light of the changed situation. We feel like researchers would feel if they had been studying American foreign policy early in the year 2001 and were overtaken by the events of September 11. Everything changed. The researchers would wonder if their findings are still pertinent. We ask the same question.

Our pre-crisis research is, however, not without value, for it measures underlying trends in the priesthood *independent of* the scandals of 2002. It tells us the (hypothetical) state of affairs apart from any impact from the revelations, charges, and media coverage. For an analyst trying to understand the priesthood in the year 2003 the task involves looking at the long-range trends depicted by the studies in this book, then adding the one-time jolt of the scandals. Although we cannot say much about the future, the trends depicted in this book are more reliable for projecting into the future than projections would be if they were based on surveys undertaken in the midst of the crisis. Our trend research measures glacial movements in the social fabric of the American Catholic Church which are largely invisible to the naked eye. The American Catholic community lives on a slow conveyor belt of change whose movement—both the direction and the speed—can be discerned only through historical and sociological research. Our pre-crisis data is useful, at least, for assisting with this task.

We are still faced with an often-asked question: Does our pre-crisis research describe the years 2003 and 2004, or not? It is hard to know, not only because things are changing from month to month, but also because we cannot easily assess (a) the strength of lay demands in America for institutional reforms and (b) the determination of high-level Catholic officials to continue business as usual without any reforms. The most we can do now is to make intelligent guesses as to what the effects of the sexual misconduct crisis will be. We will venture two guesses.

First, the priest shortage will worsen. A main reason is because of the parish priests who are now being dismissed due to past accusations of misconduct. As of autumn 2002, over 300 priests have been dismissed from pastoral duties during 2002 for this reason. Three hundred is not a large percentage of priests, but in a situation of shortage it will have an effect. In addition, gay seminarians and priests today feel more threatened now than they did in the past, due to the sometimes-heard argument that homosexuality has in some way contributed to the sexual misconduct crisis. We expect that gay men will be more hesitant than earlier to enter seminary or to continue in the priesthood. These effects of the crisis are in addition to the long-term loss of the priesthood's authority more generally. Nobody knows yet if there will be a significant drop in the number of seminarians, but within a year or two we will know.

Second, the current crisis will have a financial cost. Possibly donations will decline. An intelligent guess would be that contributions to local parishes—whose pastors have largely escaped the heat—will be less affected than contributions to diocesan appeals and to programs at the national level. It is very possible that the influence of the sexual misconduct crisis on local parish income will be negligible.

Compounding reduced contributions to dioceses is the already measurable drain on diocesan financial reserves from the costs of litigation and out-of-court settlements.

Will the crisis lead to church procedural reforms, such as a changed method of selecting priests for parishes, more lay oversight over diocesan finances, or greater lay power in diocesan decision making? People are talking about this, but nobody knows how much reform there will be. Our guess is that if it takes place, it won't be soon.

What should priests expect from all this? Again we will make two guesses. First, the influence and participation of laypersons in parish life is destined to increase, even more than we would expect merely from projecting long-term trends in lay attitudes. Thus there will be fewer priests, more lay ministers, and more widespread feelings among laypersons that they deserve a say in parish decisions. Lay organizations will become stronger than before.

Second, church offices at the national, diocesan, and parish levels will become more open and forthcoming with information. Like Americans in all religious traditions, Catholics in the future will demand more information on financial transactions, appointment decisions, and files on clergy. Laity will accelerate their requests for more information and more accountability.

In sum, we believe the work of priests will change in the future, and possibly their work will be more difficult. Institutional habits and long-held assumptions about Catholic life will need to adjust to new conditions. Seminaries and chanceries need to get ready.

COMMENTARIES

Toward a Renewed Priesthood

Most Reverend Gerald F. Kicanas

Introduction

Dean Hoge and Jacqueline Wenger have updated and expanded on a study of priesthood begun in 1970 and continued in 1985 and again in 1993. This longitudinal approach can help us gain perspective. The Church needs to encourage those doing research to gather data and participate in its interpretation. I will reflect on three aspects of this study which are pertinent to diocesan priests and have implications for dioceses and seminaries: different visions of priesthood within presbyterates, the issues and needs felt by priests, and the critical factors for living a celibate commitment.

Different Visions of Priesthood

Cardinal Francis George, O.M.I., when he was appointed as the archbishop of Chicago, initiated a program of ongoing formation for clergy in their first three years of ministry. He developed the idea after talking with Cardinal Jean Lustiger of Paris, who some years before had asked one of his auxiliary bishops to meet regularly with the recently ordained to lead them in prayer, foster fraternity, and attend to their ongoing human, intellectual, spiritual, and pastoral growth.

Cardinal George invited me to direct this new program since I had been rector at the University of St. Mary of the Lake/Mundelein Seminary, for ten years. I approached the assignment with concerns. I wondered how resistant the new priests would be to the idea. Would they feel that they were back in the seminary? Would they make time to break away from their pastoral work to attend to their own ongoing formation? Would they resent the program being required of them?

I directed the program for nearly four years while I was in Chicago. I was amazed and pleased that most of the recently ordained took the program seriously. They helped to plan the themes for the sessions and gave input on how those themes would be addressed. Over time I could see a growing fraternity among those who attended.

After the first year of the program, it became obvious that one of the sources of tension felt by the recently ordained was their relationship with their pastors. The recently ordained wanted to talk, to dialogue with their pastors, who are from a different generation of priests.

That did not surprise me, since I remembered well my first assignment in 1967 and the friction I felt with Monsignor Harry Koenig, my first pastor, a great priest, but from a different generation. He was, at that time, thirty-five years my senior. We often argued and disagreed. I remember one staff meeting, which meant in those days a meeting of the priests only. Msgr. Koenig yelled at me while the first associate refereed. I wanted to be out among the people; he wanted me to be in the rectory, on call. I went over to people's houses for dinner; he wanted me at home for dinner in the rectory. I wanted to get involved in social issues in the public arena; he wanted me to pray more often. We fought. While we shared the priesthood, we had different views of what it meant to be a priest. I learned a great deal from my first pastor, not the least of which was that I didn't have all the answers and my perspective was not the only and final word.

The format planned by the recently ordained for the meeting with their pastors involved separating the two groups, forming a group of pastors and a group of recently ordained. Each group was supposed to come up with ten adjectives to describe themselves, ten adjectives to describe the other group, and ten adjectives that pastors thought the recently ordained would use to describe them and vice versa. Then we would talk.

The results were fascinating. The recently ordained saw their pastors as liberal, dissenters, socially conscious, not prayerful, wanting things done their way. And that is exactly how the pastors suspected the recently ordained viewed them.

The pastors saw the recently ordained as conservative, courageous, having an exalted notion of what it meant to be a priest, pious, focused on thinking with the Pope, lacking initiative. This, too, was exactly what the recently ordained believed was the view of them held by their pastors.

The discussion became rather heated when we began dialoguing about the results. One of the youngest of the recently ordained cried out at one point that he had pursued priesthood at a time when his family, friends, and culture questioned why he would do that. He wanted a clear identity of what it meant to be a priest. He did not want to be one among many in the church. After all, if a lay person could do everything and was so important in the church, why should he give up so much to pursue priesthood?

There are clearly generational differences within presbyterates. Hoge and Wenger's study confirms what all of us are experiencing. Just as the older pastors found it difficult to integrate the changes after Vatican II, the older pastors today find it difficult to let go of the ways they responded to the council, some of which have not lived up to their expectations. The times continue to change and so must the pastoral response.

As I listened to the pastors and recently ordained talk to one another, I could not help but think that both articulated dimensions of diocesan priesthood that are critical. The differences do not have to be destructive, as they sometimes are. The two viewpoints, while different, are not op-posed. They can be complementary.

Diocesan priests need to walk with the people. They serve among them. They enter the lives of their people at significant levels of personal sharing and they receive profound levels of trust accorded few people. Priests are identified with the struggle of their people and speak up for them. They act as servant-leaders. But they also lead people in prayer, preside at the Eu-charist, and act *in persona Christi, capitis.* This means that they exercise cultic leadership and represent Christ present and acting in the Church. Priests play a unique and special role in the Church. They are called to preach, celebrate and guide *in persona Christi.*

One implication of Hoge and Wenger's study is that dioceses need to bring priests of different generations together for dialogue and conversa-tion about their differing views of the priesthood and the Church. That dia-logue will allow priests to get to know one another at deeper levels and find a priestly heart among those who differ from their thinking. Familiarity does not result in contempt but mutual understanding at a deeper level.

A program of ongoing formation for priests is critical to provide both an occasion for that dialogue and an opportunity leading to ever deeper under-standing of the mystery of the Church and the priesthood. Most dioceses attempt ongoing formation, but what is needed is to give ongoing forma-tion as much focus and attention as is given to initial formation. Priests need to grow from interaction through study and dialogue together.

Issues and Needs of Priests

As I talk now with priests in Tucson and before in Chicago, as I listen to priests during priests' retreats which I have given or diocesan priest convo-cations in which I have participated, I find priests differ on the issues they face and the intensity they feel about those issues. Today especially, priests are weighed down by concerns that gnaw at them and eat away at their confidence and the conviction that they matter. They wonder if they make a difference. One priest said to me lately that 2002 had been the most disheartening time in his forty years as a priest.

Hoge and Wenger's study finds ten areas identified by priests as struggles they face. The list of the topics of concern to priests (table 5.1) can provide "for national Catholic leadership an agenda which would truly serve the needs of priests."

The first thing we need to do is to face the issues and get about addressing them. There are not any easy or simple answers, but what demoralizes priests is when those issues are ignored, dismissed, or made light of.

Frank and open discussion within the presbyterate can relieve tension and can communicate an interest by the bishop in the pain and hurt of his priests. Such occasions can be moments for the bishop to listen and to teach, to understand and to give direction. Endless talk and no action can be frustrating. Identifying bite-sized issues that concern priests and that can be acted upon and resolved can give priests a sense of progress and dispel the sense of paralysis.

Former Mayor Rudolph Guiliani of New York, when he began in office, identified a specific concern that needed to be addressed: street vendors. He moved on the issue with quick and decisive action. He created a sense of momentum and showed that the city could change and improve.

I would suggest that dioceses begin with an issue that together they can seek to address. Take, for example, the image and esteem of the priesthood today, which was identified in the study as the area priests most want to discuss openly. The bishop would begin by first listening to the priests, inviting their reflections, and holding up the tradition. Then together with his priests he would look for ways to act.

Sometimes the opportunity for priests within the presbyterate to tell stories of priest mentors from the diocese who have impacted their lives can dispel any doubt that priests make a difference. Those stories are reminders of the importance of priestly ministry. Every presbyterate has its giants. Telling their stories can unify the presbyterate, inspire, and energize.

Anniversary celebrations in the diocese and even funeral Masses for dedicated, hard-working priests can be occasions to emphasize and highlight the values of priesthood.

The voice of the laity giving witness to how priests have impacted their lives can be moving. At a vocation assembly for priests in Chicago a panel made up of a married laywoman, a young teenager, and an elderly man gave witness to the gratitude they felt to priests who had contributed significantly to their lives. From listening to them you felt good about the contributions priests make.

Dioceses and presbyterates cannot face every issue all at once. Identify an area that the presbyterate can focus on for some time and get about addressing it. Movement and progress will give a sense of momentum.

This approach can reinforce what priests suggested in the study would be opportunities to help them in their ministry. Priests working together to address issues, not letting issues divide them, could lead to greater fraternity. It would bring priests more directly into decision making and help them find a spiritual dimension to their challenges.

Factors for Celibate Living

The sexual abuse issue needs to be analyzed and studied. Some feel it is media-driven and subject to serious distortion, and others feel it has silenced the voice of the Church, jeopardized the carrying out of her mission, and shaken the bond of trust between bishops, priests and people. While Hoge and Wenger's research happened before the latest sudden increase of abuse allegations, it gives some directions for responding to the present crisis whose roots go back more than two decades.

Many are attempting to explain the roots of this crisis. I believe that seminaries and dioceses can best address the concern by providing seminarians and priests with means to assist them in integrating their sexuality and strengthening appropriate strategies for chaste, celibate living. This is for everyone a life-long challenge. Seminaries today seem to be ahead of dioceses in providing this critical formation.

For a future priest to be able to live a celibate commitment in a healthy way, he needs to know himself and be able to talk freely and openly about his sexuality to appropriate people. Sexuality cannot be a hidden, secretive area of his life, but needs to be opened to the light allowing the grace of God to sustain the priest in living a chaste, celibate commitment.

In my ten years as rector of a major seminary it became customary during an admission interview with a candidate to discuss openly with him his sexual orientation and history. The candidate was asked what he understood his sexual orientation to be and invited to describe his sexual history. He was asked directly whether he had lived as a celibate and for how long. Such conversations are common today in admission interviews for seminarians around the United States.

There are candidates accepted to seminaries who indicate that they have a homosexual orientation, yet describe lifestyles that give confidence that they can live a celibate commitment. Of the five hundred candidates I interviewed in ten years, a number, consistent with national estimates for all males, identified themselves as having a homosexual orientation. Some of them were accepted into the seminary and some were not. People make widely varying estimates of the percentage of priests and seminarians who have a homosexual orientation. But so far that is purely speculative—and in the end may not be so important or helpful.

I have worked with priests in spiritual direction and during priests' retreats who know and say they are homosexual in orientation. They are living out a life of celibacy and are exemplary priests. They serve well. In Hoge and Wenger's study this is confirmed by the comments of many priests.

However, seminary rectors and bishops along with seminary faculty and members of the presbyterate need to be vigilant that a gay subculture does not form within seminaries or presbyterates. Such subcultures are divisive and unhealthy among those seeking to live a chaste, celibate life. When a person's sexuality is well integrated, he is open to all and not limited to interactions with people he perceives to be like himself. Public statements and manifestations by a priest or seminarian about his sexual orientation are most inappropriate, divisive, and implicitly narrowing to his ministry to all. The recognition that one is a sexual human being, the ongoing continued progress toward sexual integration, the ability to control impulses, and a spirituality that strives to live a moral life in keeping with the Gospel and church teachings are critical factors that need the attention of those responsible for initial and ongoing formation.

These are the dimensions that can be attended to best by creating an atmosphere where sexuality can be discussed appropriately and openly within a normal context. A seminarian or a priest needs a spiritual director with whom they talk regularly and who knows them as much as they know themselves. There are no secrets or pieces of self that are hidden.

Conclusion

Hoge and Wenger have given bishops, priests, and seminary formation staff data to digest and interpret. My conclusion from reading the study is to encourage the presbyterate in Tucson to dialogue about our different ecclesiological perspectives and visions of priesthood in respectful ways in order to broaden and enhance our perspective and strengthen our sense of common mission. I would hope that other bishops do the same.

Second, I would encourage the presbyterate to identify an issue that affects priests so that we could address it together and bring the process through to action. Consultation with others: religious, deacons, and laity may be necessary and helpful. It is critical to break down a sense of ennui that might paralyze the presbyterate.

Finally, it seems even more pressing that the diocese begin a systematic program of ongoing formation that will help priests address, among other issues, their needs as sexual beings and how those needs can be attended to in the context of living a chaste, celibate commitment.

Most Rev. Gerald F. Kicanas was appointed coadjutor bishop of Tucson in 2001. He was an auxiliary bishop of Chicago and president and rector of the University of St. Mary of the Lake- Mundelein Seminary in Mundelein, Illinois. Bishop Kicanas is Episcopal liaison for the National Association for Lay Ministry (NALM).

Faces

Rev. Canice Connors, O.F.M. Conv.

The statistics in this book have a voice of their own, and the happy inclusion of representative interviews adds emotional nuance. Attending to both, I have borrowed Donald Cozzens' popular analogy of the priesthood's "changing face" to imagine a variety of facial postures painted by the numbers and mirroring the recorded emotions.

Smiling Faces

Ah, the ear-to-ear smiles when you ask a priest if he enjoys the sanctuary, the pulpit and the parlor! The satisfiers differ somewhat within the age groupings: the post-Vatican-IIers are happier in the sanctuary doing what only a priest can (should) do. The Vatican-IIers find greater satisfaction when inviting and empowering others to get in on the pastoral action. The bottom line is that for both groups, life is better when they are on the parish grounds, not distracted with the complexities of management and the voices from "downtown." Seminaries are doing a better job in preparing for presiding and preaching but lagging in how to handle the complexity of multiple lay ministers. Is it collaboration or competition?

Shortages have shortened the waiting line for pastorships; no more nasty rectory politics. It's hard to disagree with yourself. Now that satisfactions of leadership do not have to be delayed, the question may be where do you go when you've done it all by age fifty? If you start with a small parish, move to the giant suburban one and then seek refuge in a moderate sized setting, what is left? Depleted ranks also bring some deficits. Bishops are reluctant to "lend" any of their few to national positions or to permit the pursuit of graduate degrees or professional specializations. Long gone is the hyphenated priest. The smiles may wear thin once presiding has become a well-honed skill and preaching the cycle has depleted the creative juices. Increasingly priests are seeking early retirement, not from the "pleasant tasks" but from the grind of management.

Having successfully resolved the personnel challenges of the '60s, the new problem for the priesthood may be defining the ministry of lay parish manager that does not diminish the role/status of pastor and developing a broader variety of pastoral opportunities for priests that provide the "satisfiers" apart from parish settings.

Scowling Faces

The research quantifies and verifies the growing emotional and intellectual distance separating the post-Vatican priests from the Vatican II veterans and linking the former to the pre-Vatican II elders. The cultic vs. servant-leader categories position the tension historically and theologically. But the differences are lived at the gut level. The Vatican II heroes, now mostly deceased, seared their souls in the bloody combat of ripping living liturgy and faith out of frozen rubrics and stale dogmatic formulas. Did they only win a few battles and forfeit the war? Is their best rhetoric now but sardonic parody of the smells and bells set, as restorationists find missing what they never experienced? Are the Vatican II priests reduced to resistance tactics fending off the renovations of clerical cultic islands with narrow crossovers for the laity? Or skipping the prose: What chills the blood of the aging liberals is the realization that in their youth, "the old bastards" were the conservatives. Now the young priests are becoming the conservatives and we are the old bastards. Or in Richard Cohen's version: "We were raised for one era and had to live in another, and now, tragically, we've been discounted altogether, forgotten like some lost civilization or Tiny Tim. We're accused, I suspect, of having done nothing. That, however, is not the case. We've been in therapy."

Meanwhile the younger wag the finger of guilt at those whom they believe created or occasioned the dark clouds of current shame: frivolous experimenters who by doing it "my way" unhinged themselves from the rock of Peter. The effective antidote is their concerned conservatism—a necessary ballast to right the bark of Peter. They are unashamedly CATHOLIC. Though fewer in number than previous younger sets, their morale is high, as one might predict, in skilled, highly motivated tactical forces.

The easy-to-come-by metaphors of struggle suggest that we may be dealing with the dynamics of "totalization," that tempting reduction of individuals and their histories to categories of alienation. And it is here that the focus groups do bring at least a modicum of correction. The face-to-face conversational tone softens the rhetoric and reveals the "persons" masked by the categories "cultic" versus "servant-leaders."

Surely, what is needed in every presbyterate, and especially where the post-Vaticaners are numerous, is carefully crafted conversational settings that will dissolve the stereotyping. Not all young priests are conservative re-actionaries buying up old birettas, nor are all Vatican-IIers blinded to failed liturgical follies. But laughing and chatting together will not resolve genuine differences. When carefully nurtured, the stressors of barren soil and harsh climates do yield some fine wines. Will patient analysis prove that some of the panting for certitudes is a functional anxiety generated by postmod-ernism? Do we need some kindly, informed theologians to provide friendlier interpretations and alternative intellectual strategies to shrill dogmatics? And do we need to revisit the failed strategies of reform and seek forgiveness and reconciliation for unrecognized excesses? Or better yet, do we all have to question the not-so-sacred silences that characterize presbyteral gatherings? Why is it, when there is so much pain and anxiety, that we satisfy ourselves with bantering about peripherals as if they were substantive?

Serene Faces

As Ronald Rolheiser, author of *The Holy Longing: The Search for A Christian Spirituality,* will verify, SPIRITUALITY is IN. This research spells it out in percentages that leave no doubt that priests want more time for prayer, reflection and *lectio.* The message is clear for continuing educa-tion coordinators and for the talking-heads circuit riders: focus on priestly spirituality. And how advantageous to have at hand, or nearly so, a new edition of *Spiritual Renewal of the American Priesthood.* Not to mention the NCCB publication, *Basic Plan for the Ongoing Formation of Priests,* which helpfully covers all the components of an integral spirituality.

A minor concern: will this hunger be interpreted as simply a demand for extended private prayer time, while we avoid the issue of effective common prayer? Not the monastic format of reciting office at retreats or convoca-tions (which some groups do well indeed), but praying from and out of shared experience. Composing and praying anger psalms and lamentations may both release considerable pent up emotions and forge spiritual, frater-nal bonds that transcend the classical cycle of bitch, moan, and complain.

Out of the total one hundred and fifty psalms, thirty-seven deal with anger—not the immature reactions to petty frustrations but the genuine ex-perience of encountering obstacles on the way to the kingdom of God. We also know that clergy are inclined to pass over their experiences of losses and put on a smiling face. The unattended grieving diminishes their avail-ability in the here and now of pastoral demands because they are either still caught by past pain or anxiously anticipating more of the same. Prayers of lamentation help to heal and liberate memory so that imagination can gen-erate new possibilities. The past is not forgotten, but it no longer holds the future in captivity.

Frowning Faces

Did good men really say adios due to oppressive gay subcultures? Are homosexuals destabilizing seminary environs? Then again, is it all a phobic shadow dance? The research seems to yield a firm MAYBE or perhaps a weak YES that there is a gay subculture, but it doesn't make all that much difference. Whatever the case, the issue frowns many a hierarchal brow and motivates yet another inventory of seminary closets.

Can we ever get to the real point about homosexuality? It is not about orientation, it is about integration! Or more precisely, it is definitely about psychosexual maturity. We can estimate all day long about what percentage of gay men it takes to make the priesthood a gay profession while the cutting issue is whether we have a priesthood of responsible celibates. And that laudable goal is undermined by the hermeneutics of suspicion that every homosexual priest is a potential child abuser or environmental destabilizer. The challenge is to "get on message" and stick with the demand for integrity.

Or, to go at it from an entirely different angle, is the time ripe to unmask the designed ambiguity that has been generated by a collective effort to live with the blunt, official premise on the disordered nature of the homosexual inclination? James Alison put it this way:

> Ambiguity. . . . is in fact a tone which permeates the ecclesiastical sphere of at least the three continents where I have worked, and is a serious danger to the moral and spiritual health of those who inhabit it. In countless seminaries, houses of formation, religious communities, curias and so on, an endless game of ambiguity is played which goes something like this: 'we will turn a blind eye to the obvious so long as you don't rock the boat by talking about it.' The result is swathes of the clerical caste engaged in a continuous game of emotional blackmail, for this issue can always mysteriously be raised in order to threaten or expel. . . .
>
> . . . Most of the gay majority in a Catholic seminary or house of religious formation are typically living with some or other degree of fear of expulsion, of officially sanctioned self-hatred, of bad consciences over any relationships they might find themselves in, of severe self-questioning, about whether or not they are being representative of, a body which acts in public as though it hates them. Never mind all the gossip, backbiting, intrigues, power games and delations which go along with such states of mind. . . . What sort of surprise is it that it would be destabilizing to live with a majority of gay people who are officially committed to believing that being gay is not a normal part of nature? Not only straight people, but also gay people who prize honesty are thoroughly destabilized by living in such an environment." (2001, pp. 187–89)

Contrasting Faces

The research identifies some developing distinctions between young diocesan and youthful religious clergy. A meager trend perhaps, but does it reflect an outcome from a conscious shift in the formation programs for religious that has successfully shifted the axis of vocational discernment to revolve around the issues of community charism? David Power advises us:

> Ministries for which it was at one time assumed that ordination was necessary may well look otherwise in a changed ecclesial practice. A number of institutes must deal with the fact that they have nurtured narrowly sacramental understandings of priesthood among their members in the past. They must now balance this with the need to relate ordination to mission and ministry, not to status or state of life. (In Hennessy, p. 94)

If this trend is grounded in a search for authenticity in charism, the outcome will benefit the Church in providing an alternative way of dealing with the relational issues between the ordained and nonordained. Again Power:

> Since ordination is tied to so many institutional presuppositions, it could hinder development involving the future of religious communities. In the first place, an undifferentiated ordination practice could hinder the retrieval for some religious of their original form of common life. Even those bodies in which it was, in the beginning, taken for granted that commitment to a special type of ministry meant ordination might find that the ministry can be better served in some cases by the nonordained. Greater cooperation with other nonordained ministers might take priority over ordination. (In Hennessy, p. 95)

This is a narrow interpretation of the data to be sure and one that bears the bias of some religious who believe that for many Roman Catholics the word "parish" has become synonymous with local church. All other forms of ministry are perceived as tangential to real Catholic life. For this and other reasons, the increased co-option of religious priests into diocesan and parish structures must be carefully examined.

Sad Faces

As our researchers rightly observe, the data was collected prior to the revisiting of the clergy sexual abuse of minors scandal that began gathering force in January 2002 along the Boston harbor and has since washed ashore on both coasts—a flood tide of scandal and intense questioning of hierarchical integrity. Without data, the marshland of speculation undermines confident claims but even casual observers might wonder about the slightly out-of-focus, sad face on many priests that masks low-grade depression, or worse. In the post-Dallas expulsion of those previously identified as offenders, the feeling of abandonment and the shadow of suspicion have actively invaded clergy consciousness. It is only just and right that the Church turn its attention to the long-ignored plight of the victims of clergy abuse. And no priest worthy of his oils would gainsay that priority. Yet, there is a sense of being scapegoated. The zero tolerance policy favored by the bishops strikes many priests as a way of avoiding the more relevant questioning of malfeasance within their own ranks. And, by the way, what ever happened to our theology of forgiveness and reconciliation?

Now for the what-if's. *What if* Rome does turn back or revise "the norms"? Will the second time around permit a more inclusive and extended discussion of why the clear principles of 1993 were not applied in certain dioceses? Will there be a chance for the voice of reformed abusers to be heard?

What if the *Charter for the Protection of Children and Young People* becomes particular law? What will be the impact on the relationship between priest and bishop? Paul Wilkes (in *The New Yorker,* 2 September 2002) raises the prospect of the reformer in the person of Father William Cuenin, pastor of Our Lady Help of Christians in Newton, Mass. Cuenin called into existence the Boston Priests' Forum. Will this be a revisiting of the angry '60s or something new and promising? "We looked at each other and realized that we lacked something even as basic as 'unsupervised conversation.' We live in a Balkanized world, isolated in our parishes, and we really had no opportunity to share our concerns openly, without fear of retribution" (p. 103). Current and strongly felt fears have to be spoken to, creating the safe environments. Now there's the challenge.

Uplifted Faces

> Lift up your faces, you have a piercing need
> For this bright morning dawning for you.
> History, despite its wrenching pain,
> Cannot be unlived, and if faced
> With courage, need not be lived again.

Maya Angelou composed these words as part of "On the Pulse of Morning" read at President Clinton' first inaugural. Perhaps, in the end, it is not whether present or past situations leave us smiling, scowling, or whatever, but whether or not we stop staring at each other and get about the task of looking heavenward. As Maya suggests, that demands COURAGE.

Rev. Canice Connors, O.F.M. Conv., is currently president of the Conference of Major Superiors of Men (CMSM). He is minister provincial of the Immaculate Conception Province of the Conventual Franciscans. He was former executive director of Southdown Institute and St. Luke Institute.

References

Alison, James. 2001. *Faith Beyond Resentment: Fragments Catholic and Gay.* New York: Crossroad.

Hennessy, Paul K. (ed.). 1997. *A Concert of Charisms: Ordained Ministry in Religious Life.* New York: Paulist Press.

Rolheiser, Ronald. 1999. *The Holy Longing: The Search for A Christian Spirituality* New York: Doubleday.

The Search for Identity

Dr. Susan K. Wood, S.C.L.

The focus of the present study is the existence of two types of priests today, identified as the cultic model and the servant-leader model. The authors generally find that the newest generation of priests identify themselves with the cultic model, while those priests 56-65 years old describe themselves as servant-leaders. These differences in self-identity correlate with two different ecclesiologies, the cultic model of priest loyal to John Paul II, the doctrinal teaching of the Church, and a hierarchical model of governance. The servant-leaders, on the other hand, were more democratic, more supportive of lay ministry in the Church, and more conflicted concerning the pastoral application of church teachings such as the prohibition of artificial birth control. The study helpfully substantiates statistically what many have observed more informally.

The survey forced choices between two different models of the priesthood that bear some resemblance to two of the models of the Church described by Avery Dulles in his well-known *Models of the Church*, namely the Church as institution and the Church as servant.[1] Because of the emphasis on the hierarchical nature of the Church, I believe the newer generation of priests resembles the institutional model more than the sacramental model, even though the cultic emphasis might suggest the latter. The data indicates that administering the sacraments and presiding over the liturgy is a source of joy for ninety percent of *all* priests. Thus the sacramental model may not differentiate between the two types of priest which are the focus of the present study.

Just as the fact that Dulles' models, now almost thirty years old, do not represent how ecclesiologists are currently envisioning the Church, so we

[1] Avery Dulles, *Models of the Church* (New York: Doubleday, Image Books, 1974).

might also wonder if there is an alternative view of the priesthood, suggested by more recent ecclesiologies, that might offer an alternative to the cultic and servant-leader models. Is the choice really between an ontological model and a functional model? Is it adequate to say that the priest is either essentially different from the laity or differs only by the functions he performs? I will explore these possibilities by first comparing the data of the study with Dulles' models. Then I will suggest an alternative ecclesiology and an alternative view of priesthood.

The Data Compared with Dulles' Institutional Model of the Church

As I consider the data, the conservative shift seems to represent a search for Catholic identity. The authors do not see this as nostalgia for the past, since the new generation never experienced that, but as a "longing for the time-tested, the true, and the authoritative."[2] As Mark Latcovich, vice-rector of St. Mary Seminary in Wickliffe, Ohio, noted, the sense of disconnection, disorientation, and crisis leads to the search for icons that offer stability and models from which to draw direction and inspiration. The tradition of the Church represents a rich resource to strengthen the public esteem and influence of the priesthood and to provide an identity that assures the new priest that his sacrifices are worth their effort.

The cultic model is a more visible, more clearly delineated view of the priesthood than the servant-leader model. It has many of the advantages that Avery Dulles noted in his institutional model of the Church. It provides important links between an uncertain present and an esteemed religious past. It supports a strong sense of corporate identity. It promotes a high degree of institutional loyalty.[3] It also has some of the same liabilities as Dulles' institutional model in that it tends to minimize the role of the laity and is juridical. It does not support the ecumenical movement. It binds theology too closely with the defense of official positions.[4] In short, strong priestly and ecclesial identity is achieved through a process of separation. The priest is separate from the laity, the sacred is divided liturgically from the secular, and what is Catholic is clearly set off from what is Protestant. This is supported by data in the present study which indicates that the newest generation of priests identifies themselves as receiving an ontological character which makes them essentially different from the

---

[2] Chap. 7 in the text.
[3] Dulles, 47–48.
[4] Ibid., 48–49.

laity. Anecdotes in the study describe the adoption of clerical garb such as cassocks and birettas, which further emphasize the difference between priests and laity, and the reluctance to allow children and women in the sanctuary.

According to the data, this strong identity promotes greater clerical happiness and stability. Those espousing this view of the priesthood have fewer thoughts of leaving the priesthood. A larger number would choose the priesthood again, given the option. Role clarity and visibility seem to strengthen the priesthood.

Ironically, Dulles, writing in 1974, concluded that this institutional model "is out of phase with the demands of the times."[5] This is supported by the research of Davidson and D'Antonio, which indicates that "there is no broad conservative trend among Catholics on beliefs in the areas of ecclesiology, priesthood, or liturgy. On the contrary, recent decades have seen a gradual trend in the opposite direction." The authors of the present study report that a series of Gallup polls of American Catholics between 1987 and 1999 report a modest trend toward according less authority to church leaders on moral issues, an increase in individualism and a distancing from church authority, a trend toward Catholics desiring more democratic structures and more lay participation in decision making, and increased support for a married priesthood.[6] Hoge and Wenger conclude that "the change in ecclesiology found among young priests has no counterpart among young adult laity. On the contrary, the young priests and young laity are heading in different directions on many issues." The data indicates that younger lay ministers are generally located on the spectrum between the newest generation of clergy and the rest of the laity. This certainly raises questions about the long-term effectiveness of the ministry of the new clerical generation if their conception of the Church and their role is significantly different from those they serve.

The comparison between the servant-leader model of the priesthood and Dulles' model of the church as servant is less well-defined. The model of church as servant de-emphasizes confessional proclamation and cultic celebration in order to emphasize dialogue with the world. The servant model appears to be more secular, more open to ecumenical cooperation. There is greater emphasis on social justice. Within this model the priest would be less visible and less distinct from his lay coworkers. This model supports a functional rather than ontological view of the priesthood. Priestly identity is more diffuse in this model.

---

[5] Ibid., 49.
[6] Chap. 7 in the text.

However, it must be noted that the priests in the survey rated administration of sacraments and preaching high in terms of satisfaction derived from them. Perhaps evidence for each of these models is found more in the stereotypes of the two groups than in their actual responses to the survey. For example younger priests identified the older priests as "liberals, leftist fringe, secularized, anti-establishment, and priests with a social work model." Older priests, on the other hand, found the younger priests as "liturgically conservative, institutional, hierarchical, and believers in a cultic priesthood."

New Ecclesial Paradigms

Dulles' models separated in order to distinguish. In effect, this is also the methodology of a sociological survey such as the present study. Forced choices surfaced the two groups of priests in the subjects of the study. Contemporary ecclesiology, however, synthesizes in order to integrate. Communion ecclesiology, which is dominating ecclesiology today, conceives of the church as a communion of communions. Levels of ecclesiality—the parish, the diocese, the universal Church—are communions within each level and in communion with the other levels. Communion is both synchronic, that is, a horizontal communion among levels of ecclesiality, and diachronic, that is, in historical communion with the apostolic past and eschatological future. One of the "functions" of ordained ministry is to represent and serve this communion. This is a far cry from the kind of functionality of task such as who is able to preach or administer the parish or anoint the sick.

Relationship rather than essential differences or function becomes the dominant identifier within communion ecclesiology. Ontology is not denied but is identified as an ontology of relation. A sacramental character consists in an ecclesial repositioning within the ecclesial body of Christ. A person becomes a member of the Church through baptism, is deputed to serve the mission in public witness through confirmation, and is empowered to act in a relationship of headship of the body of Christ through ordination. What differentiates the ordained from the laity is their respective positioning within the body of Christ.

Communion ecclesiology is neither hierarchic in the sense of a pryramidal structure of top-down authority nor is it democratic. Authority tends to be grounded sacramentally rather than juridically. For example, bishops have "proper, ordinary and immediate" authority because of the sacramentality of their episcopal consecration.[7] Married couples have a proper au-

---

[7] *Lumen Gentium,* 27. Quotations of *Lumen Gentium* are from Norman P. Tanner, S.J., ed., *Decrees of the Ecumenical Councils,* vol. 2 (London: Sheed & Ward; Washington, D.C.: Georgetown University Press, 1990).

thority within the marriage. The baptized have rights and responsibilities regarding the apostolate because of their sacrament and not because of a delegation from the hierarchy.[8]

I found that the choices in the survey tend to perpetuate old dichotomies between the lay and the ordained and old ecclesial stereotypes. Admittedly, neither the younger generation of priests nor the 56-65 year-olds may envision their identity within the communion ecclesiology described above. However, that only demonstrates the need to reimagine the Church and ministerial relationships. Some of the best ecclesiology and sacramental theology has not taken root in our ecclesial imaginations enough that our identities are informed by them. I will examine two statements in the questionnaire to illustrate this.

A Contemporary Theology of Ontology

The questionnaire asked priests to respond to two statements about the sacramental character conferred by the priesthood: (1) Ordination confers on the priest a new status or a permanent character which makes him essentially different from the laity within the Church; (2) There is no ontological difference between the priest and the laity, since all share in the common priesthood of Christ given at baptism; the difference is mainly one of assigned duties in the Church. The two main points are that a priest is essentially different from the laity and this difference lies in ontology rather than function.

In *Lumen Gentium* the purpose of placing chapter 2, "The People of God," before the chapter on the hierarchy was to stress what the Christian faithful all have in common by virtue of their baptism before we separate them into various distinct groups as members of the hierarchy, the laity, or religious. This is the same principle that was followed in the revised Code of Canon Law (1983) which treats obligations and rights of all the Christian faithful before describing those of the lay Christian faithful and the sacred ministers and clerics. As one bishop noted at Vatican II, the sacramental character of the priesthood does not erase the sacramental character of baptism.[9] Priests share baptism with the laity, and in that respect they are not essentially different. The issue, of course, is whether the ordained or ministerial priesthood is essentially different from the common priesthood of the baptized. *Lumen Gentium* taught that it is.[10] It is one thing, however, for the ordained *priesthood* to be essentially different from

---

[8] Ibid., 33.

[9] Bishop Franjo Seper, *Acta Synodalia* II/3, 202.

[10] *Lumen Gentium,* 10.

the common *priesthood*, and quite another for the *person* of the priest to be essentially different from the lay *person*. A ministerial priest embodies both priesthoods. Augustine captured this when he said: "When what I am for you frightens me, what I am for you consoles me. For you I am a bishop, with you I am a Christian. The former is a title of duty, the latter is one of grace. The former is a danger, the latter is a title to salvation."[11]

This leads to the second statement about the ontological difference which raises the question about the nature of the ontological change. The Catechism speaks of this as "an indelible spiritual character," not an "indelible mark," thus removing the oxymoron of a physical mark on an immaterial soul.[12] However, in doing this, it also requires a theological exploration into the nature of "character." Edward Schillebeeckx provides the best explanation of this in his classic, *Christ the Sacrament of the Encounter with God.*[13] He describes the character as an ecclesial effect of the sacrament: "a competence and commission within the visibility of the Church."[14] The person who bears a character "bears a certain relation to the visible ecclesial community."[15] This is entirely consistent with communion ecclesiology in that it describes an ontology of relationship. The sacramental character of the ministerial priesthood enables the priest to take the place of Christ in the visibility of the Church, particularly within the Eucharist, and also to personally be the representative of the whole People of God inasmuch as Christ is personally the representative of the People of God in his priestly prayer.[16]

I find the two statements in the survey to be theologically inaccurate. In the first statement, although the Church teaches that the two priesthoods, common and ministerial, are essentially different, it is dangerous to insist on the essential difference between priest and laity without at the same time stressing their commonality. To compound the problem, the second statement refers to the commonality between the two shared in baptism, but uses this to distinguish between ontology and function. A more accurate survey would have compared a theology of the two priesthoods rather than two types of persons in the Church. The two priesthoods represent different relationships within the Church. The question of ontology is un-

[11] St. Augustine, Sermon 340.1: *Patrologiae Latina* (PL) 38, 1438. Cited in *Lumen Gentium,* 32.

[12] *Catechism of the Catholic Church,* 1582.

[13] Edward Schillebeeckx, *Christ the Sacrament of the Encounter with God* (New York City: Sheed and Ward, 1963).

[14] Ibid., 157.

[15] Ibid., 158.

[16] Ibid., 171.

doubtedly a distinguishing marker for different attitudes toward the priesthood, but it needs to be posed in a more theologically accurate manner. Admittedly, "elevation" language associated with ordination also contributes to this confusion.

Perhaps this argument may appear as a fine distinction that is meaningless in the polemic heat generated by intergenerational priestly conflict. That, however, is the point: polemics breed bad theology. Henri de Lubac once commented that it is a shame to learn your catechism against someone else. Similarly, it is a shame to define priesthood over and against the laity. Just as we have too often defined what it means to be Catholic by saying that it is not what it means to be Protestant, so have we defined priesthood by saying that it is not what it means to be part of the laity. This study demonstrates the need to define both what it means to be Catholic and what it means to be priest in terms not represented by either of the two groups in the study. That will be long in coming for it entails first the constructive theological work and then the long process of filtering into the popular imagination of laity and priest alike.

Dr. Susan K. Wood, S.C.L., is a professor of theology and the associate dean of the School of Theology • Seminary at St. John's University, Collegeville, Minnesota. She is author of *Sacramental Orders* (Collegeville, Minn.: Liturgical Press, 2000) and numerous other publications.

Evolving Visions of the Priesthood:
Reflections

Dr. Zeni Fox

Introduction

Reading *Evolving Visions of the Priesthood* proved to be intellectually and emotionally challenging. Intellectually, its most helpful aspect was the way in which it confirmed so much of my personal experience as a teacher, and also offered both correction and corroboration of various things I have heard. The scope and depth of the study, especially as part of an ongoing series of studies, evoke confidence; the statistical information, analysis of trends, and the voices of individual priests are all very helpful. Certainly, what I have read will impact my work—as both context and content—of teaching both seminarians and lay graduate students. Emotionally I was challenged because I am a member of the laity, a woman, and a teacher and researcher who has worked extensively with lay ecclesial ministers, and some of the data about younger priests is not "good news" for me.

My response to the study is influenced by various parts of my story: my education as a systematic theologian and a religious educator; my experience teaching at a seminary school of theology as a pastoral theologian as well as prior experience in a parish, a diocesan office, and a national teaching center; my activities with the USCCB as advisor to several committees, especially the activities associated with the project on lay ecclesial ministry; and my work in the formation of lay ecclesial ministers, which has developed a broad network of personal relationships.

Younger and Older Priests

A key finding of the study is that there are significant differences between younger and older clergy, with a "polarization on the theology of priesthood . . . which pits older and younger priests against each other today." Very telling is the comment of a younger priest about the differences in ecclesiology between the younger and older generations that were present in the seminary: "There was almost an antagonism between the faculty and some members of my class." On the one hand, I think this can be understood in terms of the human struggle between generations. Such a struggle is multidimensional, born of the new perspectives that arise in a new time, of conflict between "fire in the belly" and the gifts of experience, and of power dynamics. But another dynamic proper to a religious tradition can be discerned. No age can fully embody the ideals of the Christian tradition; for Christians, the great task of evangelization is never achieved fully. And so a younger generation critically assesses the incompleteness of the effort to have the Gospel transform individuals and cultures, and seeks new ways of proclaiming the Gospel. The problem is when the efforts of the previous generation are judged as unfaithful rather than as simply limited and incomplete. Alternately, there is a problem when the efforts of the younger generation are seen as destructive of the life's work of those who are older. The task of mutual understanding and appreciation is both difficult and necessary. In the thirteenth century, the great flowering of the theology of Augustine and the Franciscan tradition occurred in Bonaventure's work, just when Thomas Aquinas, a Dominican, began a new theological tradition. Each is part of the Christian intellectual heritage, just as the theologies of priesthood emphasized by younger and older priests are each part of our story.

Perhaps in our time we have a dynamic similar to that found in our earliest history. Reflecting on the New Testament period, Richard Dillon has discerned two disparate movements, the first "creative and adaptive" and the later "custodial and defensive." On the one hand, he looks at Paul's writings; Paul used traditional formulae, but did not simply repeat the tradition in a rabbinic sense. Rather, he was the authoritative mediator of transmitted data for the new circumstances and needs of his churches, as were other prophetic voices of his day. On the other hand, Dillon examines other biblical writers with a quite opposite bent, who were reflecting on the gospel message in light of the fact that the Parousia had not come. Matthew, for example, had a conservative, normative concern; in the Gospel he wrote, he emphasized consolidating the tradition by investigating the constitutive past of the Church.[1] And yet neither of these two quite different perspectives existed to the exclusion of the opposite. "It was always perceived . . . that tradition is not correctly stewarded when either meaningful adaptation or faithful preservation of the *tradita* is ignored."[2]

[1] Richard J. Dillon, "Ministry as Stewardship of the Tradition" in *Catholic Theological Society of America Proceedings* 24 (1969) 41–44.
[2] Ibid., 62.

From the beginning there were "polarizations." But the Church not only survived, it was even enriched by the diversity. What prevailed was the law of love, the principle of unity. (Of course, this was not always the case, as our history of schisms and separations shows.) Today, what younger and older generations, both priests and people, need to remember is that the law of love and the principle of unity is what our founder himself called us to.

Priests' Morale

The most encouraging news in the data is that the vast majority of priests are happy in their work and that there is not a "morale crisis" in the priesthood. Granted, this finding predates the sex abuse crisis. Certainly some of the pain, anger, and sorrow in the face of the crisis would impact a study done today. However, the study shows that the greatest sources of satisfaction in the life and work of priests are the joy of administering the sacraments and presiding over the liturgy, and the satisfaction of preaching the word. Similarly, almost three-quarters of priests said that they feel "most a priest when I am 'saying Mass' (presiding at Eucharist) and hearing confessions," making this a primary aspect of priestly identity. These activities continue as central to their work and can be expected to give continuing satisfaction. On the other hand, the 25% of priests who said that the "respect that comes to the priestly office" is of great importance to their life and work may be more deeply affected by the present crisis. Furthermore, the study indicates that local conditions were a greater contribution to happiness than diocesan, regional, or international conditions. Numerous media commentaries have indicated that the majority of priests say they are not experiencing a negative response in their parishes, neither personally as priests nor financially, in terms of parishioners' giving. Media reports state that the criticisms of the abusers, and of the hierarchy for their response to the abusers and their victims, are not replicated in criticism of local parish priests. The local situation, which priests say most affects them, would seem to be supportive of parish priests.

Hoge and Wenger indicate that they had heard many times that there *is* a morale crisis in the priesthood, but their data indicate that "priests have the same level of happiness and morale as other educated men their age." Certainly, this is good news, organizationally and humanistically speaking. But spiritually too, this is a significant indicator in that peace and joy are attributes of a life lived in accordance with God's will for the individual. Fifty percent of the priests say that the "spiritual security that results from responding to the divine call" is of great importance to them; they are reflectively aware of the centrality of their response to their vocation. This is important for the men, for the laity they minister to, and for the men who will weigh the question of priestly vocation in the future. Today's priests signal with their lives the fruits of answering God's call.

Younger Priests and the Laity

The study states: "the older priests were much more in favor of empowering lay ministers than the younger ones." This conclusion is based on responses to questions about moving faster to empower lay ministers, and about the effect on parish life of more lay ministers. Approximately 50% of the men 25-35 years old express at least cautionary judgments regarding the increase of lay ministers. How does their understanding accord with that of laity on this topic?

First, in general, parish life today is characterized by extensive lay involvement. The *Notre Dame Study of Catholic Parish Life* notes the expansion of parish staffs (other than priests) and the involvement by staff of many more volunteer leaders.[3] The great expansion of ministries in parishes today is the result of this development. It is linked to something central to Christian life, a sense of community. Community is both a theological ideal for the people of God, the Body of Christ, *and* a desire of Americans in our mobile, individualized society. The Notre Dame researchers note a relationship between pastors who are enablers of the laity and a greater sense of community in those parishes.[4] Likewise, in Sweetser's analysis of successful parishes, one of the key points is the importance of shared ministry: laity, priests and religious sharing in the spiritual, educational, liturgical and leadership ministry in the parish.[5] Men who do not value the involvement of lay people in ministries risk alienation from the people, and may impact not only the exercise of many ministries and the successful nature of the parish, but also the very fabric of parish life, a sense of community.

Second, the desire for participation runs deep in American Catholics. An earlier study concludes: "the laity desire more participatory parish life, and achieving it is important to them—apparently even more important

---

[3] Joseph Gremillion and David C. Leege, "Post-Vatican II Parish Life in the United States: Review and Preview," in *Reports: A Comprehensive Survey of Roman Catholic Parishes in the United States,* conducted by the Institute for Pastoral and Social Ministry and the Center for the Study of Contemporary Society of the University of Notre Dame, ed. David C. Leege and Joseph Gremillion (Notre Dame, Ind.: University of Notre Dame, 1984–1988) 6.

[4] Ibid., 7.

[5] Thomas Sweetser, *Successful Parishes.* (Minneapolis: Winston Press, 1983) 12.

than acquiring more priests."[6] Furthermore, the most recent study shows that today *young* adults are even more desirous of "more lay involvement in church affairs at the local parish level."[7] Significantly, this is not a desire of only a segment of young Catholics. "Both left-of-center and right-of-center Catholics were equally in favor of Catholic involvement in social issues and of lay empowerment; these issues are not the agenda solely of a viewpoint held by one theological faction or the other."[8] This finding suggests that priests who do not value the involvement of lay people are in opposition to the views of those in their own cohort among the laity, as well as those of the clergy older than themselves. They may find working in the parish difficult in unexpected ways.

Younger Priests and Lay Ecclesial Ministers

The study did not differentiate lay ministry, broadly speaking, and lay ecclesial ministry, the name given to a narrower group of laity by the United States bishops. These are the men and women (over 80% are women) who work on parish staffs. The bishops have affirmed the importance of lay ecclesial ministry in the Church today, calling it "a gift of the Spirit to the Church."[9] The recent study of the impact of fewer priests also notes their importance: "While most Catholics notice that there has been a decline in the number of priests, fewer than one in four say they have been personally affected by this change. . . . Catholics most favor an increasing use of deacons and lay ministers to help meet the needs of Catholics in a time of fewer priests."[10]

What is the relationship between lay ecclesial ministers and their priest colleagues? A finding in the study is significant: About 50% of priests say they receive strong support from staff members where they minister, suggesting that those relationships are very positive. The great majority (87%) of lay ecclesial ministers report that they experience good support from their pastors. Most had served as volunteers before being hired, and were invited into their leadership positions by pastors who knew them

---

[6] Dean R. Hoge, *Future of Catholic Leadership: Responses to the Priest Shortage.* (Kansas City: Sheed and Ward, 1987) 27.

[7] Dean R. Hoge et. al., *Young Adult Catholics: Religion in the Culture of Choice.* (Notre Dame, University of Notre Dame Press, 2001) 54.

[8] Ibid., 66.

[9] *Lay Ecclesial Ministry: The State of the Questions: A Report of the Subcommittee on Lay Ministry* (Washington, D.C.: United States Catholic Conference, 1999) 20.

[10] *The Study of the Impact of Fewer Priests on the Pastoral Ministry, Executive Summary,* Document of the National Conference of Catholic Bishops, Spring General Meeting, June 2000, vii.

personally[11] (probably older priests). Because the older priests emphasize bringing people together to talk, getting people involved, valuing professional lay staff, and preparing laity to accept lay ministers, relationships with their staff are understandably good. However, they are concerned about "a movement away from some of this ease of working with laity on a par" which they see in the younger clergy, because the viewpoints of the younger priests are quite different. They focus on certain dimensions of the liturgical tradition, the need for spiritual renewal, the need to be loyal to the hierarchy, and a sacramental and cultic theology of the priest. A weakened interest in calling forth lay ministers is a dimension of this approach to ministry. This description of the views of younger priests suggests that their ministerial style will be in tension with that of lay ecclesial ministers. This has additional import in that priests have extraordinarily strong job security while lay ecclesial ministers have very little job security, and it is priests who hire and who may fire lay ecclesial ministers.

The study states that "discussions of collaboration with lay ministers tended to drift to the issue of status and role in ministry." These relationship questions are very complex. Ten years ago Murnion named some of the dimensions which need attention, including personnel matters, ministerial-professional matters or generalist-specialist matters, male-female relationship matters, and clerical-lay matters. But he concludes: "Yet, given all the personal, organizational, ecclesial, and cultural changes involved, it is a tribute to the church that the relationships are as good as they are."[12]

In 1987 Hoge had studied Catholic college students in an effort to predict future patterns of ministry. He said: "The findings can be summarized easily: the men interested in a vocation are more conservative than the other students on many issues. . . . they are institutionally conservative relative to the other students, and the distance between their views and the views of women is sometimes great."[13] This was especially true relative to those women who were considering lay ministry as their future work. The present study confirms the direction regarding priests. This study also confirms that "there is no broad conservative trend among Catholics on beliefs in the areas of ecclesiology, priesthood, or liturgy. On the contrary, recent decades have seen a gradual trend in the opposite direction." While the study suggests that younger lay ministers may have more traditional views of the priesthood than older ones, it is necessary to remember that generally speaking those studying for and those beginning formal lay ministry are

[11] Philip J. Murnion, *New Parish Ministers: Laity and Religious on Parish Staffs.* (New York: National Pastoral Life Center, 1992) 37, 58.
[12] Ibid., 64.
[13] Hoge, 1987, 128.

over 35 years of age. The lay ecclesial ministers can be expected to be more in accord with the views of other laity than the younger priests will be.

One further difference between younger priests and lay ecclesial ministers bears comment. The questionnaire used in the study stated: "It is urgent that priests achieve greater status as competent professionals in the eyes of the Catholic community." While two-thirds of the priests agreed, the younger priests were less likely to agree. Furthermore, when asked about what opportunities for growth would be helpful for their ministry, the priests rated personal life issues far ahead of various leadership skills. In fact, a significant proportion, 40%, see a tension between the priesthood as a profession or as a vocation. On the other hand, in lay ecclesial ministry circles, issues relative to professional growth are receiving significant attention. A clear indicator of this is the work done by three leading ministerial groups, NALM (National Association for Lay Ministry), NCCL (National Conference for Catechetical Leadership), and NFCYM (National Federation of Catholic Youth Ministry) on the common competencies project, an effort to delineate the professional, ministerial preparation needed for ministry.[14] (It is worth noting that the competencies work does not see a tension between vocation and profession.) The present study reports that priests sometimes feel threatened by qualified lay ministers, especially those with a competence in a particular area. If priests increasingly devalue professional preparation even as lay ecclesial ministers place more stress on this, tension may increase. All those involved in ministry education, both preparatory and continuing, need to explore ways to address this.

Women and Priests

The study indicates that some possible problems named in the survey aren't really weighing on priests today. One of these is "difficulty of working with women." On the other hand, the study includes an interesting anecdote in chapter five about a woman described as "very respectful, very helpful, very knowledgeable, knew what to do," but who was viewed negatively by priests because she was "a strong, opinionated woman."

How would women rate the problem of "difficulty working with women"? We do not have that information, but an anecdote poses the importance of the question. Some time ago a diocesan women's commission held its first listening session with women. They asked pastors to invite two women to attend—so the individuals gathered can be presumed to have

[14] Joseph T. Merkt, ed., *Common Formation Goals for Ministry* (N.p.: National Association for Lay Ministry, National Federation of Catholic Youth Ministry, Inc., and National Conference for Catechetical Leadership, 2000).

good standing in their parish and with their pastor. For a day the group prayed, worked in small groups, identified concerns, and sought consensus. The greatest concern, significantly stronger than any other, was that of priests (and seminarians) relating with women.

The empowerment of women, in the United States and throughout the world, is a vital dimension of our time in history. It has significant import for and impact on men, as well as on many structures of our society. In families and workplaces, many issues are being engaged as a result of women's empowerment. In seminaries and parishes the engagement may be weaker, because men are the primary authorities, and because they often interact primarily with other men, or with women they minister *to* or women in support roles. Engagement with "strong women" is minimized, and contributes to the tension and fear named in the study. This issue impacts not only priests' relationships with staff members, but also with empowered women of the parish. Their effectiveness and happiness in ministry may both be affected.

Implications for Ministry Education

1. Ministry education which explores the complexity of the tradition— and the diversity which has always existed within it—contributes to a constructive approach to differences and an avoidance of real polarization.

2. Ministry education which explores the life of the Church in its various expressions in our time, place and culture, and the actual experience of persons and communities of faith grounds ministry in the living tradition and in the service of the needs of the community.

3. Ministry education which invites participants into deep dialogue with each other (younger and older persons, men and women, those preparing for or practicing ordained or lay ministry) fosters understanding, relationships, and collaboration.

4. Ministry education which experientially explores realities such as power, conflict, male-female relationships, and the skills and strategies for collaboration increases the ability of ministers to work together and, therefore, to be effective and happy in their ministry.

5. Ministry education must be ongoing; seminaries, schools of theology, and ministry alone cannot achieve these goals. What is begun in those settings must continue through multiple efforts of continuing education for all ministers.

Dr. Zeni Fox is an associate professor of pastoral theology at Immaculate Conception Seminary, Seton Hall University, South Orange, New Jersey. She is author of *New Ecclesial Ministry: Lay Professionals Serving the Church,* rev. ed. (Franklin, Wis.: Sheed and Ward, 2002) and numerous articles.

Recapturing Priestly Joy

Rev. Gerald D. Coleman, S.S.

As one involved in seminary formation for my entire priestly life, I believe that I have never seen such an outpouring of interest, concern, and printed materials on the Catholic priesthood as in the 2000–2002 years. Although the majority of this literature has been occasioned by priestly sexual scandals, the research has evidenced a good deal of fascinating information, not to mention varied and at times diametrically opposed viewpoints about priests and their future. It is more than fascinating to situate and interpret these publications over against the careful research of Dean Hoge and Jacqueline Wenger.

Perhaps the book receiving the most attention is Michael S. Rose's *Good Bye! Good Men.*[1] As the subtitle indicates, the author attempts to demonstrate that Catholic seminaries have turned away two generations of vocations from the priesthood, and concludes that the priest shortage is "artificial and contrived." Rose explains, "in actuality, there are plenty of young men who exhibit . . . 'orthodoxy'—loyalty to the teachings of the church" and are not admitted to "holy orders, specifically because of their orthodox beliefs."[2]

Rose concludes that the testimony of 125 seminarians "loyal to the teachings of the Church" have met "various obstacles" which led to their "early dismissal or voluntary departure."[3] These "obstacles" are also placed in the way of orthodox applicants for the seminary due most commonly to "a biased application screening process [and] unethical psychological testing."[4]

[1] Michael S. Rose, *Goodbye! Good Men: How Catholic Seminaries Turned Away Two Generations of Vocations from the Priesthood* (Cincinnati: Aquinas Publishing, 2002).

[2] Ibid., 19.

[3] Ibid., 27.

[4] Ibid., 17–18.

In what amounts to a broad-stroked and apologetic study, based on weak to nonexistent methodology, Rose aims sharp criticism at seminary rectors, psychologists, and faculty who "focus on detecting signs of orthodoxy among seminarians,"[5] endorse homosexual practices and agendas, promote ideas and teachings which undermine Catholic beliefs in the Church's doctrine, demonstrate open contempt for proper liturgy and traditional devotions, and commit themselves to spiritual and psychological manipulation and abuse. Clearly, Rose maintains, "genuine vocations" have been frustrated and dismissed. The central point in Rose's book is that "orthodoxy begets vocations . . . based on fidelity to the Church's magisterium."[6]

According to Rose's study, what will the priests of the future be like? They will be unorthodox, disrespectful of the Church's doctrine and the magisterium, confrontational in behavior, and largely unhealthy due to either a gay orientation or solidarity with a gay subculture. It is little wonder that good and faithful Catholics who have read Rose's book are alarmed, concerned, and frightened.

Benedict J. Groeschel's *From Scandal to Hope*, while offering a generally narrow interpretation of today's seminarians and priests, does offer an important corrective to Rose's book.[7] Groeschel's work was authored during the thick of the sexual scandals arising from priestly misbehavior and is concerned mostly with the causes of this behavior. Groeschel holds for a critical and almost irrevocable link between pedophilia and homosexuality. He centers his criticism of current scandals on the permissiveness of seminaries to admit gay men to formation programs and ordination.

Groeschel roots current difficulties in the Church to the "sinister elements"[8] which he believes have entered into seminary and priestly life: permissive attitudes toward homosexuality and effeminate mannerisms and behavior which are found in varying degrees in the seminary and priesthood. Groeschel names this evil as "scandalously apparent" and identifies generally with Rose's conclusions, even though he finds Rose's writing "advocatory literature," which "overstates his case" and falls occasionally "into gossip and an overly judgmental attitude towards those that are trying to walk a middle way."[9]

In Groeschel's estimation, the future of the priesthood offers a rather "catastrophic situation."[10] The major "catastrophe" is the presence of a large

---

[5] Ibid., 27.

[6] Ibid., 337.

[7] Benedict J. Groeschel, C.F.R., *From Scandal to Hope* (Huntington, Ind.: Our Sunday Visitor, 2002).

[8] Ibid., 101.

[9] Ibid., 102.

[10] Ibid., 103.

member of campy, effeminate, and homosexually-oriented men, who inevitably create a great chasm between the priesthood and faithful Catholics.

William J. Bausch's *Breaking Trust: A Priest Looks at the Scandal of Sexual Abuse*[11] is a far more balanced and objective critique of current sexual difficulties, an analysis which gives a more optimistic view of future priests. He compares the present situation to "being on page fifty of a five-hundred page Russian novel: there's a lot more to come."[12] The future, Bausch concludes, will demonstrate a great solidarity between faithful Catholics and the many good priests which are emerging from today's seminary. Although priests in the future will be fewer in number, they will "galvanize" due to the current scandals and will be deliberate in their commitment to celibacy and faithful to church doctrine, even though there will likely be "a significantly higher percentage of homosexual priests and seminarians."[13]

Perhaps this judgment offers a reasonable opportunity to say something about the focus on homosexually-oriented men in today's seminary and priesthood. Some individuals identify priest pedophiles as homosexual "due mainly to the high percentage of priests who have been sexually involved with teenage boys." Others understand homosexuality per se as an orientation where a male is psychosexually attracted to peers of his own sex and not sexually interested in children or teenagers. In his book *Quickening Fire in Our Midst: The Challenge of Diocesan Priestly Spiritually*,[14] George A. Aschenbrenner offers a helpful corrective to the "over publicized" and "exaggerated importance"[15] of this subject. He explains, "Personal . . . honesty about sexual orientation (whether homosexual or heterosexual) is needed, as is respect for each other as united in priestly service, taking care not to get trapped in the exclusive enclave of a subculture. . . . Both in seminary and in a diocese this phenomena of an exclusive subculture is divisive and therefore it prevents appropriate communal consequences in the diocesan priesthood."[16]

In his 18 September 2002 address to the National Conference of Vocational Directors, Father Stephen Rosetti also addresses this point by stressing the concept of *communio*: "The priest is a man of . . . communion. His

---

[11] William J. Bausch, *Breaking Trust: A Priest Looks at the Scandal of Sexual Abuse* (Mystic, Conn.: Twenty-Third Publications, 2002).

[12] Ibid., 52

[13] Ibid., 56.

[14] George A. Aschenbrenner, S.J., *Quickening the Fire in Our Midst: The Challenge of Diocesan Priestly Spirituality* (Chicago: Loyola Press, 2002).

[15] Ibid., 123.

[16] Ibid., 122.

priesthood is devoted to the body of Christ, and tied to the body of the Eucharist. He is to reconcile and love the many parts of the one body—the many faces that make up the church, and to shepherd them into a single whole which is Christ. . . . Your job and mine is to teach and form our seminarians and priests to be men of communion. If the passing of this generation reveals that we have done so, we will have done our job well."[17] In other words, a seminarian or priest must always be a "man of communion" and never of division. If his sexual identity creates division, he should not be in a seminary or in the priesthood.

Aschenbrenner's conclusions are clearly optimistic, showing that today's seminarians and tomorrow's priests are "recapturing priestly joy" and offer a deep sense of priestly spirituality and celibate commitment. Today's seminarians, he summarizes, deeply devotional in character, will inevitably be priests very different from the small percentage of priests who have caused the crisis of sexual abuse: they are making a concerted effort to be "different" from the priests who have fallen into dysfunctional behavior, and they will emerge as priests who are spiritually balanced and doctrinally mature. Although a small number of these future priests will be theologically narrow in both teaching and manner, they will instill into the priestly culture a spirit of joy and a commitment to a deep spirituality.

George Weigel penned *The Courage to Be Catholic: Crisis, Reform and the Future of the Church*[18] in the midst of clergy sexual abuse, and he attempts to demonstrate how this crisis happened and what might emerge. He places a great deal of emphasis on the negative impact which the gay subculture has created in seminaries and the priesthood itself, a crisis which has led some priests toward pedophilic behavior. Weigel believes that it is absolutely necessary to crush the gay subculture by carefully banning men with a homosexual orientation from the seminary and the priesthood. While recognizing that "classic pedophilia" is rare among Catholic priests, he concludes that the primary form of sexual abuse by Catholic clergy in recent decades has been the homosexual molestation of teenagers and young men.[19] He further maintains that future priests have been formed by a certain level of "intellectual deceit and self-deception they learned in the seminary"[20] and will lead lives of behavioral deceit and self-deception. The only viable priest in Weigel's future landscape is one who is qualified intellectually and committed spiritually.

---

[17] Stephen Rosetti, "The Priest as a Man of Communion," *Origins* (2002) 289.

[18] George Weigel, *The Courage To Be Catholic: Crisis, Reform, and the Future of the Church* (New York: Basic Books, 2002).

[19] Ibid., 36.

[20] Ibid., 158.

In *The Changing Face of the Priesthood: A Reflection on the Priest's Crisis of Soul,* Donald Cozzens outlines the many ways he sees changes in today's seminarians and priests, specifically: a deficiency of background in a Catholic ethos, family difficulties that have caused certain dysfunctional behavior, cultural diversity, language inhibitions, and homosexuality.

In *Sacred Silence,*[21] Cozzens places more emphasis on denial patterns that create enormous problems in facing the many crises found in today's Church. He also cautions that many men in the seminary and priesthood have been either consciously or unwittingly caught up in a gay subculture and permitted their sexual orientation to become a dominant feature of their self-definition. At the same time, Cozzens identifies with James Whitehead's analysis of the priest as "orchestrator and representative of the community's faith" and concludes that the *alter Christus* of the future will be a priest among the people rather than a priest over the people, a differential which demands that a priest be rooted in a solid sense of his own identity. This description does not deny the priest's role as *alter Christus,* but rather repositions its meaning in a more horizontal than vertical manner. Situating this assessment in light of Cozzens' evaluation of the "masks" and "faces" of denial that exist in today's Church, Cozzens concludes that the priest of the future must be willing to face the many levels of denial in the Church, and break the sacred silence that surrounds these denials. If today's seminarians and future priests are willing to face this task, he concludes they will witness a "sacred speech" that will earn them the right to be seen as an *alter Christus.*

In a rather focused work edited by Paul Thigpen, *Shaken by Scandals*[22] presents an array of authors who analyze today's seminarians and offer hints about tomorrow's priests. In a central chapter, Michael Novak claims that "there is coming an awakening of a great love for orthodoxy."[23]

This "Great Awakening" is rooted in the belief that God will give the Church true and authentic shepherds and gift the Church of the future with a wholesome and newly-found joy. The conclusion of Novak and the other authors is that despite the many difficulties and problems in today's Church, Catholics will demand honesty and integrity, demanding that future priests be committed to truthfulness, self-integrity, and orthodoxy. Importantly, however, this understanding of "orthodoxy" is entirely different

---

[21] Donald B. Cozzens, *Sacred Silence: Denial and the Crisis in the Church* (Collegeville, Minn: Liturgical Press, 2002).

[22] Paul Thigpen, *Shaken by Scandals: Catholics Speak Out About Priests' Sexual Abuse* (Ann Arbor: Servant Publications, 2002).

[23] Michael Novak, "Something Good is Coming: The Great Awakening Ahead," in Thigpen, 60.

from that of Michael Rose who identifies orthodoxy with such traits as historicism, liturgical rubrics, and blind obedience. Michael Novak has set a much wider stage which calls today's seminarians and tomorrow's priests to honor the very best of the Catholic tradition, and reinsert into the Church a sense of joy in the depth of Catholicism. When this hope is coupled with the other studies mentioned here, it is crucial that today's seminarians and tomorrow's priests understand wisely and fruitfully the best of the Church's tradition.

Father Howard P. Bleichner's 2002 commencement address at St. Mary's Seminary in Baltimore, claims that just as 11 September 2001 altered "the shape of the future," priestly sexual abuse has rocked the church in much of the same way. Bleichner is reminded of the opening line of Dickens' *A Tale of Two Cities*: " These are the best of times and the worst of times." A sign of the "best of times" is found in the consistent reconstruction of the last twenty years that has profoundly touched today's seminaries and priesthood: a papal visitation from 1981–1990, a worldwide Synod on priestly formation in 1990, and *Pastores Dabo Vobis* in 1992, the most comprehensive document on priestly formation in a century. Bleichner concludes with a poignant and telling reference: "The pope's very frailness—slow and hesitant steps of an old man—underscores how much an act of will . . . and intention . . . presents a 'counter-image' to the negative elements that have marked recent problems in the priesthood and the church."

These "hesitant steps" are a striking image of the need to push forward from the recent past marked by ambiguity and abuse. In *Pastores Dabo Vobis,* John Paul II observes that "The priest, . . . is called to be a 'living image' of Jesus Christ" (no. 43). The Pope describes this imitation of Christ: "to know the depths of the human heart, to perceive difficulties and problems, to make meeting and dialogue easy, to create trust and cooperation, [and] to express serene and objective judgments." It is important then, that the priest mould his human personality in such a way that it becomes a bridge and not an obstacle for others in their encounter with Jesus Christ."[24]

The critical question now emerges: Is "The New Vision of the Priesthood" of Hoge and Wenger realistic? Will the current "season of uncertainty" produce priests that authentically model the qualities set forth in *Pastores Dabo Vobis*?

The Hoge-Wenger research indicates the tremendous decline (about 12-14% per decade) in the ranks of diocesan and religious priests, a decline that has created a large number of no-priest parishes in the United States, along with an increasing number of permanent deacons and lay ministers:

[24] Ibid. See also Bishop John Nienstedt, "The Distinct Yet Related Parts of Priestly Formation," *Origins* 32 (2002) 336–38.

that is, an increase in "professional lay ecclesial ministers (professional lay ministers today are about 82% female) in parishes."[25] The study's conclusion is self-evident: "in the next few years the number of lay ministers will exceed the number of priests working in parishes." These statistics are especially revealing when one considers that the number of Catholics in the United States has risen continually over the past century, a growth that one would expect to continue, partly due to the "new immigration" and partly due to the "higher fertility levels of recent immigrants."[26] While the decreasing number of priests is apparent, the average age of priests has been rising, the average in 2001 being sixty. The vision for the future of the priesthood is problematic, then, especially when one places these numbers in the context of fewer seminarians in U.S. seminaries.

The Hoge-Wenger study importantly points out the improved seminary training over a thirty-year period, coupled with a "less rebellious and confrontational type of seminarian."[27] The priest of the future is one who will have various areas of satisfaction: for example, joy in administering the sacraments, presiding over liturgy, preaching, creating personal relationships and community bonds, and to a lesser extent, living the "common life" with like-minded priests. This analysis of today's seminarians promises a future priest who will meet the qualities of *Pastores Dabo Vobis* by offering a corrective to the problems that the Church has experienced in the last half-decade. Celebrating the sacraments, offering Mass, and being a priest for the people will produce in tomorrow's priest a "priestly stature" that should be interpreted positively rather than negatively. Is there a morale crisis in today's seminarians and future priests? The Hoge-Wenger study answers in the negative: "Newly ordained feel needed today, and they are happier and more energized than they were three decades ago." Today's seminarians and young priests are aware of the "loneliness of priestly life" but are taking good measures to counter this loneliness, especially evidenced in deep personal prayer and commitment to peer support groups.

While seminarians and young priests reject the concept of "priest-as-professional," they strongly believe in a "new priestly status" which comes with ordination. Although not specifically referenced by Hoge and Wenger, this belief may be rooted in the conciliar teaching: "By their vocation and ordination, the priests of the New Testament are indeed set apart in a certain sense within the midst of God's people" (*Presbyterorum Ordinis*, 3).[28] While seminarians and younger priests are more conservative than they

---

[25] Chap. 1 of this book.
[26] Ibid.
[27] Ibid., chap. 3.
[28] Walter M. Abbott, ed., *The Documents of Vatican II* (New York: Guild Press, 1966).

were in 1970, the Hoge-Wenger study concludes that a "pre-Vatican attitude is returning" but only in the sense of a "new conservatism" best interpreted as devotional and sacramental. This fact demands a proper theological formation, therefore, in order to prevent the future priest from adopting a pre-Vatican posture translated as rigid, clerical and closed-minded. Future priests will be "unapologetically Catholic," but lacking for the most part a belligerent attitude or style.

Does the Hoge-Wenger study evidence sufficient data to conclude that, even in the midst of the recent crises facing the priesthood and the Church, seminarians and future priests will be men of communion? All evidence points to the fact that they will engage people and enter respectfully into their lives. They will not reprimand or belittle, insult, or look down on people, or treat them as inferior. All of this is very good news for the future of the presbyterate in the United States.

Rev. Gerald D. Coleman, S.S., is president/rector of St. Patrick's Seminary in Menlo Park, California. He is author of *Homosexuality: Catholic Teaching and Pastoral Practice* (New York: Paulist, 1995) and numerous articles.

Trees, Trains, Trends, and Tugs-of-War: A Reflection on Priesthood Today

Rev. Nick Rice

If a parish priest had to pick a figure from Scripture that would best reflect what is happening to ordained priesthood today, who would it be? For some, Job would come to mind! He could easily be seen as one who was tired, dejected, full of unanswered prayers, sitting on piles of parish problems and mountains of debts, deprived of sheep and cattle because they were all sent to cover diocesan assessments. Perhaps, for others, it would be Peter, saying to the Lord, "I really didn't want this job anyway, but you called me, and I keep throwing out nets that come back empty!" Try to talk to the Lord about problems and concerns, and he's told, "Get behind me! You're thinking only in terms of this world and not like God." Or maybe it's like the disciples trying to feed the five thousand on the hillside. "Lord, there are so many to take care of, so many expectations, and I have so little to give them!" The only advice Jesus has is to tell them to sit down and take a break.

For many priests right now, the figure might be Zaccheus. He was going on about his life, but his curiosity about Jesus got the best of him, and that would forever change his life. He went out on a limb, wanting to observe Jesus from a safe distance, blindly oblivious and totally unsuspecting of what he would be called to do. Whatever it was, as in the case of the other fishermen, tax collectors, net menders, it would involve something much larger than a challenge to his particular talents as a businessman.

This image is a meaningful one, because it can serve as a paradigm of the evolution of ordained priesthood for our era. In very real and sometimes painful ways, priests have been called to "come down" from that tree limb of clerical position and prestige, from a privileged position into which practically all church ministry on the local level has been folded. It was "curiosity about Jesus" that probably prompted most to seek this position of service. It may also have been an attraction to the privileged role and dignity that was accorded this ministerial post.

Whatever it was, as we look back on this historical development of the "clerical priesthood," in many ways it had become like Zaccheus, a little above the maddening crowd of the world, "in it but not of it," for some "observing Jesus from a safe distance" of the sanctuary of rather formidable rectories. And then the voice is heard, "Come down from that tree. I want to have dinner and talk with you!" At first the reaction has to be, "How wonderful he noticed me! I've been singled out!" (or some reaction to being personally called to be a "priest").

But the journey down the tree has not been one without splinters and injuries. The prospect of being this close to the Lord has sometimes proven uncomfortable. The challenge to "come down" and be part of the human crowd seeking a messiah for our modern challenges has felt like a betrayal of being "specially called" to some. Whatever the case, the paradigm is rich because of the second part of the invitation, "I mean to dine at your house tonight." This represents our corporate priesthood, the profound challenge to become "disciples of the Lord" before we become "church anything." The image of the Lord walking in our world today among the needy masses, looking up at the priesthood as it has evolved, and saying lovingly, "Come down! We need to talk!" provides a mental picture of what is happening today.

The ordained priesthood is going through a painful, but necessary, purification and redefinition today. It is not pleasant to be called down off that "limb," and there are various ways to respond to that invitation, but we refuse to "come down" at our own peril. The peril is that we miss the opportunity, as priest and as church, to move from "curiosity about the Lord" to passionate involvement with those people who walk the streets looking for the face of God, whose life experiences cause them to look more to the dust of the streets than to the safety of the tree branch.

The New Journey

Since the end of Vatican II, the American priesthood has been on a journey, an effort at self-discovery and redefinition. By leaving what we knew and were comfortable with, we have struck out into unknown territory serving a new vision of church. Even the slightest glance at the parish of the late 1990s compared to the parish of the early '60s shows the tidal wave of change that has engulfed us and prompted us to look at ourselves in a new way. We just never expected that all this change would affect us as much as it has.

With fewer men being ordained, with the Catholic community growing in numbers and diversity, with the body of priests growing older, with an expanded set of pastoral and professional expectations, and with a community that has a different set of needs than in the past, we have spent a lot of time focused on how we will be able to respond adequately. We are walking in both familiar and new territory. The question we are grappling with now is probably the most basic: "What does it mean to be a priest?"

Our priesthood is first of all a call to discipleship with Jesus. It is an important form of discipleship in our Church. This discipleship means a personal and often costly following of Jesus, which affects every dimension of life. Priests are called to represent Christ to the Christian community—in the words of Henri Nouwen, "to be living reminders of Jesus." As priests, however, we are not just called to be disciples, but also leaders. We are to bring Jesus' call to discipleship to others, to form them, to teach them how to be disciples. An important dimension of priestly leadership is being able to sustain a vision of a renewed church in a difficult time of transition such as our own. John Courtney Murray remarked at the end of Vatican II that

> the Council had set afoot in the church a process described as 'Renewal and Reform.' Renewal is of the intellect. It's when you set out where you plan to go, and you design the plan in grand strokes and broad themes. It sets a vision before you. Reform, however, is an affair of institutions, changing them to serve the larger vision you have sketched.

Murray predicted that the challenge that the post-conciliar Church would face is that its vision of renewal would run ahead of its capabilities of reform.

Father Bryan Hehir maintains that the gap between renewal and reform is the gap that must be filled by leadership. "Leadership is the only way you can mediate between a living vision that is large and grand, and institutions that are not yet ready to support the vision."

How do we handle our lives and our responsibilities while the Church grows into a new understanding about ecclesial ministry? It could be that wrestling with a ministerial change that seems overwhelming is the sacrifice we priests of today must make to live through an age of transition. Perhaps priests today have to be men with enough courage to usher the Church into a new age and to pay the price of such an enormous task. It may be that a recognition of the situation in priestly vocations today will give the Church just cause to pronounce the passing of the present form of priesthood, to grieve, and then let go of the priesthood that used to be. However, even priests who can envision and hope for the future priesthood will grieve some of the elements lost from the past form of priesthood.

Our mettle has been severely tested by the sexual scandals of the past ten years. We all somehow feel its shadow fall over us. But we were being challenged and tested even before that. The conciliar documents, especially *Lumen Gentium* and *Presbyterorum Ordinis,* began to reframe the priests' identity. Many documents from the National Conference of Catholic

Bishops of the United States named the changes that were taking place as a "renewed identity" unfolded. This new research by Dean Hoge and Jacqueline Wenger documents some of the movements taking place in the ordained ministry now.

The fact that this book comes out in the aftermath of the sexual abuse crisis and the *Charter for the Protection of Children and Young People* of Dallas only lends importance to its findings. The results coincide with the findings of the survey done from June to October 2002 by the *Los Angeles Times* (www.latimes.com/home/news/polls). The fact that the data overlaps on so many issues lends credence to both.

The Gap

Anyone who has ever traveled on the London subway has heard the same refrain every time the doors open—"Mind the gap! Mind the gap!" The "gaps" that need to be minded in our church life today are well-documented in this new book. The gaps between the "younger" clergy and the "older" clergy, between differing ecclesiologies, between the episcopacy and the presbyterate, between priests and people, between differing visions of Vatican II, between a "cultic" priesthood and a "servant" priesthood; all of these must receive focused attention.

The "gaps" that need attention are not entirely new ones, but what is new is the amount of the gap. The gap that has grown between recently ordained and older men in priesthood holds serious consequences to a unified sense of common mission, and it can be a serious challenge even to the comfort of each when sharing a rectory together.

A "gap of credibility" has increased between many priests and the institutional church on such serious issues as birth control, issues of human sexuality, candidates for ordained ministry, and some sacramental practices. The lack of serious pastoral consultations with the priests in the "pastoral trenches" has caused many to face the future with increased skepticism about whether or not "the Church" really understands the challenges facing priests in days to come.

Priests identify one of their major challenges as "representing official church positions" about which they have serious conscience reservations themselves, in addition to seeing these teachings virtually ignored by many Catholic laity. In our day, credibility is no longer simply given to the church or to the priest. We can no longer depend on the "Catholic culture" to communicate beliefs, systems, and life practices.

The document refers to another gap that is identified rather strongly— the one between priests formed and nourished by the captivating vision of a church identified in the documents of Vatican II and those priests for whom Vatican II is simply part of an historical moment of development with much good, but also many mistakes. Some older priests who have given their life's energies and years of ministry to unfold the vision of Vatican II, at the explicit direction of the Church, wonder why there seems to be an institutional retrenchment, part of which is expressed in the movement back to a more "cultic" priesthood.

The difficulty comes when "cultic" priests seek to pastor "servant" parishes. Despite this simplistic categorization, the truth, nonetheless, is that most parishes and most lay leadership have been formed in the guiding principles of Vatican II. The post-Vatican elements in a new vision of the priesthood claimed by many recently-ordained, can only be understood if priests together engage honestly in the tasks of sharing their hearts' convictions as well as their intellectual or theological convictions. This process requires a healthy amount of humility on the part of all, but not to engage in it invites the possibility of a presbyterate characterized by passive-aggressive behavior. The gap must be attended to, but no one should have the illusion that the rule "priests belong in the sanctuary and people belong in the pews" can any longer be the guiding theology that identifies priesthood—if it ever did. It is critical now that we "mind the gaps" through serious prayer and dialogue, through research and pastoral practice documentation, through an increased sense of common mission and purpose, and through patience and humility.

Many priests today feel like they are the ones being put at the end of a kaleidoscope, and that they are being twisted and turned in dizzying directions by all the shifts and changes in church life and the identity of the priesthood. Thrown on top of all this is the sexual abuse crisis and its result that what was once experienced as a noble, sacrificial way of life is now viewed with suspicion, a lack of trust, and a demand for greater accountability.

While the new survey shows some of the trends and movements in the identity of the Catholic priest today, it does not begin with the most basic question of all—namely, "What is the very mission of the Church in the world and our society in particular?" Any serious effort to "name the mission" will reveal that we do not have the luxury of identifying two separate expressions of ordained priesthood—one cultic and one servant. While history documents that different emphases are stressed at different times, it also shows us that to stress one at the exclusion of the other ends up with a dualism that divides the Church and dilutes its mission.

While we can identify some of the societal and ecclesial elements that sway ordained priesthood toward a primary cultic or a servant-leader emphasis, there has never been a period when times and circumstances in different places of the world would not bring about one emphasis or another. In our time and circumstances, some thirty years after the Second Vatican Council fathers spoke of a new vision of the mission of the Church in our modern world, the identity and ministry of the priest would be gradually redefined in light of that mission. Just as we spoke of different "models of the church" during this defining time, so we see different expressions of priesthood evolve.

Since the documents of Vatican II did not lay out a blueprint for development of this "new priesthood," what we have witnessed is a priesthood trying to adjust and redefine itself through the process of implementing the council's changes in the understanding of "the people of God," the laity's baptismal call to ministry, the role of liturgy and catechetics in forming believers for mission. The very clear lines between "the world" and "the Church" became blurred, as a simplistic dualism could no longer serve to identify where God was acting and where the Church was called to serve.

The symbolic "communion rail" between the sanctuary (the Church) and pew (the world) was removed, and we were left to wrestle with the questions of where God's holiness abides, who controls the access to grace, the role of the priest as the custodian of the great mysteries, and how to attract and train all the evangelists, teachers, healers, community builders, table servers and footwashers that would be needed to carry out this much larger role of the Church as it challenged itself anew to minister to the whole world.

If this mission is accepted and understood in a serious way, we do not have the luxury of identifying ourselves as either "cultic" or "servant leader" priests. Naturally, when it looks like the "sanctuary" is being abandoned or invaded, some will want to reemphasize its importance. Naturally, when the "pew" is just beginning to find its voice and vocation as persons responsible for the transformation of society, there is the danger of co-opting the role of the priest and deemphasizing the "sanctuary or cultic." There is no major balance that somehow produces the "perfect priest," so there will always be the tensions and pulls toward one emphasis or another. Most often both groups can easily quote church documents and papal messages to justify where each chooses to stand, but if this is carried to an extreme of "either/or" then it is the Body of Christ that suffers.

Part of the challenge pointed out by the results of this survey is also named in the instruction from the Vatican Congregation for the Clergy, "The Priest, Pastor and Leader of the Parish Community," where it quotes the address of Pope John Paul II to the plenary session (23 November 2001):

> In recent times, the Church has experienced problems of 'priestly identity', deriving sometimes from an unclear theological understanding of the two ways of participating in the priesthood of Christ. In some areas, these difficulties have progressed to the point of losing that profound ecclesiological balance which is proper to the perennial and authentic Magisterium.
>
> At the present time, however, circumstances are such that it is possible to overcome the danger of 'clericalizing' the laity and of 'secularizing' the clergy.

The generous commitment of the laity in the areas of worship, transmission of the faith, and pastoral collaboration, in the face of shortages of priests, has tempted some sacred ministers and laity to go beyond that which is permitted by the Church and by their own ontological sacramental capacities. This results in theoretical and practical underestimation of the specific mission of the laity to sanctify the structures of society from within.

This same crisis of identity has also brought about the 'secularization' of some sacred ministers by the obfuscation of their absolutely indispensable specific role in ecclesial communion. (http://faithleap.home.att.net/priestin-structions.htm; from www.zenit.org)

Research can identify trends and movements. Very seldom does it recommend solutions to perceived problems. This is the role of faithful, humble, and deeply pastoral leaders who can "bridge the gaps" by their common sense and uncommon holiness. Sometimes, in unlikely circumstances, one looks for wisdom in unlikely places! In these times, it makes eminent sense to add to serious theology and skilled research, the common sense and humor of Garrison Keillor in *The Meaning of Life:*

To know and to serve God, of course, is why we're here, a clear truth that, like the nose on your face, is near at hand and easily discernible but can make you dizzy if you try to focus on it hard. But a little faith will see you through. What else will do except faith in such a cynical, corrupt time? When the country goes temporarily to the dogs, cats must learn to be circumspect, walk on fences, sleep in trees, and have faith that all this woofing is not the last word. Time to shut up and be beautiful, and wait for morning. Yahooism, when in power, is deaf, and neither satire nor the Gospel will stay its brutal hand, but hang on, another chapter follows. Our brave hopes for changing the world sank in port, and we have become the very people we used to make fun of, the hold and hesitant, but never mind, that's not the whole story either. So hang on.

What keeps our faith cheerful is the extreme persistence of gentleness and humor. Gentleness is everywhere in daily life, a sign that faith rules through ordinary things: through cooking and small talk, through storytelling, making love, fishing, tending animals and sweet corn and flowers, through sports, music and books, raising kids—all the places where the gravy soaks in and grace shines through. Even in a time of elephantine vanity and greed, one never has to look far to see the campfires of gentle people. If we had not other purpose in life, it would be good enough to simply take care of them and goose them once in a while. (In *We Are Still Married* [New York: Viking, 1989] 217)

Rev. Nick Rice is a priest of the Archdiocese of Louisville. He is pastor of Our Lady of Lourdes Parish in Louisville and was president of the NFPC from 1994–1997.

Appendix

This appendix includes detailed tables noted in the text and other items from the 2001 survey which are not reported there.

Table A.1
Description of Sample Members (In percents)

Number of cases:	All (1279)	Diocesan (858)	Religious (421)
Present age:			
39 or less	8	10	5
40–49	14	16	12
50–59	24	26	20
60–69	24	23	25
70 or more	30	26	39
Mean age:	60	59	64
What was your age when you were ordained?			
27 or less	54	63	35
28–30	18	15	22
31–35	17	12	28
36 or more	11	10	15
Mean age:	29	29	31
What is your current position?			
Pastor with special work outside the parish	12	15	4
Pastor without special work outside the parish	25	33	8
Full-time diocesan administration or religious community administration	4	3	7
Full-time parochial vicar	10	10	8
Parochial vicar with special work outside the parish	2	3	2
Educational apostolate	8	2	20
Hospital chaplaincy	2	2	3
Prison chaplaincy	0	0	1
Ministry with a special group	2	2	3
Social service apostolate	1	1	2
Retired	16	19	12
Other	17	11	31

Table A.2
Eleven Sources of Satisfaction (In percents)

	All	Diocesan	Religious
There are many sources of satisfaction in the life and work of a priest. Would you indicate how important each of the following is as a source of satisfaction to you? (Percent saying "great importance")			
1. Joy of administering the sacraments and presiding over the liturgy.	90	94	82
2. The satisfaction of preaching the Word.	80	80	79
3. Opportunity to work with many people and be a part of their lives.	67	65	72
4. Being part of a community of Christians who are working together to share the Good News of the Gospel.	62	59	68
5. Opportunity to exercise intellectual and creative abilities.	55	53	59
6. Spiritual security that results from responding to the divine call.	51	51	51
7. Challenge of being the leader of the Christian community.	47	53	34
8. The well-being that comes from living the common life with like-minded priests.	35	26	52
9. Satisfaction in organizing and administering the work of the Church.	34	38	27
10. Respect that comes to the priestly office.	25	29	16
11. Engaging in efforts at social reform.	23	20	30

Table A.3
Twenty Problems Facing Priests (In percents)

	All	**Diocesan**	**Religious**
There are many problems which face priests today. Would you indicate how important the following problems are to you on a day-to-day basis? (Percent saying "a great problem to me personally")			
1. The way authority is exercised in the Church.	24	23	27
2. Too much work.	17	19	13
3. Unrealistic demands and expectations of lay people.	13	16	8
4. Loneliness of priestly life.	13	14	12
5. Being expected to represent church teachings I have difficulty with.	13	12	16
6. Celibacy.	11	12	8
7. Uncertainty about the future of the Church.	10	10	8
8. Relationship with the diocesan bishop of the diocese in which you work.	8	9	6
9. Relationships with superiors or pastor.	7	7	7
10. Difficulty of really reaching people today.	7	7	6
11. Theological change in the concept of the priesthood.	5	5	3
12. Lack of opportunity for personal fulfillment.	4	5	3
13. Relevance of the work that priests do.	4	4	2
14. Lack of a clear idea of what a priest is.	3	4	3
15. Absence of challenge in priestly work.	3	3	3
16. Conflict with parishioners or laity about issues of the day.	3	3	2
17. Difficulty of working with women religious.	3	3	2
18. Too little work.	2	2	2
19. Difficulty of working with women.	1	1	1
20. Difficulty in sharing authority.	1	1	1

Table A.4
Sources of Support in Priestly Ministry (In percents)

	All	Diocesan	Religious
In your priestly ministry, How much support do you experience from each of the following? (Percent saying "strong support")			
1. From your family	59	62	55
2. From non-priest friends	50	50	50
3. From staff members where you minister	49	52	42
4. From parishioners	43	48	32
5. From fellow priests	29	28	32
6. From your bishop	24	29	14
7. From the Vatican	13	14	10
8. From the presbyteral council	5	6	2
9. From the National Conference of Catholic Bishops	3	3	4
10. From the National Federation of Priest's Councils	2	3	2
11. (If religious priest) The leader(s) of your religious institute			38
12. (If religious priest) Your local religious community			37
13. (If religious priest) The Conference of Major Superiors of Men			5

Table A.5
Trends in Attitudes about the Priesthood and the
Church Today (Percent who agree in each survey)

	1970	1985	1993	2001
1. Ordination confers on the priest a new status or a permanent character which makes him essentially different from the laity within the Church.	71	68	70	77
2. There is no ontological difference between the priest and the laity, since all share in the common priesthood of Christ given at baptism; the difference is mainly one of assigned duties in the Church.	18	22	26	23
3. The idea that the priest is a "man set apart" is a barrier to the full realization of true Christian community.	33	32	28	26
4. I feel that I am most a priest when I am "saying Mass" (presiding at Eucharist) and hearing confessions.	72	62	70	73
5. What is lacking today is that closeness among priests which used to be present.	52	45	52	55
6. It is urgent that priests achieve greater status as competent professionals in the eyes of the Catholic community.			65	67
7. Priests today need to be more involved with broad social and moral issues beyond the parish level.			72	74
8. The Catholic Church in the U.S. should continue to welcome Episcopalian priests who want to become active Roman Catholic priests, whether they are married or single.			70	72
9. Priests who have resigned from the priesthood should be invited to re-apply for permission to function as priests again, whether they are married or single.	51	48	52	52

	1970	1985	1993	2001
10. Celibacy should be a matter of personal choice for diocesan priests.	54	53	58	56
11. The Catholic Church needs to move faster in empowering lay persons in ministry.			70	73
12. Parish life would be aided by an increase in full-time professional ecclesial lay ministers.				72
13. Priests' attitudes on church issues can never have an effect in our present institutional church structures.			34	33
14. Priest members of presbyteral councils need more influence if the councils are to be effective in enhancing priestly ministry.			63	60
15. More effective organizations of priests are needed to serve the needs of the priesthood today.			54	53
16. I think it would be a good idea if Christian communities such as parishes were to choose their own priest from among available ordained priests.	31	27	25	23
17. I think it would be a good idea if the priests in a diocese were to choose their own bishop.		52	50	47

Table A.6
How important is open discussion? (in 24 areas)
(Percent saying "very important to me")

	All	Diocesan	Religious
1. The image and esteem of the priesthood today.	62	64	58
2. Psychosexual maturity of priests.	51	46	59
3. Support for living the celibate life.	49	47	53
4. Sharing ministry with laity.	47	46	49
5. Problems of overwork.	43	43	43
6. The policy of mandatory celibacy.	42	42	42
7. Problems of sexual misconduct by priests.	42	38	48
8. The process of selecting bishops.	41	41	42
9. Multiculturalism and race relations.	39	34	49
10. Problems of rectory or community living.	32	32	32
11. Sharing ministry with deacons.	31	34	24
12. The lack of professional standards.	31	32	28
13. Quality of representation as a priest nationally.	30	36	17
14. Ministry to priests with HIV/AIDS.	30	28	33
15. Parishes with lay administrators.	29	31	36
16. Mandatory laicization of priests.	29	29	30
17. The admission of self-declared homosexuals to the priesthood.	28	26	32
18. Policies on living arrangements.	27	33	14
19. Differences in sexual orientation of priests.	26	23	32
20. Recruiting priests from foreign nations.	25	27	22
21. Quality of representation as a priest at the diocesan level.	24	26	18
22. Ordination of women.	23	22	26

	All	**Diocesan**	**Religious**
23. Clarification and standardization of salaries.	16	21	4
24. The issue of ethnic or national parishes.	15	16	14

NOTE: The percentage saying "I don't want it discussed" is not shown here. It was very low on most items. The items on which it was highest were #22 (ordination of women), 22%; #17 (admission of self-declared homosexuals into the priesthood), 12%; #6 (mandatory celibacy), 7%; #19 (differences in sexual orientation of priests), 6%; and #16 (mandatory laicization of priests), 5%.

Table A.7
Four Questions about Sexuality Issues (In percents)

	All	**Diocesan**	**Religious**
Is there a homosexual subculture in your diocese or religious institute?			
Yes, clearly	19	18	21
Probably but not clearly	36	36	36
No	17	17	17
Don't know	28	29	25
In the seminary or seminaries you attended, was there a homosexual subculture at the time?			
Yes, clearly	15	17	12
Probably but not clearly	26	26	26
No	44	40	51
Don't know	15	17	11
In your opinion, have the recent media stories of sexual misconduct by Catholic priests hindered your ministry, or have they had no effect?			
Hindered greatly	10	11	6
Hindered slightly	45	46	44
Had no effect	36	34	38
Don't know	9	8	11
Helped	1	1	1
Have these media stories of sexual misconduct affected how much you encourage men to consider the priesthood?			
Yes, much less encouragement	6	7	4
Yes, slightly less encouragement	20	20	19
No effect	70	69	73
Don't know	4	4	4

Table A.8
Attitudes about Presbyteral Councils (In percents)

	All	Diocesan	Religious
Are you acquainted with the topics and issues discussed in the presbyteral council in your diocese?			
Yes, quite	48	61	19
Yes, slightly	34	32	38
No	18	7	42
How interested are in you the work being done by your presbyteral council?			
Very interested	26	32	13
Somewhat interested	51	53	46
Not interested	16	13	24
Don't know	7	2	17
How effective do you think your presbyteral council is in representing priests?			
Very effective	13	16	9
Somewhat effective	43	50	27
Somewhat ineffective	16	18	11
Very ineffective	11	12	7
Don't know	18	4	46

Table A.9
Confidence in Leadership (In percents)

	All	Diocesan	Religious
How much confidence do you, yourself, have in the decision making and leadership of the following?			
1. Your diocesan bishop			
Great deal	24	28	16
Quite a lot	32	33	29
Some	29	26	33
Very little	14	12	17
Don't know	2	1	5
2. The National Conference of Catholic Bishops			
Great deal	8	8	7
Quite a lot	28	29	26
Some	41	40	42
Very little	20	20	21
Don't know	3	3	4
3. The presbyteral council in your diocese			
Great deal	6	8	1
Quite a lot	24	27	17
Some	35	40	26
Very little	23	23	22
Don't know	12	2	34
4. The National Federation of Priests' Councils			
Great deal	3	2	2
Quite a lot	14	15	13
Some	33	36	27
Very little	31	34	24
Don't know	20	13	34
5. Your diocesan pastoral council			
Great deal	3	4	1
Quite a lot	14	16	9
Some	28	31	22
Very little	33	38	24
Don't know	22	12	43

	All	**Diocesan**	**Religious**
6. (If religious) The leader(s) of your religious institute			
Great deal			25
Quite a lot			42
Some			23
Very little			10
Don't know			1
7. (If religious) The Conference of Major Superiors of Men			
Great deal			6
Quite a lot			23
Some			29
Very little			21
Don't know			21

Table A.10
Comparisons with Other Professionals (In percents)

	All	Diocesan	Religious
Think of the professional persons you know—for example, doctors, lawyers, and educators. How do you think you as a priest compare to them in regard to the following attributes?			
a. Depth of knowledge and skill.			
I have more	14	13	15
I have about the same	73	75	70
I have less	10	9	11
I have much less	1	1	1
Don't know	2	2	3
b. Autonomy to make decisions.			
I have more	18	17	18
I have about the same	43	44	43
I have less	26	25	28
I have much less	11	12	9
Don't know	2	2	2
c. Responsibility for an undertaking.			
I have more	23	25	20
I have about the same	60	60	60
I have less	12	11	14
I have much less	4	4	4
Don't know	1	1	2
d. Commitment to serving the needs of people.			
I have more	57	59	54
I have about the same	40	39	42
I have less	1	1	1
I have much less	0	0	1
Don't know	1	1	2
Do you feel a tension between seeing the priesthood as a profession or as a vocation?			
Yes, great tension	12	15	7
Yes, slight tension	28	30	24
No	57	52	66
Don't know	3	3	3

Table A.11
Six Questions About the Priesthood (In percents)

	All	Diocesan	Religious
In the future if you would be asked to restrict your work to sacramental and liturgical duties, would you be satisfied or dissatisfied?			
Very satisfied	22	25	18
Somewhat satisfied	22	25	17
Neither satisfied nor dissatisfied	10	9	10
Somewhat dissatisfied	17	16	18
Very dissatisfied	26	22	34
I don't know	3	3	3
To what extent do you feel you are utilizing your important skills and abilities in your present assignment?			
Not at all	2	3	2
Comparatively little	9	10	6
To some degree	22	23	20
Fairly much	67	64	72
(If religious priest) Do you feel a tension between your present ministry and the charism of your religious institute?			
Yes, great tension			5
Yes, slight tension			15
No			79
Don't know			1
Which of the following statements most clearly reflects your feeling about your future in the priesthood?			
I will definitely not leave	79	78	81
I probably will not leave	16	17	15
I am uncertain about my future	4	4	4
I probably will leave	1	1	1
I have definitely decided to leave	0	0	0

	All	**Diocesan**	**Religious**
If celibacy for priests became optional, do you think you would ever get married?			
Certainly yes	4	5	2
Probably yes	8	10	5
Uncertain	12	13	9
Probably no	29	31	26
Certainly no	47	41	58
If you had your choice again, would you enter the priesthood?			
Definitely yes	67	68	66
Probably yes	21	19	24
Uncertain	8	9	6
Probably not	3	3	4
Definitely not	1	1	0

Table A.12
Seventeen Statements about the Priesthood
and the Church Today (In percents)

	All	**Diocesan**	**Religious**
1. Ordination confers on the priest a new status or a permanent character which makes him essentially different from the laity within the Church.			
Agree strongly	48	53	37
Agree somewhat	29	30	27
Uncertain	6	4	9
Disagree somewhat	10	8	15
Disagree strongly	7	5	12
2. There is no ontological difference between the priest and the laity, since all share in the common priesthood of Christ given at baptism; the difference is mainly one of assigned duties in the Church.			
Agree strongly	11	8	15
Agree somewhat	12	11	14
Uncertain	7	7	7
Disagree somewhat	17	16	21
Disagree strongly	53	58	43
3. The idea that the priest is a "man set apart" is a barrier to the full realization of true Christian community.			
Agree strongly	9	8	13
Agree somewhat	17	17	16
Uncertain	10	8	14
Disagree somewhat	27	28	26
Disagree strongly	37	39	32
4. I feel that I am most a priest when I am "saying Mass"(presiding at Eucharist) and hearing confessions.			
Agree strongly	41	45	32
Agree somewhat	32	32	31
Uncertain	4	4	3
Disagree somewhat	16	13	22
Disagree strongly	8	6	12

	All	**Diocesan**	**Religious**
5. What is lacking today is that closeness among priests which used to be present.			
Agree strongly	19	22	12
Agree somewhat	36	38	33
Uncertain	24	18	36
Disagree somewhat	16	16	15
Disagree strongly	5	6	4
6. It is urgent that priests achieve greater status as competent professionals in the eyes of the Catholic community.			
Agree strongly	24	23	25
Agree somewhat	43	42	46
Uncertain	15	14	17
Disagree somewhat	12	15	7
Disagree strongly	6	6	5
7. Priests today need to be more involved with broad social and moral issues beyond the parish level.			
Agree strongly	27	24	34
Agree somewhat	47	47	46
Uncertain	16	18	11
Disagree somewhat	8	9	7
Disagree strongly	2	2	2
8. The Catholic Church in the U.S. should continue to welcome Episcopalian priests who want to become active Roman Catholic priests, whether they are married or single.			
Agree strongly	40	40	39
Agree somewhat	32	30	37
Uncertain	14	14	14
Disagree somewhat	7	8	7
Disagree strongly	7	8	4
9. Priests who have resigned from the priesthood should be invited to reapply for permission to function as priests again, whether they are married or single.			
Agree strongly	31	32	28
Agree somewhat	21	19	26

	All	Diocesan	Religious
Uncertain	15	14	17
Disagree somewhat	13	14	11
Disagree strongly	21	21	19

10. Celibacy should be a matter of personal
    choice for diocesan priests.

Agree strongly	35	35	33
Agree somewhat	21	18	27
Uncertain	10	9	11
Disagree somewhat	10	11	8
Disagree strongly	24	27	20

11. The Catholic Church needs to move
    faster in empowering lay persons
    in ministry.

Agree strongly	38	34	47
Agree somewhat	35	36	32
Uncertain	11	11	9
Disagree somewhat	10	12	6
Disagree strongly	6	6	6

12. Parish life would be aided by an
    increase in full-time professional
    ecclesial lay ministers.

Agree strongly	38	37	41
Agree somewhat	34	34	34
Uncertain	15	15	16
Disagree somewhat	7	9	4
Disagree strongly	5	6	4

13. Priests' attitudes on church issues
    can never have an effect in our
    present institutional church
    structures.

Agree strongly	10	11	7
Agree somewhat	23	25	20
Uncertain	22	21	25
Disagree somewhat	28	26	31
Disagree strongly	17	17	17

14. Priest members of presbyteral councils
    need more influence if the councils are
    to be effective in enhancing priestly
    ministry.

	All	Diocesan	Religious
Agree strongly	26	29	19
Agree somewhat	34	35	33
Uncertain	30	24	42
Disagree somewhat	7	9	3
Disagree strongly	3	3	3

15. More effective organizations of priests are needed to serve the needs of the priesthood today.

	All	Diocesan	Religious
Agree strongly	16	16	14
Agree somewhat	37	37	39
Uncertain	30	28	33
Disagree somewhat	12	14	9
Disagree strongly	5	5	4

16. I think it would be a good idea if Christian communities such as parishes were to choose their own priest from among available ordained priests.

	All	Diocesan	Religious
Agree strongly	7	7	8
Agree somewhat	16	16	16
Uncertain	21	17	28
Disagree somewhat	21	23	18
Disagree strongly	35	37	30

17. I think it would be a good idea if the priests in a diocese were to choose their own bishop.

	All	Diocesan	Religious
Agree strongly	22	22	22
Agree somewhat	25	23	29
Uncertain	15	15	16
Disagree somewhat	15	16	14
Disagree strongly	23	25	19

References

Alison, James. 2001. *Faith Beyond Resentment: Fragments Catholic and Gay.* New York: Crossroad.

Alison, James. 2002. *Being Wrong and Telling the Truth: A Gay Perspective.* Lecture given at St. Joseph's in the Village, London. 30 May.

Appleby, R. Scott. 1990. "Part I: The Transformation of the Roman Catholic Parish Priesthood." In Jay P. Dolan, et al. *Transforming Parish Ministry: The Changing Roles of Catholic Clergy, Laity, and Women Religious.* New York: Crossroad. Pp. 3–107.

Bacik, James J. 1999. "The Practice of Priesthood: Working Through Today's Tensions." In Karen Sue Smith, ed., *Priesthood in the Modern World.* Franklin, Wis: Sheed and Ward. Pp. 51–65.

Caplow, Theodore, Louis Hicks, and Ben J. Wattenberg. 2001. *The First Measured Century.* Washington, D.C.: American Enterprise Press.

CARA Report. 2001. Vol. 7, no. 1. Published by the Center for Applied Research in the Apostolate, Washington, D.C.

Catechism of the Catholic Church. 2001. http://www.ziplink.net/cgi-bin/cgi-wrap/kerygma/a.pl.

Cohen, Albert K. 1970. "A General Theory of Subcultures." In David O. Arnold (ed.), *The Sociology of Subcultures.* Berkeley: Glendessary Press. Pp. 96–108.

Coleman, Gerald D. 2002. "Human Sexuality and Priestly Formation." *Seminary Journal* 8, no. 1:16–23.

Congregation for the Doctrine of the Faith. 1986. *Letter to the Bishops of the Catholic Church on the Pastoral Care of Homosexual Persons.* http://www.vatican.va/roman_curia/congregation/cfaith/documents/rc_con_cfaith_doc_1986.

Congressional Information Service. 2002. "Attitudes Toward the Legality of Homosexual Relations, Selected Years 1977–1999." *Sourcebook of Criminal Justice Statistics.* 2000. Lexis-Nexis Online Statistical Universe.

Cozzens, Donald B. 2000. *The Changing Face of the Priesthood.* Collegeville, Minn.: Liturgical Press.

D'Antonio, William V., James D. Davidson, Dean R. Hoge, and Katherine Meyer. 2001. *American Catholics: Gender, Generation, and Commitment.* Walnut Creek, Cal.: AltaMira Press.

Dolan, Jay P., R. Scott Appleby, Patricia Byrne, and Debra Campbell. 1990. *Transforming Parish Ministry.* New York: Crossroad.

Fetto, John. 2002. "Gay Friendly?" *American Demographics* 24:16.

219

Fichter, Joseph H. 1968. *America's Forgotten Priests: What They are Saying*. New York: Harper and Row.

Froehle, Bryan T., and Mary L. Gautier. 2000. *Catholicism U.S.A.: A Portrait of the Catholic Church in the United States*. Maryknoll, N.Y.: Orbis.

Garneau, James F. 2002. "Trust Replaces Suspicion: Causes and Results of Polarization among Clergy in Contemporary U.S. Catholicism." Unpublished paper. Columbus, Ohio: Pontifical College Josephinum.

Gillis, Chester. 1999. *Roman Catholicism in America*. New York: Columbia University Press.

Gordon, Milton, M. 1970. "The Concept of the Subculture and its Application." In David O. Arnold, ed., *The Sociology of Subcultures*. Berkeley: The Glendessary Press. Pp. 31–38.

Greeley, Andrew M. 1972. *The Catholic Priest in the United States: Sociological Investigations*. Washington, D.C.: United States Catholic Conference.

Hedin, Raymond. 1995. *Married to the Church*. Bloomington: Indiana University Press.

Hemrick, Eugene F., and Dean R. Hoge. 1985. *Seminarians in Theology: A National Profile*. Washington, D.C.: United States Catholic Conference.

Henneberger, Melinda. 2002. "Vatican Weighs Reaction to Accusations of Molesting Clergy." *The New York Times,* 3 March. Lexis-Nexis Online Statistical Universe.

Hennesey, James, S.J. 1981. *American Catholics: A History of the Roman Catholic Community in the United States*. New York: Oxford University Press.

Hennessy, Paul K., ed. 1997. *A Concert of Charisms: Ordained Ministry in Religious Life*. New York: Paulist Press.

Hoge, Dean R. 2002a. *The First Five Years of the Priesthood*. Collegeville, Minn.: Liturgical Press.

_____. 2002b. "Report on Survey of 2002 Priestly Ordinations." Unpublished report. Washington, DC: Catholic University, Life Cycle Institute.

Kemper, John C., S.S. 2002. "Religious Formation Today: The Blessings and the Challenges." *Seminary Journal* 8, no. 1:34–40.

Kennedy, Eugene C., and Victor J. Heckler. 1971. *The Catholic Priest in the United States: Psychological Investigations*. Washington, D.C.: United States Catholic Conference.

Latcovich, Mark. 2002. "Seminarians in the 1990s." Unpublished report. Wickliffe, Ohio: St. Mary Seminary.

Lattin, Don. 2000. "Berkeley Seminary Center Sets Precedent." *San Francisco Chronicle,* 16 September, sec. A.

Lonsway, Francis A. 2001. "The Entering Student Questionnaire: A Study of Five Years of Use." Unpublished paper. Pittsburgh, Pa.: Association of Theological Schools.

Los Angeles Times. 2002. "Most Priest Say Bishops Mishandled Abuse Issue." 20 October, sec. A.

_____. 2002. "Young Priests Hold Old Values." 21 October, sec. A.

Martin, James. 2000. "The Church and the Homosexual Priest." *America* 183:11–15.

Marzheuser, Richard. 1999. "A New Generation is on the Rise in Seminaries." *Seminary Journal* 5, no. 1:21–31.

McDonough, Peter and Eugene C. Bianchi. 2002. *Passionate Uncertainty: Inside the American Jesuits*. Berkeley: University of California Press.

Morin, Richard, and Dan Balz. 1966. "Americans Losing Trust in Each Other and Institutions." *Washington Post*. 28 January. Pp. A-1, 6.

Morris, Charles R. 1997. *American Catholic: The Saints and Sinners Who Built America's Most Powerful Church*. New York: Random House.

Murnion, Philip J., and David DeLambo. 1999. *Parishes and Parish Ministers: A Study of Parish Lay Ministry*. New York: National Pastoral Life Center.

National Conference of Catholic Bishops Committee on Priestly Life and Ministry. 1989. "Reflections on the Morale of Priests." *Origins* 33:497–505.

National Federation of Priests' Councils. 1994. *Project Future Directions: Survey Reports*. Chicago: National Federation of Priests' Councils.

Okure, Aniedi. 2002. "Lay Ministers' Views of New Priests." Unpublished paper. Washington, D.C.: Catholic University of America.

Ouchi, William G. 1981. *Theory Z*. New York: Avon Books.

Peters, Thomas J., and Robert H. Waterman. 1988. *In Search of Excellence*. New York: Warner Books.

Putnam, Robert D. 2000. *Bowling Alone*. New York: Simon and Schuster.

Schmalzbauer, John. 2000. "Catholics and Evangelicals in the 'Knowledge Professions': From the Margins to the Mainstream." Paper presented to the Association for the Sociology of Religion, Washington D.C., 12 August.

Schoenherr, Richard A., and Lawrence A. Young. 1993. *Full Pews, Empty Altars*. Madison, Wis.: University of Wisconsin Press.

Schwartz, Robert. 1989. *Servant Leaders of the People of God*. New York: Paulist Press.

Smith, Karen Sue, ed. 1999. *Priesthood in the Modern World*. Franklin, Wis.: Sheed and Ward.

Sweetser, Thomas P. 2001. "A Letter to the American Catholic Bishops from Your Pastors." *America* 185:18–20.

Thornton, Arland. 1989. "Changing Attitudes toward Family Issues in the United States." *Journal of Marriage and the Family* 51:873–93.

United States Census Bureau. 2000a. "America's Families and Living Arrangements." *Current Population Reports*, 2000. Washington, D.C.: Census Bureau.

United States Census Bureau. 2000b. *Statistical Abstracts of the U.S., 2000*. Lexis-Nexis Online Statistical Universe.

Walsh, James, et al. 1995. *Grace Under Pressure: What Gives Life to American Priests*. Washington, D.C.: National Catholic Educational Association.

Weigel, George. 1993. "The Human Rights Revolution, *Pacem in Terris* 1963." In George Weigel and Robert Royal, eds., *Building the Free Society: Democracy, Capitalism, and Catholic Social Teaching*. Grand Rapids, Mich: Eerdmans. Pp. 69–87.

Wheeler, Barbara G. 2001. "Fit for Ministry? A New Profile of Seminarians." *Christian Century* 118:16–23.

Yang, Alan S. 1997. "Trends: Attitudes Toward Homosexuality (in the Polls)." *Public Opinion Quarterly* 61:477–507.

Index